BACK TO THE
DRAWING BOARD

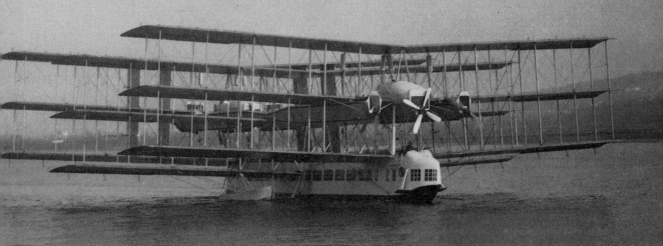

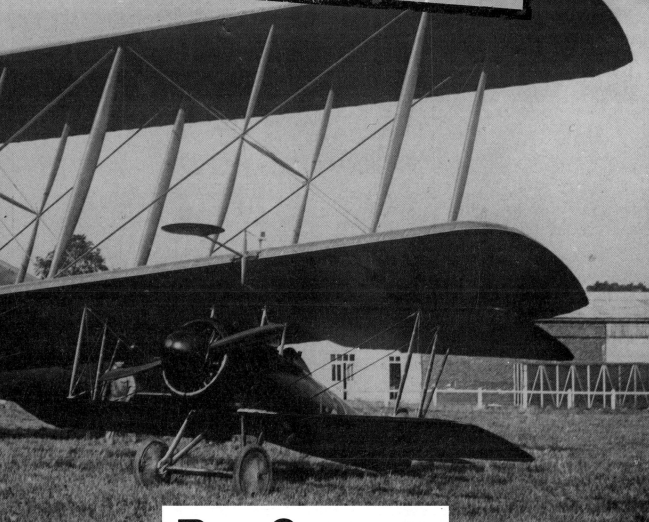

BACK TO THE DRAWING BOARD

BILL GUNSTON

Airlife

ACKNOWLEDGEMENTS

As so often before, I am deeply indebted to Phil
Jarrett for providing the bulk of the photographs.
Those of Soviet aircraft have been kindly lent by
Nigel Eastaway, chairman of the Russian Aviation
Research Trust.

First published in the UK in 1996
by Airlife Publishing Ltd

British Library Cataloguing in Publication Data
  A catalogue record for this book
  is available from the British Library

ISBN 1 85310 758 1

Typeset by Hewer Text Composition Services, Edinburgh
Printed in England by Butler & Tanner Ltd, Frome and London

Airlife Publishing Ltd

101 Longden Road, Shrewsbury SY3 9EB

CONTENTS

INTRODUCTION

I am sure that nobody has ever *tried* to design a bad flying machine. Of course, every 'absolute' claim ought to be hedged about with exceptions and qualifications. For example, in 1911–18 it was indeed common for designers to create aeroplanes that would not fly. Often called 'Penguins', these were designed to be steered across fields by *ab initio* pupils so that they could begin to get the feel of things without the extra worry of the vertical dimension. In contrast, these stories are about aircraft that failed to perform as expected, or which were simply dangerous.

Inevitably, this book will be compared with an earlier volume entitled *The World's Worst Aircraft*. Its author, James Gilbert, is a long-time and respected friend. I hope he will remain one if I suggest that a high proportion of the aircraft he scorned were in fact not bad aircraft at all, but part of bad programmes.

For example, Igor Sikorsky's *Ilya Mourometz* bombers were impressively bold and successful achievements for over eighty years ago. Their combat record was something to be very proud of. Much later the Brabazon, Princess, Convair jetliners and B-70 were beyond criticism in their aerodynamics, structures, systems and flying qualities. In no sense whatsoever were they 'bad aircraft', except to an accountant. It just so happened that, having been launched with the highest of hopes, they emerged into a changed world where the customers preferred something else.

The mighty 'Brab', designed when the Atlantic seemed very wide indeed, would have had to compete against the DC-7C, L-1649 and jet 707, which were not even dots on the horizon when the huge Bristol was proposed. The Princess would have had the same problem, made even worse by the fact that, when it flew, long paved runways had replaced the civil flying-boat bases. The CV-880 could not compete against Boeing's so-called 'bargain basement' 720, and persisting with the CV-990 was just throwing good money after bad. But they were fine aircraft, and the handful that were built had long and successful careers.

One could equally claim that the Vanguard was a 'worst aircraft' because Vickers-Armstrongs sold just forty-three of them, about 500 fewer than they had hoped. In fact it was an excellent aircraft,

designed and developed very quickly, with great skill and at well below the estimated cost. It failed in the market-place because, whereas in 1956 it had seemed to be the obvious next stage beyond the Viscount, by the time it emerged in the early 1960s everyone took it for granted that turboprops were obsolete. Vickers tried to get rid of the propellers with a derived Vanjet, but never got it off the drawing board.

Sadly for Vickers, we realise today that the turboprops were not obsolete at all. Indeed, in 1989 Canadair caused raised eyebrows when they launched the RJ (Regional Jet) in order 'to compete in a segment of the market at present dominated by turboprops'. The Vanguard was a fine aircraft which just happened to be either five years too late or thirty years too early!

All aeroplanes are critically dependent upon their engines, and it shows what a fascinating field aviation is to note that the newest and most efficient transport aircraft have turbofans or propfans or turboprops, the latter including pushers with scythe-bladed propellers at the back. Each design team would be happy to provide convincing arguments why theirs is the best way to do it. But there are plenty of examples from the past of propulsion systems which, though they seemed the best answer at the time, eventually came to nothing. In 1955 the USAF funded work on two mighty strategic bombers. The NPB (Nuclear-Powered Bomber) promised to be huge and slow, but it would hit any target on Earth, and come from any direction. The CPB (Chemically Powered Bomber) might be as big and expensive and have a shorter range, but it would dash over its target at Mach 3. The USAF paid a billion or two to decide it didn't want either. As Churchill said, 'You can always rely upon Americans to do the right thing, after they've tried everything else.'

Back in April 1933, when a mere thousand dollars was several times the average annual wage, a Travel Air biplane took off, leaving a thin trail of steam. Driving the propeller was a 150-horsepower compound V-twin *steam engine*. The brothers George and William Besler advertised it as smooth, quiet, efficient and safe, and able to turn in either direction, but unfortunately the list of drawbacks was even longer. Until recently the

Captain Geoffrey de Havilland in the cockpit of one of his greatest creations, the BE.2a. This was one of the best aeroplanes of 1912.

diesel appeared to be another failure, but as the very latest engine for light aircraft to appear in the Russian Federation is a completely new and very efficient diesel perhaps I had better reserve judgement. In any case this is a book about aircraft, rather than engines.

Another proof of the fact that – contrary to the predictions of supposed experts in 1919, 1945 and 1978 – aeroplane design has never got into a rut is seen in the extraordinary diversity of configurations that have flown, many of which are flying today. I almost put a chapter in this book on aeroplanes with circular wings, either a ring or a disc, but there have been too many. In any case, though they had nothing to commend them, these amazing ring-wings mostly flew, and made normal landings.

Again, if ever there was a candidate for 'back to the drawing board' it was the Blohm und Voss BV 141 of World War II. On one side of the centreline was a crew nacelle, almost entirely transparent. On the other side was a long tube with the engine at the front and the tail at the back, the tailplane being on one side only. Admittedly, the 141 saw only limited service as an observation aircraft with the Luftwaffe, but that was not because of its flying qualities. Its problems had nothing to do with the starkly amazing asymmetric configuration.

As Professor C.E.M. Joad always said, to every question put to him, 'It all depends on what you mean.' Take any dozen aviation buffs, or chief designers, or pilots, or airline finance directors, or maintenance engineers, or Chiefs of Staff, and you will get a dozen different definitions of a bad aeroplane. When I began to write a list of aircraft to be included in this book I quickly realised I had to think deeper and comprehend what the design team were trying to do.

For example, two of the obvious candidates to go on my list were the Gee Bee racers and the Messerschmitt Me 209 V1. These were among the most tricky, unpleasant and downright dangerous powered aircraft ever designed. But another criterion on which to judge an aircraft is what it achieved. Did it do its job, and accomplish what the designer intended? On that basis these two nasties score 100 per cent. They were designed to win races and break world records, and they did precisely that. Indeed the Me 209 V1 set a piston-engined speed record that nobody could break for over thirty years. Beyond question, these near-lethal aircraft cannot be called failures.

Yet answering the question 'What did it accomplish?' can often be quite difficult. For example, two of the greatest fighters of all time were the Sopwith Camel and Messerschmitt 262. They would stand very high in a book about flying successes. Yet they killed almost as many of their own pilots as they did of the enemy, and in the case of the Me 262 this was doubly serious. In the final year of World War II the Luftwaffe had thousands of almost new 109Ks, 190Ds and other formidable aircraft lying around unused. In contrast, they had a desperate shortage of pilots, especially combat-ready pilots, and those killed in Me 262s were the best of the lot.

The Me 262's ancestor, the Bf 109, was the most important German fighter from the first day of World War II (when it was effectively the *only* front-line German fighter) to the last. When it first flew in May 1935 it was potentially the best fighter in the world, smaller than the Hurricane and Spitfire (which both came later), with great performance and very easy to make. Repeated upgrades kept it competitive, yet it fell far short of what could have been achieved. I was lucky enough to fly both the E and G versions, and I was astonished at their serious deficiencies, some of which seemed to be easily rectifiable. I am sure that any Bf 109 submitted to Britain's Boscombe Down would have been rejected out of hand. So how did Luftwaffe aces rack up fantastic scores on such a flawed fighter? Simply by long familiarity, which made them masters of their trade. So there we have an aircraft simultaneously among the best and the worst.

We see something similar, but more diverse, in the post-war products of de Havilland Aircraft. This famous firm had a magic all its own. If you were an 'old boy' from the DH Technical School you were convinced there was nothing else in sight – all other aircraft companies were inferior. Inevitably, perhaps, this made the firm arrogant. For example, we were invited to witness the first flight of the Alvis-engined Beaver 2. In those days every paper had an air correspondent, and at least thirty media people came to witness this trivial event. A local reporter stood up and said, 'But it's been flying nearly a week,' whereupon Martin Sharp – in a sharp voice, too – said, 'You have just witnessed the first flight, you will all report it correctly.' If you know you are infallible, you can behave like this.

Trouble is, de Havilland ought instead to have hung their heads in abject shame. It was that great American the late David A. Anderton who first opened my eyes to their disgraceful post-war record. He just said, 'Every damn DH airplane comes unglued.' If there is one fault in an aircraft that is absolutely unforgivable, it is catastrophic structural failure in the air, and de Havilland made a habit of it. Nobody would dream of putting the types involved in this book, because eventually they were made to hold together, but I did include one of the most beautiful of their pre-war types, for almost the same reason.

In studying aircraft design prior to about 1960 one cannot help noticing how some design teams, such as those led by Andrei N. Tupolev or Ed Heinemann, could produce a long succession of outstanding aircraft without a single bad one, while other designers had desperate struggles with everything they did. For example, Blackburn Aircraft appear frequently in these pages, but all their later disasters were to a large degree caused by trying to follow official specifications, which almost guaranteed useless aircraft. (How incredible that in following naval specification NA.39 Blackburn should have created the Buccaneer, so little appreciated as the greatest attack aircraft of its generation.)

Since 1960 important aircraft have tended to be created by huge faceless teams sitting in front of computer displays. The increase in manpower and the billion-fold increase in the speed of calculations result in each of today's aircraft taking not ten weeks but ten years.

Indeed, in the earliest days of aviation a new design might take a mere ten days. When World

War I began, a completely successful little fighter was designed, built and flight-tested near Southampton in seven. In that wonderful pioneering era many flying machines simply failed to fly. Nobody was shocked, just disappointed. A bit more power, plus some hit-and-miss 'tweaking', often did the trick. Even when the beast had been persuaded to rise from the ground, to quote Sir Thomas Sopwith, 'We used to crash a lot, but it was fun.'

On the other hand, there are plenty of examples of aircraft where repeated modifications made them worse. To this day, it is common to find that the production aircraft are so burdened by improvements that they are slower, shorter-ranged and have a lower ceiling than the prototype. There is little point in putting into this book pre-1914 aircraft that refused to leave the ground, but after about 1920 such a fault became inexcusable. The USA has even had one or two since 1970.

To be fair, these latter-day failures have been the result of aiming at a difficult objective. There is a small element of excuse for an unsatisfactory aircraft if the design targets are exceptionally challenging. For example, in the closing stages of World War II the Germans were faced with the frantic need to stem the onslaught of Allied bombers, and this led to such creations as the Me 163B, Ba 349 and BV 40. I put the BV 40 in this book because the idea of an engineless fighter is so novel, but the others were far more dangerous to their pilots than they were to the enemy. Whether with imagination this could have been foreseen is arguable.

At about the same time the Japanese got themselves into a similarly beleaguered situation, and fought back with *kamikaze* attacks on Allied ships. Such assaults began with lash-up conversions of existing fighter and attack aircraft, but soon specially designed 'delivery systems' were produced. The MXY-7 *Baka* is outside the scope of this book, because it was a manned suicide missile which did just what it was intended to do. On the other hand, the Nakajima Ki-115 *Tsurugi* (Sabre) was an ordinary aeroplane, but designed to fly suicide missions carrying a heavy bomb. If you are not coming back you don't bother about time between overhauls, or landing flaps, and your undercarriage (hardly 'landing gear') can be crude welded tube without shock absorbers, jettisoned after take-off. Thus it would be pointless to evaluate the Ki-115 on the same basis as other aircraft.

In the same year, 1945, the USAAF contracted with McDonnell Aircraft for a tiny jet fighter to be carried in the bomb bay of a B-36. It was to drop out over enemy territory, fight off hostile interceptors and then hook back on, fold its wings and tuck itself away for the long ride home. The resulting XF-85 Goblin was one of the oddest fighters in history. It was quite a good little machine in some respects, but seriously deficient in speed, endurance and firepower. What finally killed it was the difficulty, not to say danger, of trying to hook back on to a kind of trapeze. But when you think about it, how could such a machine be expected to win over a fighter able to use a 12,000-ft runway? In deadly combat this stumpy midget was surely always going to come off a good second.

Again, in the pioneer days of VTOL (vertical take-off and landing) the objectives were so difficult that compromises were inevitable. Quite a lot of contrasting VTOLs have made it on to these pages, either because they were so dangerous to fly, or because (with hindsight, of course) they can be seen to have been non-starters. On the other hand, two gigantic early bombers are not included. The US Army Barling was simply a poor performer. The British Tarrant Tabor suffered from the fact that, at low airspeeds, such as at the start of a take-off, there was no way of countering the nose-down overturning moment imparted by the pull of the two highest engines on the topmost wing. Frankly, this surely ought to have been foreseen.

One of the stories, dealing with a little racer of 1922, makes the comment that just after World War II so-called tailless aircraft were all the rage. To try to find out how such machines should be designed, Britain tested several tailless gliders. One of these, the General Aircraft GAL.56, was judged to be the worst aircraft ever tested by Captain E.M. 'Winkle' Brown, who in my opinion is the greatest living pilot. Limiting the count strictly to pilot-in-command, and treating a dozen or two marks of Spitfire and Seafire (for example) as one aircraft, he has 487 types in his log books.

He was one of many people I questioned about the famous comment supposed to have been made in a wartime Boscombe Down evaluation: 'Entry to this aircraft is difficult. It should be made impossible.' This was doing the rounds fifty years ago, when I was in uniform, and everyone knew that it was in the assessment of the Botha, except for those who insisted it was written about the Buckingham. In fact, I am persuaded that this is an apocryphal story without basis in fact.

Of course, in writing a book like this the author has to rely for the earliest types on the available written record. This can be inaccurate, or at least misleading. It is all too easy to clutch at a statement as gospel merely because it was published at the time. I apologise to the memory of any designer whose work I have castigated unfairly on the basis of something written by an uninformed or partisan chronicler who, for whatever reason, did not quite present the whole picture. In addition, there are dozens, if not hundreds, of types of aircraft which had a very short active life, being scrapped or just left to rot for reasons which have not been handed down to us.

Sadly, it does not matter what you are like but what people say or think you are like. When I began to write this book people in New York, Washington and Florida were scared to visit London, because they thought they might be blown up. It would have done little good to explain that they were far more likely to be murdered in their own cities! In the same way, in the years immediately following World War I, almost every American knew that two of the most dangerously flawed aircraft in the sky were the DH.4 and the Bristol Fighter. The fact that thousands of both types had put up a splendid record in British service was hardly noticed. 'Give a dog a bad name' is nowhere truer than in aviation.

Even today damning reports appear from time to time about aircraft which are either commercial rivals or else merely 'foreign'. I don't mean hostile foreign but friendly foreign, which really makes American hackles rise. In the 1970s, when the Tornado was called the MRCA, it was rubbished by US magazines because it posed a possible commercial threat. For the same reason, I now read in [US] *Air Force Magazine* that the Eurofighter 'doesn't measure up . . . an existing fighter might be a better buy [but] going with a foreign fighter would throw thousands of Germans out of work'. See what I mean about getting the wrong idea from something written at the time?

Of course, contemporary records occasionally give an impression of false goodness. Of all the Allied planemakers in World War II the most publicised failure was Brewster Aeronautical Corporation. Their SB2A dive bomber (British name Bermuda) and F2A fighter (Buffalo) were total disasters, and when Brewster were asked instead to make the outstanding Chance Vought Corsair they failed miserably even at that. Yet on 23 December 1941 the British Ministry of Aircraft Production sent them the following cable: 'All pilots praise the Buffalo's fine speed and manoeuvrability. An RAF pilot reconnoitring over Thailand was attacked and pursued by five Japanese naval aircraft and seven Messerschmitt 110s [*sic*] but outpaced and outwitted all of them. Other Buffalos piloted by Australians in the Penang raid shot down four out of nine Japanese dive bombers.' One wonders what such rubbish was meant to accomplish.

Countless good aircraft have come to grief through being called upon to operate in an unexpectedly harsh environment. In World War II plenty of Allied aircraft, especially those with tail wheels, proved unable to stand up to prolonged operations from Soviet front-line airstrips paved with boards or tree-trunks. The Fairchild Cornell trainer may have been safe at sea level, but when I flew one in Southern Rhodesia on a hot day at an airfield 4,860 ft above sea level I nearly abandoned the terrifyingly long take-off. The DH Mosquito was one of the greatest war-winners, but post-war service in the tropics added it to the list of DH aircraft which came unglued – in this case, literally.

And so on. There is no slick assessment that will sort aircraft into good and bad. And in any case the purpose of this book is not to instruct but to entertain – but it might make people think a bit.

ROYAL AIRCRAFT FACTORY BE.2

In the Introduction the point is emphasised that there are all sorts of bad aeroplanes. Very often a good design, hailed universally as a major step forward, has later proved to be either obsolete in an era of fast-moving technology or else utterly unsuited to an environment which nobody had the foresight to imagine at the time of its design. The BE.2 and its successors came into the second category.

The problem lay in the fact that in 1911–12 there was nobody in Britain in any position of authority who had any experience of aviation, or understanding of what aeroplanes might do (or very quickly be developed to do), or imagination of what might happen in any future war. Every officer was steeped in the doctrine of either the Army or the Royal Navy. A few of the most junior were flying enthusiasts, and were even seeking permission to learn to fly at their own expense, but the generals, admirals and Ministers of the Crown regarded flying machines as things in which no gentleman would show any interest. There is abundant evidence that their minds were virtually closed to any kind of discussion on the subject. The official view is encapsulated in two quotes. From the Admiralty: 'Their Lordships foresee no practical application for flying machines in naval service.' From the Secretary of State for War: 'We do not consider that aeroplanes will be of any possible use for war purposes.'

It is important to remember this background of total ignorance when reading the story of the BE. Put another way, it is the easiest thing in the world to be wise after the event. Having said that, anyone in any way responsible for British defence (in the widest sense) might have been expected to pay some attention to the important roles played by aeroplanes in conflicts in North Africa, the Balkans and Mexico in 1911–12, and to important bombing and gunnery trials in France, Germany and Italy. Had they done so, the inevitability of war in the air – air/ground, ground/air and air/air – would have been self-evident.

What happened was that in May 1912 the Royal Flying Corps was established, and military trials were announced to decide which aeroplane was best suited to equip the RFC. These trials were the kind of things officials and senior officers love to get their teeth into. Enormous effort was ex-

pended arguing about the details, whilst overlooking the really important things. One of the latter was that the Royal Aircraft Factory at Farnborough possessed far more aircraft design expertise and experience than the rest of the country combined, yet, because the Factory was supposed to be forbidden actually to design or make aeroplanes, it was not allowed to take part in the trials! So the £5,000 first prize went to S.F.Cody's utterly obsolete machine, which won solely because of its reliable and powerful engine.

By far the best aircraft at the trials was the BE.2, but officially it was not allowed to take part because it had been designed at the Factory by Geoffrey de Havilland. To modern eyes it may look archaic, but seen against Cody's contraption it was positively futuristic. It was in all respects a classic example of the conventional aeroplane, with biplane wings, an enclosed fuselage, tractor engine and propeller on the nose, simple tail at the back and undercarriage with two wheels at the front and a skid at the tail. The engine was a 70-hp Renault air-cooled vee-8 driving a four-blade propeller. There were two cockpits in tandem, the pilot being behind the observer. Lateral control was effected by warping (twisting) the wings, and the tail comprised a fixed tailplane, hinged elevators and a rudder, there being no fin. Skids projected ahead of the wheels to protect against nosing over, and the lower wings were likewise protected by curved skids near the tips.

BE stood for Blériot Experimental, which simply meant that it was a tractor machine, not a pusher. The original BE.1 had been created by ostensibly 'repairing' another aircraft, but as the original machine had been a primitive Voisin pusher we can see that the 'repair' was merely a way of getting round the rule that Farnborough was not allowed to make aeroplanes. When the excellence of the BE.2 was recognised, Cody's machine was forgotten. About 150 BE.2, 2a and 2b aircraft were delivered by seven contractors. It would be an exaggeration to state that no two were alike, but there were numerous small or large differences. Though used mainly as trainers, these early BEs saw much action in 1914–15, dropping bombs of up to 100 lb and with the observer armed with a pistol, revolver, carbine or even a machine-gun.

The BE.2e, an example of which is seen here, was the most numerous version of all. It was just as lethal as its predecessors; unable to manoeuvre in combat and with the observer still in the front cockpit.

What happened next was that E.T. Busk, a young Cambridge graduate, joined the staff of the Factory, was taught to fly by de Havilland, and then carried out a courageous and exhaustive programme of research into the stability of aeroplanes. Among other things this resulted in the BE.2c, a development of the BE series with exceedingly strong natural stability. Externally the 2c did not look very different, apart from having stagger (upper wing ahead of the lower), dihedral (wings sloping up from root to tip), four ailerons instead of warping, and a fixed fin. There was no reason to doubt that, when it first flew in June 1914, the 2c was the best aeroplane in Britain. In particular, its strong natural stability was clearly a great advantage in the only role that could be foreseen for military aircraft, namely reconnaissance. Major Sefton Brancker took the new prototype up to 2,000 ft over Farnborough, set the nose towards Netheravon, closed the throttle, took his hands off the controls and wrote a recon report of everything below, never touching the controls again until he was 20 ft from the grass of Netheravon airfield.

Accordingly, when Britain found herself at war on 4 August 1914, the BE.2c was ordered in unprecedented numbers. Over the next two years it was developed into the 2d and 2e, but all were to the same basic highly stable design. More than 3,200 were built in Britain by twenty-two contractors, and others were built in Australia. In the first half of the war the BE was by far the most numerous front-line aircraft of the RFC, equip-ping Nos. 2, 4, 5, 6, 7, 8, 9, 10, 12, 13, 15, 16 and 21 squadrons. It would have been an excellent reconnaissance aircraft, but for one small factor that had been overlooked: there were also other aeroplanes in the sky, adorned with black crosses.

Before the war several writers had suggested that a country at war would try to interfere with the aerial operations of its enemy. Some even envisaged exchanges of fire between airships. Nobody really put their finger on the problem and pointed out that the more inherently stable an aeroplane was, the easier it would be to shoot down. The RFC was to learn this basic fact in the hardest possible way from the late summer of 1915. Until then aerial fighting had been occasional, experimental and often indeterminate. What changed matters was the entry to service of the Fokker E (*Eindecker*) monoplane. Small, low-powered and not much faster even than a BE, these possessed one deadly new attribute: a machine-gun (or even two or three) fitted with an interrupter gear, so that the pilot could aim the whole aircraft at the enemy and fire straight ahead, through the disc of the propeller.

The monoplane's agility and firing accuracy made it into a deadly killing machine. It shot down British aircraft in droves, but BEs suffered more casualties than all other types combined. If a BE encountered an *Eindecker* it was almost certainly doomed, unless it could try to escape by flying into a cloud – though this was likely to be almost as lethal, for without blind-flying instruments a pilot swiftly became disoriented. The BE did not have the speed to run away, could not escape by climbing (it took forty-five minutes to reach its ceiling of 10,000 ft), could not manoeuvre out of the enemy's aim and could not shoot back. With the pilot in the rear cockpit, the observer had to sit in front, where any attempt to fire a gun was thwarted by the upper wing, propeller, struts and wires. Every conceivable kind of armament installation was experimented with, to no avail. No. 6 Squadron even tried lowering a weighted cable, hoping to entangle it with an enemy's propeller. The score on this occasion was, inevitably, Fokker 1, BE 0. British newspapers described the BE as 'Fokker Fodder'.

One might have expected the pilot and observer to change places. In fact the BE.2d usually had dual controls, but it was still almost always flown from the rear. The final BE.2 variant, the e, reverted to having pilot controls in the rear only. Strangely, BE.2c aircraft of the Belgian air force were modified to put the observer in the rear, and to have a proper armament scheme of a synchronised Vickers and pivoted Lewis, yet they seem to have fared little better than their defenceless British brethren.

Amazingly, production of the later BE.2 versions continued until July 1917, long after the skies over the Western Front had become filled by the Fokker, Albatros, Halberstadt, Roland and Pfalz fighters of the gaily coloured Circuses. To continue to send BEs to that theatre would have been obscene, and in fact by 1917 almost all were in less deadly kinds of employment.

'Thus,' writes historian Jack Bruce, 'these unwilling warriors – for the BE was originally designed to be merely a stable aeroplane, not a fighting aircraft – ended their days in comparative peace. But they achieved a kind of immortality, for they were regarded as the embodiment of the Government-designed aeroplane, mass-produced by official order, yet inefficient, ineffective and inferior for all military purposes. To blame the BEs themselves would be to misjudge them, for they were safe and reliable flying machines, lacking only the performance and manoeuvrability necessary to survive the ever-increasing intensity of aerial warfare. The fault lay with those who continued to order the BEs and, worse still, send them to war long after they were obsolete.'

WIGHT TWIN AND QUADRUPLANE

One should not be too critical of aircraft designed over seventy years ago, especially as during World War I the belligerent nations needed every aeroplane they could get. This meant that large numbers of designs were put forward by people with little or no previous experience of flying machines. The Wight types, however, were designed by Howard T. Wright, who had been flying and (to some degree) designing before the war. For some reason he eschewed normal aerofoil profiles in favour of an odd section of his own which had pronounced camber near the leading and trailing edge and an almost flat middle portion. It can easily be shown that this is inefficient.

Wright was taken on in 1912 by J. Samuel White & Co., the famous Cowes boat-builders, to organise and manage an aviation department. This opened on the first day of 1913, by which time Wright, assisted by T.C. Letcher, had already completed the design of the first product, the Pusher Seaplane. It was a large machine held together by a forest of struts, and I am certain it was never able to take off, even on the power of its 160-hp Gnome engine. In the early 1950s I was

delighted to meet E.C. Gordon England, one of the most famous early pilots, who test-flew all the Wight aircraft (the name Wight, by the way, was a play on White, Wright and the Isle of Wight). He told me that, even when fitted with the 200-hp Salmson Canton-Unné water-cooled radial the original seaplane had a pathetic performance. Despite this, seven were supplied to the Royal Naval Air Service, and two of these made reconnaissance flights over the Turkish forts along the Dardanelles. When one considers that these missions were probably flown within a mile of thousands of Turkish guns at a speed of some 55 mph, the courage of the pilots is obvious.

Among various tractor and twin-fuselage machines Wight then built for the RNAS a further batch of big pusher seaplanes. These were to be torpedo carriers, and so were powered by the 225-hp Sunbeam Mohawk water-cooled vee-12. One machine, possibly the first, No. 831, took off from Calshot on 10 October 1914 and laboriously managed to climb to 3,000 ft in 25 minutes. It was later called the Type A.II Improved Navyplane, and on 22 March 1915 Squadron Commander J.L. Travers

RNAS No. 1451 was the third Wight Twin. Like the others, with torpedo (as seen here) and a full load of fuel it was unable to take off.

took No 831 out from Calshot on a trial with a torpedo. It proved to be unable to taxi faster than 20 knots and thus was quite incapable of getting anywhere near leaving the water.

Wight produced several further seaplanes and the odd landplane, of which the most generous assessment must be that they were undistinguished.

But their final effort was enough to cause even their test pilot to 'ask that he might be excused'. England was a man of courage and experience, and he probably knew a lot more about aircraft design than Mr Letcher, who was really responsible for this supposed single-seat fighting scout. The seeming brilliance of the Sopwith Triplane, first flown in

This is how the Wight Quadruplane Scout looked when it was built.

late May 1916, apparently made the Wight management think four wings would be even better. Koolhoven's effort in the Armstrong Whitworth FK series (see page 22) was merely unsatisfactory; the Wight was almost certainly dangerous in its original form.

In this original form, while the length was 20 ft 9 in, the upper three wings all had a span of 19 ft and the bottom wing somewhat less. An odd feature was that the front and rear struts between the three upper wings, and the steeply inclined cabane struts, were all faired together with fabric, while all struts lower down were exposed. The wings, which had Wright's 'double camber' aerofoil, were individually very small, and the fact that the span was less than the fuselage length was extraordinary for 1916. The fuselage fitted between the two middle wings. On the front was a fully cowled 110-hp Clerget rotary, while at the back was a fin and rudder that looked obviously too small. The upper three wings had ailerons. Strangest of all, the wheels were recessed into the leading edge of the bottom wing, which meant that the aircraft had to have a gigantic tailskid to keep it in a roughly 3° attitude on the ground (in surviving photos the tail is being propped up even higher). Gordon England thought there was a good chance that, even at high power, the aircraft would never take off, the balance between angle of attack and skid drag proving incapable of solution.

Accordingly the Quadruplane was modified to the extent that it became a new aircraft. At least, the fuselage, wings, tail and undercarriage were all completely different. Gordon England did summon up the nerve to fly it in early 1917. I forget the exact wording, but when I asked him how much he flew it he certainly implied, 'As little as possible.' Later it received yet a third set of wings, with the tips and interplane struts sloping in from top to bottom. Jack Bruce records, 'It . . . was reported to have been written off at Martlesham on 2 February 1918. The wonder is that it lasted so long.'

Front gunners: SPAD A and BE.9

Of all the ways in which it is possible for a machine-gun to be installed at the front of an aeroplane, the most hair-raising is to provide a cockpit for a gunner immediately in front of a tractor propeller on the nose On first consideration this sounds impossible, yet it was a feature of several designs of the 1914–18 period, one of which was put into service in some numbers. The objective was to combine freedom to fire ahead with the better performance possible from a tractor propeller.

The most important aircraft in this class was the SPAD A series. It is hard to believe that these machines came from the drawing board of the gifted Louis Béchereau. He had previously designed the world-record Déperdussin racers, and his other SPAD fighters were masterly examples of design, over 15,000 being built. The crucial difference is that the later SPADs were fitted with gun interrupter or synchronising gear, to enable a machine-gun to fire ahead through the disc swept by the revolving propeller. Though several such mechanisms had been submitted to the French and British governments from 1912 onwards, these vitally important proposals had merely been filed away and ignored.

So in early 1915 Béchereau was among those who decided to fasten a small cockpit in front of an otherwise conventional fighting scout. To get the centre of gravity in the right place this meant moving the 80-hp Le Rhône engine as far back as possible, so that, to clear the propeller, the inboard leading edges of the biplane wings had to be cut away. Immediately in front of the propeller was mounted a lightly constructed nacelle containing a cockpit for a gunner able to aim a Hotchkiss or Lewis pivoted to a pillar on the extreme nose. The back of the nacelle was flat, and in the centre was a ball-bearing which located the front of the propeller shaft. Of course, this made it impossible to start the engine by a Hucks vehicle, with a drive shaft engaging in dogs on the front of the propeller. For major access the nacelle could be unbolted from the upper wing and pivoted forward from the brackets on the undercarriage.

That such an unpleasant and clearly dangerous concept should have been adopted by the Aviation Militaire is remarkable. In fact forty-two SPAD A2 aircraft were put into French front-line service. (Incidentally, a photograph shows one bearing the name *Ma Jeanne* and, as a strut obscures the fuselage immediately to the left of the first word, the author was instantly reminded of an Me 262 which bore the name *Wilma Jeanne*.) But the most determined users of the A2 were the Imperial

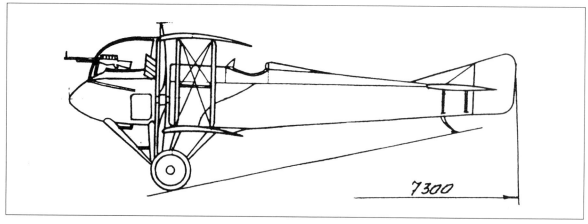

A Russian drawing of the SPAD A2.

Russian Air Service, which received fifty-seven and flew them intensively.

The A2 first flew on 21 May 1915. Powered in its production form by a 110-hp Le Rhône rotary, it reached just over 80 mph at sea level and 72 mph at 5,000 ft. The difficulties for the gunner were obvious. A simple wire guard was supposed to stop him from losing fingers or hands, but in the event of a nose-over landing he could hardly avoid serious injury. At least one Russian was killed in this manner, rather surprisingly during operations on skis from compacted snow. Despite this the Russians also bought twelve of a slightly developed version, the A4.

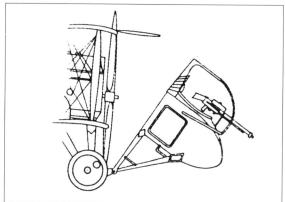

To get at the engine, the gunner cockpit of the SPAD A2 could be bodily pivoted forwards.

Known as 'the Pulpit', the BE.9 was predictably unpopular.

Britain's only attempt at this configuration came from no less a source than the Royal Aircraft Factory. The BE.9, also flown in early 1915, was basically a BE.2c with the engine moved as far back as possible in order to permit a nacelle for an observer/gunner to be added in front of the propeller. This nacelle, like that of the SPAD, was pivoted to the landing gear at the bottom and incorporated a ball-bearing for the front of the propeller shaft. Surprisingly, it was not connected anywhere else, except by thin bracing wires to the upper wing. As in the SPAD, it interfered with engine cooling and seriously degraded performance, maximum speed of the BE.9 being only 63 mph. I cannot resist quoting from *Wind in the Wires* by Lieutenant D.W. Grinnell-Milne, of RFC No. 16 Squadron:

"There was no communication possible between front and back seat; if anything happened, if the pilot were wounded, or even if nothing more serious occurred than a bad landing in which the machine tipped over on its nose, the man in the box could but say his prayers: he would inevitably be crushed by the engine behind him.

"One of these machines was attached to the Squadron in which I served; but by the merciful dispensation of Providence it never succeeded in defeating an enemy craft. Had it done so I have no doubt that brains of the Farnborough Factory would have rejoiced in their war-winning discovery, hundreds of 'Pulpits' would have been produced and in a short while we should not have had a living observer in France to tell the experts what it was like in that little box – for I feel sure no civilian expert ever risked his own life in it. However, even in 1915 when almost every new machine was looked at with delighted wonder, it was recognised that in the BE.9 unsuitability of design had reached its acme. The 'Pulpit' was soon returned to the depot."

BLACKBURN TB

The first aircraft to be designed for warlike purposes by Blackburn Aircraft – then of the Olympia Works in Leeds – was the TB, or Twin Blackburn. It had twin wings, twin engines, twin fuselages, twin cockpits, twin vertical tails and twin floats. It was designed in early 1915 to meet an Admiralty requirement for a long-range aircraft able to range far out over the North Sea by night and destroy Zeppelin airships. In some respects, considering how little was known about the design of combat aircraft in 1915, the TB was a creditable achievement. Unfortunately, like many Blackburn aircraft, it was never fitted with engines of adequate power. It also suffered from numerous other deficiencies, and though most could with a bit of thought have been rectified, the TB made no contribution to the war effort.

The TB was, of course, a wooden aircraft with fabric covering, except for the pontoon-type floats which were almost entirely wood. Each float was directly under its own fuselage, the floats being unconnected. As was usually the case in 1915, there were also two auxiliary floats at the tail. Blackburn was at the time in production with the BE.2c, and the TB rear fuselage and tail incorporated BE parts. The engines were meant to be the 150-hp Smith Static, an outstanding 10-cylinder radial. This never went into production, and – though several alternative engines of similar power were available – the decision was taken to fit the 100-hp Gnome Monosoupape. Thus, performance was reduced from exceptional (for 1915) to merely adequate, maximum speed being 86 mph and cruising speed about 70. Nine TBs were delivered to the RNAS, the last having 110-hp Clerget engines.

Lack of power restricted the weapon load to a single box of twenty-four Ranken darts. These were essentially small incendiary bombs with tails containing spring-loaded arms which, after the head had pierced an airship's envelope, arrested the dart so that it could ignite escaping gas. This box was in the cockpit of the observer, who had no means of communicating with the pilot in the other fuselage except by hand signals. This virtually precluded the exchange of any but the most obvious messages. Moreover, despite the fact that there were four ailerons, the wings deflected so that the control cables became slack, and if by any chance the pilot did manage to move the ailerons they did little except twist the wings (lateral control deficiencies rear their head constantly in this book). According

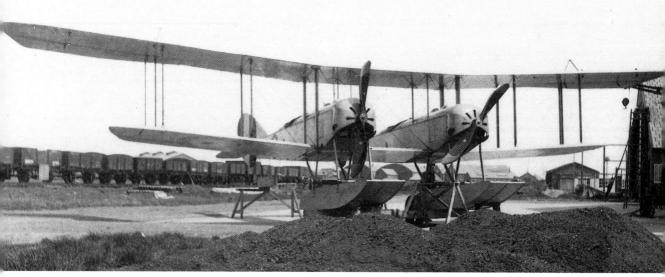

Two views of the first Blackburn TB, on the Isle of Grain.

to A.J. Jackson's 'Putnam' *Blackburn Aircraft since 1909* there was also a disconcerting amount of relative movement between the fuselages.

But for sheer hilarity, one can picture a TB being started. To quote Jackson:

"Starting on the water needed discipline, courage and agility, for a pool of excess petrol, which formed on the float when the Gnome was primed, promptly ignited when the engine fired. The observer's job was to lie on the lower centre section and put out the fire on the pilot's side with an extinguisher, scramble into his own cockpit to start the second engine and then leap out again to extinguish the fire on his own float."

DUFAUX FIGHTER

Several oddities resulted from the urgent need in 1916 to produce aircraft that could fire a machine-gun straight ahead, or in the forward hemisphere (for example, the 1916 escort and BE.9/SPAD A). There were also other ways, quite apart from the obvious one of a traditional pusher layout. Various designers found ways of making what looked like a conventional aeroplane but with the propeller behind the wings, revolving around the fuselage. Kasyanenko's No. 5 fighter of 1917 had the propeller behind the tail!

One designer who consistently achieved what at first glance looked impossible was Alphonse Gallaudet. Most of his aircraft for the US Navy had a normal fuselage and tail, with either one or two engines amidships between the biplane wings. They were geared to an internally toothed ring encircling the fuselage, and the four propeller blades were mounted on the outer face of this ring. I mention them not in a critical vein but to show that the basic idea worked. A broadly similar concept was patented in 1916 by the famous Swiss designer-pilot Armand Dufaux. He proposed that the aft end of the fuselage should be joined to the rest of the aircraft by a single tube. The outer surface of this tube was to provide a bearing for the hub of the propeller, which was to be extended forwards in the form of a gear driven by the engine.

Dufaux then put the idea into practice. His Société pour la Construction et l'Entretien (maintenance) d'Avions built the Dufaux scout in the first three months of 1916. It was quite a small biplane, noteworthy at first glance for its apparent absence of engine. Closer inspection revealed a 110-hp Le Rhône rotary mounted rather low in the fuselage, its cylinders spinning just in front of the rear spar of the lower wing. It was geared to a large two-blade propeller which rotated on the tube connecting the rear fuselage, and through which passed the controls to the rudder and elevators. Having the engine mounted internally amidships made the fuselage fairly portly. At the front it was wide enough for a pilot seated on the left and a gunner seated on the right, with a Lewis gun firing ahead. He could aim over a wide arc covering much of the forward hemisphere.

Apart from the main tube, the only connection

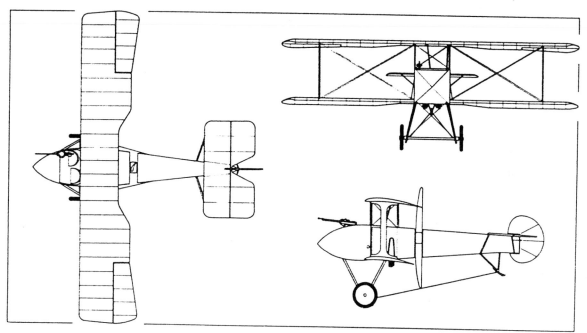

Three-view drawing of the Dufaux.

between the tail and the rest of the aircraft was a pair of thin tie-rods linking the bottom of the main undercarriage to the tailskid. These prevented the main tube from being overloaded in a heavy landing or, especially, when taxying over bumpy ground. The most that can be said of the Dufaux is that it did not suffer structural failure (so far as we know). Its performance was mediocre. It would have been better to have made it smaller and fixed

the gun to be fired ahead by the pilot. Even then, it is hard to see what advantage over a traditional pusher the clumsy and dangerous arrangement offered. Any modern designer would dislike the lack of redundancy in an aircraft structure whose two parts were connected by a single tube – a tube, moreover, carrying all the varied loads imparted by the propeller and the transmission from the spinning rotary engine.

THE 1916 ESCORTS: ARMSTRONG WHITWORTH FK.12, SOPWITH LRTTR AND VICKERS FB.11

This is another case in which I appear to pour scorn on harassed designers who were trying their best in an environment of ignorance. By 1916 the Fokker monoplanes were making life extremely difficult for the Allies, and especially for the pilots and observers of the luckless BEs. To get anything done at all, everyone who flew had to be surrounded by escorts. Jack Bruce cites the case of a BE of No. 12 Squadron which on 7 February 1916 was detailed to fly a reconnaissance mission escorted by 'three other BE.2cs, four FE.2bs, four RE.7s and a Bristol Scout – 12 machines in all'.

Not unreasonably, the War Office in London thought it was about time they issued a requirement for a long-range escort fighter. Of course, it was common knowledge that the main – indeed almost the only – reason for the Fokker's superiority was that it had a machine-gun firing straight ahead, past the blades of the revolving propeller.

One might have thought the instant response should have been to produce a more powerful British fighter with a similarly mounted gun with an interrupter or synchronising gear. Had the War Office searched wherever it was that inventors' proposals were allowed to gather dust, they would have found at least four such inventions submitted from 1911 onwards. Alternatively, of course, one could use a pusher engine, the tail being carried on widely spaced booms as on many pre-1910 aeroplanes, thus leaving the nose free for a forward-firing gun. The Airco DH.2 and Vickers FB.5 'Gunbus' were existing examples of RFC pusher fighters, and to achieve real ascendancy over the Fokkers all these needed was a modicum of redesign with more powerful engines.

Instead the mandarins of Whitehall became mesmerised by the conception of a larger aircraft with an endurance of seven hours and carrying

The Vickers FB.11 was remarkable only for its 'howdah' gunner nacelle on top.

With the LRTTr, Sopwith combined several odd features.

gunners able to fend off attackers without the aircraft itself having to manoeuvre. This avoided the need for a fixed gun with interrupter gear. Manufacturers were invited to use the new '250 hp Rolls-Royce', the vee-12 engine later named Eagle. Seven companies responded to the January 1916 specification, and I would love to have seen the drawings of the rejects!

There were three winners, and all built and flew their proposed designs. The least unconventional was the Vickers FB.11. At first glance it looked much like an Avro 504 or any other normal tractor biplane. There were differences, however. For one thing, it was large, the wings having a span of 51 ft, an area of 845 sq ft (compared with 434 sq ft for the DH.4 bomber, for example) and being 9 ft apart vertically. Second, though this was a mere detail, the superb engine was totally enclosed in a metal cowling with an air inlet at the front to cool the water radiator, which was inside the fuselage behind the engine, the hot air escaping through louvres in the sides of the fuselage. Like its two rivals, the FB.11 was a three-seater, with a pilot and two gunners. In the fuselage the pilot was fairly well aft, under the trailing edge of the upper wing, with the rear gunner immediately behind him, with a Lewis on a Scarff-ring mounting. The other gunner sat in solitary state in a nacelle projecting ahead of the centre of the upper wing. (Such nacelles were called 'howdahs' after the equally lofty canopied seats used on elephants.) He also had a Lewis on a Scarff-ring, covering the upper part of the forward hemisphere. He could climb up without a ladder, using recesses or projecting steps, though at one point this involved holding the

exhaust pipe, which one hoped was cold. Once in place he was 14 ft up, which must have been quite exciting even before take-off.

More seriously, there was no way the top gunner and pilot could communicate. Despite its fine engine, the FB.11 needed fifty-five minutes to climb to 10,000 ft, at which height its maximum speed was 81½ mph. Cruising speed is not recorded, but was obviously unimpressive, and lateral control was described as 'poor'.

Second of the proposed escorts was the Sopwith LRTTr. At this time Sopwith was one of the few companies with a track record of numerous successful designs, fresh examples of which were appearing every few weeks. Despite this, nobody thought to assign a logical series of designations, and this particular aircraft's odd appellation was short for Long-Range Tractor TRiplane. In configuration it was similar to the Vickers, apart from being a triplane and having an odd landing gear. It was really an early example of what we today call nose-wheel or tricycle gear, except that there were four wheels. In those days boys used to race 'soap box' carts running on wheels from discarded prams, and this seemed to have influenced the designers at Canbury Park Road. The Rolls-Royce engine was installed quite normally, with a frontal radiator. Oddly, despite being a triplane, the span was 53 ft, even greater than that of the Vickers. All struts were faired by fabric, there were six ailerons, and under the central part of the bottom wing was a hand-wheel-driven air-brake. Centred on the top wing was the nacelle for the upper of the two gunners. Study of photographs suggests that he needed a

In its original form the Armstrong Whitworth FK.12 was so weird the company refused to let it be flown.

ladder to get aboard. Bruce says that his gun commanded 'the entire upper hemisphere', but in fact his Lewis would have been pivoted on a pillar in front and thus would always have had to fire ahead. Nothing is known of the LRTTr's performance, but it was clearly an unimpressive and sluggish machine, and, said Bruce, 'probably dangerous'.

The third of the successful submissions, by Armstrong Whitworth, was even stranger than the others. It was built in two versions sufficiently different to be regarded as two quite separate designs, but both appear to have been designated FK.12. The designation implied that it was the twelfth design for the company by Frederick (Fritz, popularly known as 'Cully') Koolhoven, a Dutchman who later had his own company at Rotterdam. Right up until the Luftwaffe flattened his works on 10 May 1940 he was quite happy to offer unconventional answers to problems. The fact that the FK.12 is not his only entry in this book speaks for itself, and if the FK.11 had been completed I'm sure that would also have made the grade, because it would have had fifteen wings!

Both FK.12s were triplanes, with the middle wing much greater in span (62 ft) than the others. The relatively tiny fuselage was centred on the middle wing, but only just came as far as the leading edge. It is difficult to imagine how the structure was arranged, because the big engine sat right in the place where the spars should have been,

the four-blade propeller being inches in front of the leading edge. The quite small top and bottom wings had only a single bay of interplane struts and no ailerons. The radiators were tall rectangles fastened to the front of the struts joining the fuselage to the top wing. Beneath the nose a massive strut led down to twin wheels under the middle of the bottom wing. Under the outer interplane struts were small auxiliary wheels to stop the contrivance tipping over. Under the fuselage just behind the trailing edge of the bottom wing was a large pylon structure carrying a skid which kept the tail up. Against all this, the tail seemed disarmingly normal.

The pilot sat just behind the trailing edges. Looking straight ahead he had a fine view of the radiators, and of the two enormous gunner nacelles, which were mounted above the middle wing just beyond the disc of the propeller. It is difficult to see how the gunners could have got aboard or dismounted without a ladder. The aircraft was 17 ft high, and no inbuilt steps were apparent. Each gunner was to have had a Lewis on a pillar mounting. They would have had a good field of fire, which included each other. Each nacelle had a strong curved arch on its inner side which was presumably to protect the gunner's head in the event of the aircraft nosing over and the top wing collapsing.

In fact, this could never happen, because Captain I. Fairbairn-Crawford, AW's aircraft general manager, flatly refused to allow the FK.12 to be flown. This almost certainly precipitated Koolhoven's departure a few months later. The designer was, however, permitted to try again and make a second FK.12 with some of the more obvious deficiencies removed. The No. 2 aircraft, serial 7838, had two bays of interplane struts joining the top and bottom wings, a much larger fuselage mounted between the bottom and middle wings, a conventional nose with tractor propeller well out in front, a completely different tail and a new undercarriage with two pairs of wheels (still with track no wider than the fuselage), skids under the bottom wing to prevent rolling over, and a normal tailskid. The gunners' cockpits were in much smaller nacelles slung entirely beneath the middle wing and projecting ahead.

This time, perhaps with misgivings, Captain Fairbairn-Crawford allowed the FK.12 to be flown. Both Peter Legh and Lieutenant R. Payze carried out brief testing. It is hardly surprising that neither liked the aircraft, and its performance was disappointing. In any case, by this time the RFC was receiving sensible aircraft, such as the Sopwith 1½-strutter with a synchronised Vickers firing ahead and a Lewis at the back.

Incidentally, there were several other British aircraft at this time with gunners in 'howdah' nacelles on top, but the 1916 escort suggestions included particular oddities.

Even the completely different second FK.12 was a strange beast.

BIG BLÉRIOTS: THE TYPES 67, 71–75, 115 AND 125

In 1909 an early aviation reporter wrote, 'Priced at £400, Monsieur Blériot's monoplanes represent not only value for money but also the very best and most modern type of flying machine to be had at any price.' This was probably fair comment. Apart from rather weak and unreliable engines, the Type XI Mod (Cross-Channel) was an excellent, clean monoplane which represented a landmark in aeroplane design. But then something seemed to happen to our Louis. His aesthetic taste certainly deserted him, and towards the end of World War I he, or rather his hired designers, produced a series of four-engined aircraft which were quite astonishing in their ugliness.

It may be insidiously easy to follow a logical series of steps in going from the original requirement to the finished aircraft, without stopping to consider if the thing looks right. One can argue until the cows come home about this, but most designers of my acquaintance have adhered to the general belief that 'If it is right, it looks right.' The reverse is also usually true: 'If it looks wrong, then it is wrong.' These big Blériots were designed quite logically. How do you get lots of power from low-powered engines? Use several engines. How do you minimise the stability and control problem after engine failure? Mount all the engines as close to the longitudinal axis as possible.

The original requirement was a 1916 French *Concours des Avions Puissants* (competition for powerful aeroplanes). The objective was a bomber with such speed and firepower that it would need no escort. To be frank, nearly all the designs and prototypes built to this requirement were visibly also-rans, but Blériot deserves special mention for persisting with, if anything, even more bizarre aircraft. The aircraft built to compete in the *Concours* was the Type 67. A biplane with long, untapered wings, it had four engines arranged in a square, two on the top wing and two on the lower, all of them tractors. To minimise the asymmetric problem the engines on each wing were placed as close together as possible, the propellers almost touching. This in turn meant that the fuselage had to be halfway between the wings, and as the lower wing was quite high off the ground this meant that, even with an outsize tailskid, the fuselage sat at a very steep angle. One cannot criticise the tail, with two horizontals and three verticals, because that was par for the course with large machines in 1917, but one might think thirty-two struts rather an excessive number to link the upper and lower engines.

The most fundamental weakness, however, was

Seen here with a SPAD XV, the Blériot 75 was one of the better-looking of this grotesque family.

The ill-fated first Blériot 115.

that the Type 67 was hardly an *avion puissant*. The engines were 100-hp Gnome 9b rotaries. With only 400 hp available with which to overcome the built-in headwind, the first Blériot bomber reached just 70 mph at full throttle. I do not know the bomb load, but it must have been hardly worth bothering about.

Nothing daunted, Blériot's Ingénieur Touillet rightly decided that more power was needed. Accordingly Types 71–75 followed, though they were not all constructed, and certainly not in numerical order. The 74 Bn4 (Type 74 night bomber, four seats) was originally planned around four Gnomes, but fortunately reason prevailed and it was actually completed with 220-hp Hispano-Suiza vee-8s. Tested in 1919, it proved to be almost as useless as its predecessor. Cruising speed was only a little better at 65 mph, handling character-istics were described as 'malicious', and it offered the choice of either fuel for a short range or a small bomb load and no fuel. In parallel the Type 71 was built, with the same layout and engines, but little is known about it.

Trying to do better, Touillet was at the same time designing a larger bomber, the Type 73. Doubtless he really did his best with this air-craft, which had four of the excellent Hispano 8Fb engines of 300 hp each. The objective was to carry 1 tonne (2,205 lb) of bombs for a useful range. Sadly, the result was grotesque, resembling a high-pooped galleon riding on a large pram at each side. For a change the fuselage was brought down beneath the lower wing, but the tail was kept in the same place, resulting in the bizarre upswept aft end The struts linking the upper and lower engines were greatly simplified, but their mid-points were joined by a clumsy rectangular frame of a configuration which showed that the structure was technically as bad as the aerody-namics. Whether the Type 73 Bn3 ever reached its brochure maximum speed of 81 mph is uncertain, but there is no doubt that the claimed figures for weights and bomb load (for useful ranges) were a pipe-dream. In any case, this monstrosity had a short life, because on 22 January 1919, on the 73's second or third flight, when it was en route to the

Few aircraft have appeared more grotesque – at least to my eye – than the big Blériots. This example was the ill-fated Type 73, reminiscent of a high-pooped galleon riding on a pair of perambulators. (Malcolm Passingham.)

Blériot factory at Buc for modifications, it broke up in the air. The pilot, wartime ace Armand Berthelot, was killed.

Later the Type 74 was re-engined with 300-hp Hispanos, and improved in various other ways. Blériot also built a civil transport version, the 75 Aérobus, or Mammoth, noteworthy for its bizarre whale-like bulged fuselage.

By 1923 Blériot had progressed to the Type 115 airliner. This looked relatively sensible, the only odd features being the projecting bay windows round the nose for the navigator, and the two open cockpits above the eight-seat passenger cabin! The engines were 180-hp Hispano vee-8s. The prototype suffered a jammed aileron when barely a month old, and crashed. The second, which repeated the same F-ESBB registration, actually won a prize at the 1923 *Grand Prix des*

Avions de Transport, but the prize money was reduced by 30 per cent because it could not average 100 kph (62 mph)!

Much later, in 1931, the Blériot 125 appeared. This passenger transport had a monoplane wing, in the centre of which was a nacelle housing two 550-hp Hispano-Suiza engines in the then-popular tandem push/pull arrangement, with the three-seat crew cabin in the middle of the nacelle. Under the wing were two giant bulging fuselages, extended at the back to carry the tail. Each fuselage seated six passengers, who could see the other six but were unable to communicate with them, or with the crew. Designer Léon Kirste spent the whole of 1931–33 trying to make this final disaster fly well enough to qualify for a Service Technique certificate. He failed, and the 125 was scrapped in 1934.

SUPERMARINE NIGHT HAWK

An author is always on tricky ground when he writes about something of which he has no personal knowledge. I never knew Noel Pemberton-Billing, nor any of his aircraft. I will leave it to the reader to decide whether the Night Hawk ought to be in this book or not.

P-B was one of the many 'larger than life' characters who populated the world of aviation in the first half of this century. He did everything imaginable, with colossal drive and enthusiasm. When World War I broke out he said to his small team at Woolston, Southampton, 'Right, we must build a small scout. Nobody goes home until it's finished.' And they didn't. The design process occupied all of twenty-four hours, and eight days later Victor Mahl made the first flight. What's more, the PB.9 was a very fine little aircraft and had quite a long career. But P-B was also a naval officer, company chairman, Member of Parliament, author, military planner, pilot (having taken a whole day off to learn and qualify), aircraft designer and ceaseless critic of what he forever saw as an inept government.

He was the very last person to see a problem and fail to do something about it. In 1915 it was all too obvious that Britain had essentially no defence against raiding German airships. In one night P-B worked out that what was needed was a kind of aerial cruiser that could 'lie in wait for Zeppelins', carried out all the preliminary design, and began to

complete the working drawings. This time the aircraft was far bigger and more complex than the PB.9, and no doubt P-B was ashamed that the design and construction of the PB.29 took seven weeks.

The PB.29 was a large quadruplane, underpowered by two 90-hp Austro-Daimler water-cooled engines. The lack of power was not considered serious, because the idea was that the aircraft would climb up to airship height and then potter about, with the ability to remain over the same spot in a breeze of 28 mph. A Lewis machine-gun was to be mounted above the top wing, but before this was installed the machine crashed at Chingford, not necessarily because of any fault.

Chingford – today a sea of houses – was in those days a Royal Naval Air Station, and the RNAS thought P-B's concept worth taking further. The result was the PB.31E Night Hawk, and it first flew in February 1917, at RNAS Eastchurch. Anyone seeing it for the first time – especially if it was airborne – must have gasped.

The Night Hawk was the ultimate expression of P-B's anti-airship weapon platform. It was again designed as a slow-flying night patroller, but it was far more refined than its predecessor. It was again a quadruplane, with wings of high aspect ratio for maximum efficiency at very low speeds. To ensure good lateral control at speeds around 40 mph it had eight ailerons. The fuselage joined the two middle

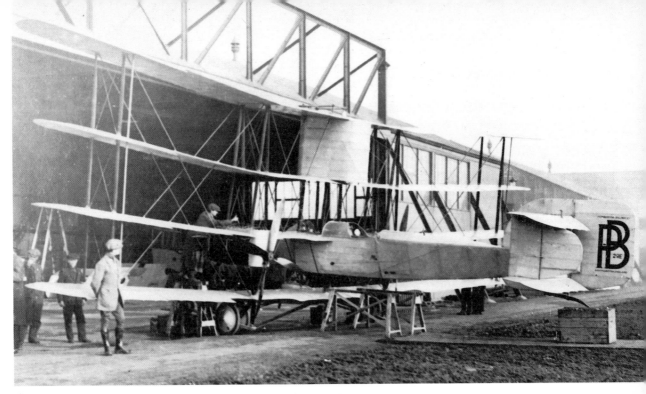

Pemberton-Billing's first attempt at a Zeppelin-killer was the PB.29E.

wings, but the pilot was inside a large enclosure with windows all round which extended up to the top wing. Steps up this enclosure led to an open 'howdah' at the top from which could be fired a Davis recoilless gun. The size chosen was the 1.5-pounder, and twenty rounds were carried. Immediately behind the Davis was a Scarff-ring mount for a Lewis machine-gun, and a second Lewis was on another Scarff mount in the nose, ahead of the pilot. P-B once claimed there were four Lewises, and also described a 'special revolver', like today's rotary missile launchers, with which an incendiary flare could be dropped 'every 20 feet, so that in straddling a 65-ft Zeppelin at least three would strike'.

The Night Hawk was full of other innovations. Perhaps the most outstanding was a powerful (2.25 kW) searchlight in the nose. The generator was driven by a 5-hp ABC flat-twin engine, whose exhaust heat helped to keep the cabin warm. The searchlight could be aimed almost anywhere ahead of the aircraft by a lever in the front gunner's

Just completed at the Woolston, Southampton, factory, the PB.31E bore national insignia.

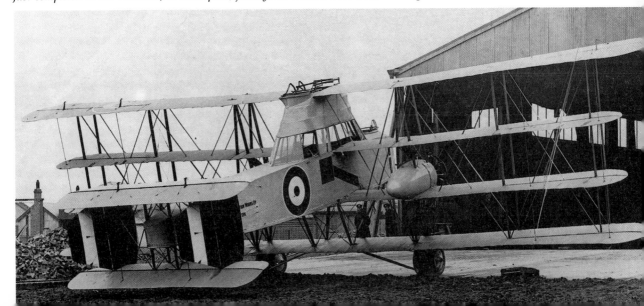

cockpit. The light was to assist in landing at night, when the wide track of the main undercarriage was also an advantage. P-B said there was a sleeping berth for off-duty members of the five-man crew. In fact the weight schedule allowed for a crew of only three, all of whom were needed all the time, and no bed was installed. This could have been hard on an eighteen-hour mission, especially in winter. A ton of petrol was carried in nine tanks, any of which could rapidly be isolated following damage. All flight and engine controls, and all petrol pipes, were said to be 'carried outside the fuselage in armoured casings'. Altogether it sounds a true battleship of the skies, yet P-B calculated that two 100-hp Anzani 10-cylinder radials would provide adequate power.

In his classic *British Aeroplanes 1914–18* J.M. Bruce says, 'It seems probable that the non-adoption of this big quadruplane was attributable to the successes achieved in the autumn of 1916 against enemy airships by standard types of Service machines armed with standard weapons.' A more likely, or at least additional, reason would seem to be that this fantastic battlewagon was one of the most useless aerial weapons ever created. Whereas P-B himself stipulated the requirement as 'a machine able to reach at least 80 mph . . . to climb to 10,000 feet in 20 minutes . . .' the official trials with the only Night Hawk to be completed showed the maximum speed to peak at 60 mph at 6,500 ft (being 55 mph at sea level and slightly less at 10,000 ft) and to need a full sixty minutes to climb to 10,000 ft, which could be regarded as the practical ceiling. Thus, this Zeppelin destroyer was actually slower than its quarry, and had a ceiling only half as high. To destroy an airship it would have had to encounter one at the same place, height and time by sheer chance. Should this incredible event have come to pass, the airship could have risen at five times the Night Hawk's best rate of climb merely by dropping ballast.

Who'd have thought that one member of the design team would later produce the Spitfire? His name was Reginald Mitchell.

KENNEDY GIANT

This story throws light on the way major defence contracts were managed during World War I, at least in the new and challenging field of aviation. It is said, 'In the country of the blind, the one-eyed man is King.' It certainly appears that in the opening months of that conflict anyone with even the faintest semblance of a track record in aircraft design could – if he was obviously 'a gentleman' – get himself a juicy contract to design and build at least the prototype of some wonderful new warplane.

There appears to have been only the most cursory cross-examination of the would-be constructor in order to establish precisely what he had accomplished in the past, or what his qualifications might be. Even more surprising, it is clear that not very much interest was shown in the numerical specification of the proposed aircraft, or what it was intended to accomplish.

To be frank, eighty years ago it was difficult to assess a proposed design. If a smooth-talking individual could produce a three-view and some suggested figures for dimensions, weights and performance, I am persuaded that – if they seemed plausible – these would immediately have been accepted at face value. Indeed, there is no evidence that Mr C.J.H. Mackenzie Kennedy produced even as much as this when he said to the War Office in London, 'I can build you a giant bomber, the biggest aeroplane in the world.'

He related how he had assisted Igor Sikorsky with the design and construction of the fabulous series of IM (*Ilya Mourometz*) reconnaissance bombers in the Russia of Tsar Nicholas II. He had certainly been there. In 1905 he had arrived with little but five pounds in his pocket and a lot of innate *savoir faire*. Starting from scratch he had made a host of useful connections, which he increasingly translated into valid business, though his Aeronautical Machines Co. made only copies of Voisin aeroplanes, plus the odd machine to a customer's own design.

Sikorsky told me that Kennedy had never actually worked for him. There seems little doubt that, having carefully studied the IM designs, Kennedy decided to try his luck back in Britain with the proposal that he should build something similar. He met an astute businessman named Hamilton Edwards, and it was he who signed the contract of 7 July 1915. This required delivery of 'One Sikor-

One of the less-familiar photographs of the Kennedy, showing its final form.

sky, No. 2337, four 200-hp Salmson'. This water-cooled radial engine was inadequate for the huge biplane Kennedy proposed, and it was notorious for its high drag.

Kennedy Aeroplanes Ltd was established in palatial offices at 102 Cromwell Road near the South Kensington museums. Here Kennedy produced simple drawings of a giant bomber made of wood, with steel plates at the joints and a mix of ply and fabric skin. Struts and wires abounded. The fuselage was a rectangular box, the nose hardly projecting ahead of the unequal-span wings. Had Kennedy known about the Dorner Rs I flying-boat he would certainly have made the span greater than 142 ft, in order to make good his claim of 'world's largest aeroplane'. Tucked well in on each side above the lower wing were the engines, in push/pull tandem pairs. At the back were a huge lifting tailplane (the centre of gravity being behind the centre of lift) and a tiny rudder. Underneath was a vast assemblage of struts holding the wheels and skids.

Kennedy wisely subcontracted the actual design and manufacture, mainly to the newly formed Fairey Aviation Co. and to the Gramophone Co. (later HMV, then EMI). Both were at Hayes, Middlesex, and the completed parts were trucked to Northolt, where the Kennedy Giant was put together in the open in the winter of 1916–17. At one point, when the monster was being man-oeuvred on soft ground, it broke its back. At last, around June 1917, Lieutenant Frank Courtney – then an instructor at Northolt – was ready to make the first test flight. He probably had his doubts even before he got on board, but what actually happened was that the tailskid stayed scraping along Mother Earth, no matter how hard the engines and wings tried to lift up front. Later there was some argument about whether the entire aircraft did briefly part company with *terra firma*. Certainly it never flew in the accepted sense, though getting the main wheels off the ground did qualify for the War Office's payment for 'One Sikorsky'.

Obviously the centre of gravity (CG) was much too far aft. Kennedy decided the simplest answer was to add weight up front, so he made the nose 8 ft longer, which improved the appearance. He also greatly enlarged the rudder, which clearly needed doing. An aerodynamicist would say that to drive the ailerons by push/pull rods carried on trunnions about 2 in above the wing leading edge was the most certain way of ruining wing lift, but the rods stayed. One who did not stay was Courtney; he had had enough, and wanted to survive to become one of Britain's most famous test pilots. Nearly forty years later, at his home at La Jolla, California, he told me, 'I did not have the slightest doubt that, had I ever got the Kennedy properly into the air, I would have been unable to bring it back to the airfield for a controlled landing.' In any case, thought Courtney, it was never going to make the slightest contribution to the war effort.

It may be unfair to be too critical of the Giant, or Super Sikorsky as it was also dubbed. I am sure that No. 2337 was designed and built in good faith, and there is every reason to believe that Kennedy genuinely wanted to create a bomber capable of

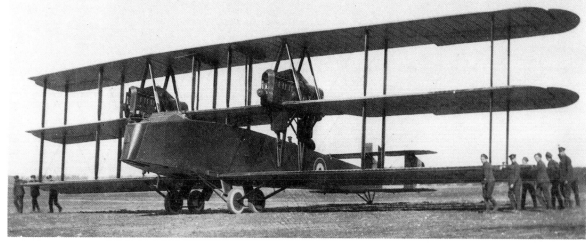

First of the Bristol triplanes, the Braemar Mk I bomber.

being put into service in numbers. Could he have been expected to comprehend that such a task was beyond his capability? In practice, perhaps he was just another of that prolific species who love to invent something, and who then immediately start inventing something else and forget about the first objective. Even before the first attempts to fly the

Giant, Kennedy was busy with a more modern bomber, with a much smaller and more sensible airframe with gunners in the extreme nose and tail. But, as any aircraft constructor will tell you, to stay in business (which Kennedy didn't) you have to do more than build a prototype; you have to sell in quantity.

Unlike the publicised Pullman, not many photographs of the Tramp exist. This was the No. 1 aircraft. The engines were in the fuselage, which was the main reason why neither ever flew.

BRISTOL TRIPLANES:
BRAEMAR, PULLMAN AND TRAMP

Like Sopwith and several other firms which had made large profits during World War I, the British & Colonial Aeroplane Co. was wound up in 1920 to escape a huge tax bill, and replaced by the Bristol Aeroplane Co. While this was going on, their chief designer, W.T. Reid, was working on a series of large triplanes. Their basic aerodynamic design might be criticised as obsolescent, but in fact they were not bad flying machines. They rate inclusion here because of the suggestion that they should be powered by steam turbines!

The original requirement, in 1917, was for a long-range heavy bomber. The basic layout was drawn by Reid's predecessor, Captain Frank Barnwell. It seems strange to us today that, having built in a colossal 'headwind' with the clumsy triplane layout, he should then have put the four engines inside the fuselage, driving a large tractor propeller on each wing. This was partly to save drag, but also in order that the engines should be accessible to the crew in flight. In another of my books, for PSL, *Giants of the Sky*, there is quite a long section on the enormous German bombers with such a layout, which had much to commend it when such things as pipe connections and valve springs were likely to break on every flight. The other side of the coin was that the clutches, gears and shafting were very heavy and prone to give as much trouble as the engines themselves. So on balance the idea was unattractive.

Reid, at that time Barnwell's assistant, was almost certainly right when he altered the bomber to have four Siddeley Puma engines in conventional tandem push/pull nacelles on the middle wings. The result was the Braemar I, first flown on 13 August 1918. It naturally suffered from faults, though none was serious, and in many ways it was a good aircraft. Modern designers of bombers, used to wing loadings around 200 lb/sq ft, will be intrigued to learn that the Braemar I had 1,905 sq ft to support a maximum weight of 16,500 lb, or 8.66 lb/sq ft.

A Mk II Braemar was built with Liberty engines, achieving the commendable speed of 125 mph, but it swung on take-off, collided with a hangar and was wrecked. It is easy to criticise, but one would

have thought any swing could have been controlled by coarse rudder and shutting down the engines on the outer side. Be that as it may, the war ended and the third aircraft was completed with a fourteen-seat passenger fuselage; it was named the Pullman. The pilots sat in an enclosed glazed nose, similar to that of the Kennedy. It was to be another ten years before pilots got over their prohibition of an enclosed cockpit, and even then they insisted on a large axe being handy so that they could never be trapped.

Well, that might have been that. Even with only fourteen seats the Pullman was too big for the infant airlines of 1920, and Bristol might have got on with something more sensible. Incidentally, its landing speed of 50 mph was judged far too high, so it was not entered in the August 1920 Civil Aircraft competition. Unfortunately, the designers (and presumably the White family, who ran the company) had become excited by the idea of giant airliners, and got the bit between their teeth. Reid could hardly wait to get back to his drawing board in March 1919 and prepare the three-view of a Pullman enlarged for fifty passengers. Two months later this was cut back to only forty seats, which was only about eight times the number actually needed on the busiest trunk routes, such as London–Paris. Fortunately these big Pullmans were never built, but Bristol somehow got the Air Ministry to pay for two further giant triplanes, called Type 37 Tramp, described as 'spares carriers' – whatever that meant. These were just empty freighters, powered by four of the same Puma 6-inline water-cooled engines as the Braemar I, but with the engines grouped in an internal engine room. Siddeley-Deasy supplied the gears, shafts and clutches to drive the 14-ft four-blade tractor propellers.

Both Tramps were built, receiving RAF serials J6912 and 6913. They then spent more than two years on the ground, first at Filton and then at Farnborough. They never flew, because the complex transmission systems to the propellers never reached a satisfactory stage of reliability – despite more than 48,000 hours having been logged in Germany on twenty-two different types of transmission system handling the same or greater power, in many types of large bomber.

Even this might not have got the big triplanes into this book. What made inclusion inevitable was the bizarre belief that these, or even bigger, aircraft might be powered by *steam turbines*. Expressed baldly like this, the notion sounds like lunacy, which is what it was, but there are two ways of looking at most questions. According to Chris Barnes, in his 'Putnam' on Bristol aircraft, 'In February 1919 Captain Barnwell had discussed the use of flying-boats as ancillaries to ocean liners with the Royal Mail Steam Packet Co., who had pressed strongly for a steam-turbine power unit if feasible.' The idea was that the Royal Mail liners sailing to South America should carry a giant flying boat on board. About 1,000 miles from Rio or Buenos Aires, the flying-boat would be loaded with one ton of mail and then lowered by crane over the side, to take off and reach its destination two days

before the ship. The basic idea was actually put into use by Deutsche Luft Hansa in 1929, using Heinkel seaplanes.

Not unnaturally, the Royal Mail marine engineers knew very little about piston aircraft engines, but a great deal about huge steam turbines. In their opinion, steam turbines would be quieter and safer than existing aircraft petrol engines. Their boilers would also burn cheaper fuels. The fact that Barnwell, and presumably the Bristol directors, took such an idea on board passes my comprehension. The company even discussed the design of a turbine with Fraser & Chalmers, and of a boiler with Bonecourt Waste Heat. The Braemar I was to be used as the steam-turbine test-bed. Nobody appeared to consider that a steam-turbine propulsion system for an aeroplane was an absolute non-starter, for at least nine basic reasons (one of which was that no sufficiently light system existed or could be created).

Christmas Bullet

This small biplane scout (fighter) was one of that select group of aircraft which became famous because they were so dreadful! Its perpetrator was also one of those aviation pioneers who, knowing his technology was far in advance of the rest of the world, kept it secret and spent much of his time making outrageous claims and pouring scorn on the ignorant folk who failed to appreciate his brilliance.

William H. Christmas was a medical doctor who unfortunately became interested in aircraft design. He believed wings should be highly flexible, like

those of a bird. According to his claims he built and flew various aircraft in Virginia and Maryland (burning one to preserve its secrets) before setting up the Christmas Aeroplane Co. in Washington in 1912. He kept refining his design and at last, in early 1918, contracted with Continental Aircraft on Long Island to build two small scout aircraft noteworthy for having a small lower wing and a large upper wing, but no struts except on the tail and landing gear.

Doctors command respect, so he had little difficulty in obtaining financial and political

The much-modified second Bullet, with Dr Christmas in the black coat between his sponsors Alfred and Henry McCorey.

support, and in July 1918 received a 185-hp Liberty 6 (half a Liberty vee-12) on loan from the army. With this the first Bullet – also called the Continental Scout, the Christmas Strutless biplane and the Cantilever Aero Bullet – was completed in mid-January 1919. Christmas persuaded a pilot just back from the Western Front, Cuthbert Mills, not to heed the advice of the Bullet's constructors and to 'take it up'. Watched by his mother, Mills did just that. The wings flexed beautifully for a few seconds and then parted company with the fuselage. Mills was killed instantly, while the Army was more angry at the loss of its engine.

Undeterred, the good doctor exhibited the second Bullet at a New York air show in March 1919, the placard stating that it was good for 200 mph and was 'the safest, easiest-controlled plane in the world'. This time he got hold of a 200-hp Hall-Scott engine, and the unsuspecting test pilot was

Captain Allington Jolly, RAF. Jolly took off and flew straight into a barn, like his predecessor being killed instantly.

In August 1919 Dr Christmas testified before Congress, not only claiming that his plane could fly 60 mph faster than anything else in the sky, but also that, before the USA entered the war in April 1917, the German government had offered him *one million dollars in gold* to go there and take over their aircraft designs. He also commented that he could not fulfil any US government contracts for at least a year, because his plant was so swamped with orders, mostly for export.

Fortunately Christmas got on with his medical practice and built no more aircraft. He lived to be ninety-four. I hardly considered this story worth including, because I am concerned in this book to look at aircraft designed and built by professionals, but I was told by many friends, 'You just can't leave it out!'

CENTRAL CENTAUR

The history of aviation is liberally sprinkled with ironies. A favourite is for an aeroplane of supreme crudity to have a good career, while a refined and far better design proves a disaster. So it was with

the Centaur 2A and IV, though in fact the two designs were unrelated.

Central Aircraft was formed in 1916 in Kilburn High Road, London. After the war it designed a

The Centaur 2A cabin aircraft, which lasted just four months.

simple biplane about as large as an Avro 504, called the Centaur IV. Eight were built, all with seats in the same cockpit for a pilot and two passengers. They were aircraft of totally disarming crudity. Maximum speed varied from 70 to an alleged 75 mph, cruising speed being around 58 mph. Yet, except for one which crashed early on, in 1920, all had extremely active and successful lives, and some survived in Belgium until 1938!

In contrast, the Centaur 2A was a much bigger and seemingly better aircraft, with none of the stark 'home-made' look of its smaller relation. Powered by two Beardmore 6-inlines of 160 hp,

two were built. The first had open cockpits for a pilot and six passengers, while the second had a cabin for seven passengers. Again they were no great performers, with a cruising speed of 60–65 mph, but at least they looked a professional job. Yet the open version crashed in its eleventh month with crossed elevator cables, while the cabin aircraft spun in, killing all six people on board, four months after its first flight. Perhaps one could say neither crash really reflected on the design of the aircraft, though with so low a performance an aircraft can never be very far from a stall/spin.

BAT Baboon and Crow

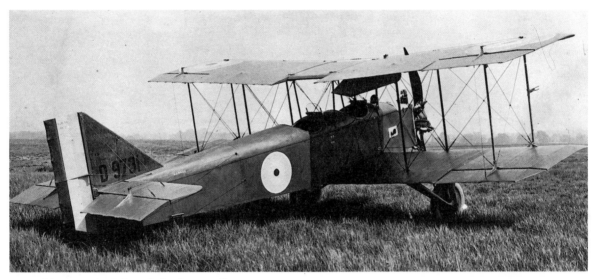

From this aspect the Baboon looks almost ordinary.

We have already met Fritz 'Cully' Koolhoven, a large Dutchman who had a long and generally successful career in aviation, because of the quadruplanes he designed for Armstrong Whitworth (see page 22). From that company he moved to BAT (British Aerial Transport). One of his designs for BAT was the FK.24 Baboon. To create this he was assisted by Robert Noorduyn, who later designed the famous Noorduyn Norseman. Together the two of them managed to create the most crude and ungainly aircraft imaginable. Nobody would ever have thought the Baboon the product of a professional team at a major company. An elementary trainer, it had all the hallmarks of having been

knocked together from scrap material in a back yard. On the other hand, it did fly. Perhaps I am comparing apples with oranges, but let's just look at how the Baboon compares with a modern two-seater (the Rand Robinson KR-2 home-built): engine, Baboon 170 hp ABC Wasp, KR-2 90 hp Volkswagen; maximum speed, Baboon 89 mph, KR-2 220 mph; range, Baboon 145 miles, KR-2 2,000 miles. BAT's chief test pilot, Major Christopher Draper, even won a race with the Baboon. It was from Hendon aerodrome to Bittacy Hill and back. Where's Bittacy Hill? It is one mile east of Hendon aerodrome, with the National Institute for Medical Research on top. You could walk there from the aerodrome in a few minutes!

A few months later, in 1919, Koolhoven produced the FK.28 Crow. This was a single-seat ultra-light, precisely in the style of the Santos-Dumont Demoiselle of 1907. The pilot sat in what looked like a soapbox, suspended by four struts directly under the wing. On the front of the wing was the engine, and behind it two booms holding the tail. In theory it should have had quite a good performance. Plenty of today's home-builts can cruise at 80 mph and climb at 650 ft/min on less than the 40 hp installed in the Crow. Perhaps the 1919 engine, an ABC Gnat, failed to give its advertised power. For whatever reason, Koolhoven was very unhappy about allowing Major Draper to fly the Crow. Eventually, in autumn 1919, Draper was allowed to fly this early ultralight. With the throttle firewalled he just managed to get airborne. In stark terror he kept flying for a complete circuit. In the 1950s he told the author, 'I was sorely tempted just to land in the next field, but I somehow managed to get round, dodging the trees and even people; I couldn't have climbed over them.' The Crow was scrapped soon afterwards.

In 1922 Koolhoven began work with his own firm at Waalhaven, Rotterdam. Several of his many designs achieved some success, but he made at least one further mistake. At the 1936 Paris Salon he exhibited a mock-up of the FK.55. This odd fighter had the 720-hp Lorraine vee-12 engine mounted on the centre of gravity under the high wing, driving contra-rotating propellers via a long shaft as in the Airacobra. The pilot sat above the shaft in the nose. There was nowhere to put the landing gear, so when the prototype was actually built it had fixed gear. Test pilot Thomas Coppers flew the FK.55 on 30 June 1938. Obviously something was very wrong, because he landed immediately, and the FK.55 never flew again.

BLACKBURN SIDECAR

In the months immediately following both the world wars there was a great upsurge of popular belief in a wonderful new world. In this world the common man would have a car and, would you believe, probably an aeroplane. Newspaper articles pictured the sky filled with light or ultra-light aircraft which would somehow take off and land at, shall we say, 78 Acacia Avenue, Suburbia. Not many of these proposed aircraft actually got built, but one of the 1919 crop was the Blackburn Sidecar.

It is easy to criticise after the event, but the mind boggles at the way this small monoplane was arranged. Of wooden construction, with wire bracing and fabric and ply covering, it seemed unnecessarily clumsy. Pilot and passenger sat side

Blackburn seriously wondered if they could fill the sky with Sidecars.

by side high above the wing, yet there was an enormous depth of narrow fuselage below the wing as well. At the back the control wires were joined to a rudder and to a horizontal tube carrying left and right tailplanes, there being no fixed surfaces. On the nose was a 40-hp ABC Gnat flat-twin engine, fed by a 14-gallon tank under the seats.

The single Sidecar was built at Blackburn's Olympia (Leeds) works in early 1919. In April it was on show at Harrods in London, while mannequins modelled a range of expensive 'flying clothing'. The Sidecar was then featured at Heelas' store in Reading. In August it appeared on the newly opened British civil register, as G-EALN, but not a lot more was heard of it. Presumably attempts were made to fly it, but if so these were unsuccessful. In 1921 the Sidecar was acquired by Blackburn's London manager, B. Haydon-White, who had the Gnat replaced by a far heavier 100-hp ten-cylinder Anzani radial. It still never flew, and was dismantled shortly afterwards. One wonders if Robert Blackburn ever seriously thought it might be made by the hundred.

SAUNDERS KITTIWAKE

In the period following World War I it was possible for companies to survive on a diet of one-offs: aircraft of which only a single example was built. Of course, it helped if each had a customer, but perhaps half the 1,500-plus different types produced in the 1920s had not even that in view.

The Saunders Kittiwake, for example, was built to compete in the 1920 Air Ministry Commercial Amphibian competition – which it missed by taking too long to build. In those distant days the Air Ministry actually encouraged aviation by offering prizes for the best aircraft in particular categories, which even included ultra-lights.

Whether one is building for a competition or for a customer or merely speculatively, it is often hard for a designer to find the right level of technology between the pedestrian and uncompetitive on the one hand and the highly advanced and thus possibly troublesome on the other. In this case designer F.P.H. Beadle produced quite an attractive little machine, smaller than most of its rivals, and distinguished by several unconventional features.

For example, he designed the complete lower hull to be quickly detachable from the rest of the aircraft so that it could easily be repaired following damage (which was common in those days to marine aircraft). He made the hull out of the company's patented Consuta plywood sewn by copper wire, which Saunders had employed ever since the pioneer Bat Boat of 1912. The landing wheels could be retracted manually into boxes under the planing bottom.

Another odd feature was that the wings were thin, very close together, joined by a row of single struts along the main spar and, not least, fitted with manually driven hinged leading and trailing edges. This variable-camber mechanism, another company patent, was expected to provide for improved lift and control at low speeds. It meant that the ailerons had to be put somewhere else, such as halfway between the wings, pivoted to the struts. The superimposed bay windows facing ahead, each with large flat vertical panes, were also unusual, and hardly conducive to low drag.

The Kittiwake was designed for two crew and seven passengers. Gross weight was to be 6,000 lb (2,722 kg), and the engines were 200-hp ABC Wasps. Captain Norman Macmillan, who was already making a name for himself as a test pilot, flew it from Cowes on 9 September 1920. As he climbed from the sea he was shocked to find

The Saunders Kittiwake was unnecessarily innovative, and I believe that the gap/chord of the wings was too low.

the leading-edge flap structure coming apart, and he put the Kittiwake straight back on the water. There followed urgent repairs and inspections, before the amphibian was flown again. Eventually it made several flights, mostly in the hands of F.W. Merriam, but in July 1921 it was scrapped because it had attracted no commercial interest. None of its unusual features was used again.

CAPRONI CA 60

In the wonderful pre-1910 era, when a thousand inventors had a thousand different ideas about how a flying machine should be designed, it was only to be expected that many of the aeroplanes actually built should have been bizarre creations, which any modern designer would instantly recognise as failures. By the start of World War I, however, the general arrangement of wings just behind the centre of gravity, partnered by a down-loaded tail, had become almost universal. At the end of

One marvels at how Caproni could have created the Ca 60 in 1920, when quite a lot was known about aeroplane design.

that conflict, some 100,000 aeroplanes later, at least designers were no longer groping in the dark.

It is therefore astonishing to discover one of the Italian Caproni companies, immediately after the war, solemnly designing a gigantic flying boat which even at the time could be seen to be nonsensical. Few records survive of why this was done. It appears to have been the personal brain-child of Count Gianni Caproni, and it was certainly not built for a customer. Huge as it was, this strange creation was planned merely as the proof-of-concept prototype for an even bigger flying boat intended to carry 150 passengers across the Atlantic.

Briefly digressing, such an objective should have been recognised as utter nonsense. A quarter of a century later Britain struggled to create a vehicle to fly just twelve passengers across that ocean (see the Avro Tudor story, page 123), and 150 non-stop remained an impossibility until the Tu-114, 707-320 and DC-8. Of course, Caproni may have been thinking of alighting repeatedly in the Atlantic storms to refuel from convenient ships – who knows?

The creation that was built was designated Ca 60, but it was more popularly known as the *Transaereo* (which doesn't seem to mean much), *Noviplano* (nine wings) and *Capronissimo* (Caproni greatest). Great it certainly was. Though the span was a modest 30 metres (98 ft 5 in), the fact that there were nine untapered wings resulted in the wing area being 750 sq m (8,073 sq ft), or twice that of a B-52. At a time when typical passenger aircraft, such as the DH.16, had a total installed horsepower of 320, the Caproni monster had just ten times as much.

This power was supplied by eight Liberty engines, three tractor and one pusher at the front and one tractor and three pusher at the back. For some reason the engines on the centreline had four-blade propellers. But the obvious flaw in the design was that there were sets of triplane wings, at the bow, amidships and at the stern. We do not know what possessed Caproni to choose such an arrangement.

The eminent annual *Jane's All the World's Aircraft* was hardly given to offering criticism, but reported:

The longitudinal moment of inertia is colossal – which in any case would call for extremely powerful longitudinal stabilising and control surfaces. But the distribution of the load is such that all three sets of wings must be nearly equally loaded, a condition entirely opposed to the generally accepted principles of stability, and the longitudinal control is apparently supplied by an opposed use of the ailerons of rear and front planes. As a result the machine was, it may be surmised, not merely unstable but also uncontrollable longitudinally.

Designed and built in 1920, the creation was launched into Lake Maggiore on 21 January 1921. Writing in an early edition of *Aeroplane Monthly*, Giorgio Apostolo made the comment, 'The whole structure would not have looked out of place sailing up the English Channel with the Spanish Armada.' Following flotation tests, chief pilot Semprini – who in his best-known photograph looks seriously thoughtful – took the monster into the air for a tentative hop on or soon after 4 March 1921. It is recorded that at a height of about 60 ft the contraption majestically nosed over and flew straight into the lake.

People speculated on the reason. Some said the hundreds of sandbags, simulating sixty passengers, might have shifted in flight, but they could only have slid towards the tail, causing the machine to rear up and stall. Others said Semprini could have pulled out, but that the bow wings collapsed. The author doubts that either of these things happened. We do not have to look for such explanations; *Jane's* hit it on the head.

Fortunately Semprini climbed out of the wreckage. Caproni ordered the Ca 60 to be repaired, but while this was being done it caught fire and was destroyed. One wonders about the insurance situation.

NID 37 *TYPE COURSE*

One of the most notable French designers was Gustave Delage, who joined the Nieuport company in January 1914. He was responsible for many thousands of nimble little fighting scouts which were notable for being sesquiplanes (sesqui = 1 ½), in that they were biplanes with one wing (the upper, in this case) much larger than the other. He had a conviction that this would somehow be the best compromise between the speedy monoplane and the agile biplane.

Predictably, once the war was over Delage sought to beat his rival Béchereau by creating the fastest racing aircraft in the world, and he briefly succeeded. To compete in the annual Coupe Deutsch race the Air Ministry funded two Nieuport-Delage racers, one of which was exhibited at the 1921 Paris *Salon*. The structure was a delight, the finely streamlined fuselage being a monocoque (devoid of any skeleton inside the skin) assembled from multiple glued veneers of tulipwood. Inside the nose reinforced brackets carried the Hispano-Suiza HS 42 vee-8 engine of some 300 hp, cooled by two of the outstandingly effective Lamblin 'lobster-pot' radiators hung under each side of the nose. Lower still was the ultimate in sesquiplane technology in the form of the *aile inférieure*. This was little more than an extended fairing round the undercarriage axle, extended beyond the wheels to give extra lift.

Delage got it right, though the *aile inférieure* probably did little but add drag. On 26 September 1921 famed pilot Sadi Lecointe made four timed runs to set an official world speed record at 330.275 kph (205.23 mph). But in the Coupe Deutsch race something catastrophic happened, and Lecointe was extremely lucky to find himself in a field surrounded by pieces of wreckage but without serious injury. There seems little doubt that the cause was flutter of the wings or ailerons, though it was suggested that the propeller might have hit a bird.

Delage thereupon went back to the drawing board and for the 1922 Coupe produced an even faster racer, the NiD 37 *Type Course* (racing version). There was also a *Type Chasse* (fighter version), which was exhibited at the 1922 Paris *Salon*. This had a much larger wing which, as events were to show, was probably a good idea.

Painted white and red, the 37 *Type Course* looked even stranger than its predecessors, with a beautifully smooth bullet-like fuselage, tiny cantilever wing, small tail and a broad *aile inférieure* which carried the wheels. The engine, a Wright-Hispano H-3 reputedly good for 407 hp, was this time cooled by a single big Lamblin under the nose. The pilot was perched above the rear of the engine; one report even said his pedals were actually attached to it.

When all was ready Lecointe, recovered from his crash, opened the throttle and raced across the Villesauvage airfield. When the *Type Course* showed no sign of flying he hastily closed the throttle and prayed that the tailskid would drag the machine to a halt. He made several further attempts to get the racer into the air, but when the carburettor caught fire, scorching his feet, he decided he had had enough.

Perhaps fortunately for Lecointe's safety, the NiD 37 Type Course refused to fly.

Semiquaver Alula

In the years following World War I dangerous aeroplanes lay thick upon the landscape. This particular one never crashed – at least, not in its dangerous form – but that was more by luck than judgement.

The story really began in the middle of the war, when A.A. Holle, a Dutchman resident in England, began inventing what he claimed to be improved types of wing. The first was tested on the Holle Varioplane, a parasol monoplane using parts of other aircraft. The wing was fitted with remarkably large split flaps, described as a variable-camber device. This was sound in concept, and can fairly be regarded as ahead of its time. The trouble started when he invented, and patented, his second wing, named Alula after the auxiliary slat-like digit on the leading edge of bird wings. No such refinement was present on Holle's wing.

Its only plus factor was its graceful appearance – at least, to anyone ignorant of structures or aerodynamics. In plan it was almost what today is called a delta, with taper on the leading edge to a pointed tip. From head on the Alula wing looked dangerously thin, curving down from a horizontal centre section to tips which, if anything, were curved slightly upwards. In side view the inner sections had pronounced positive incidence, but this was washed out until the tips had slight negative incidence. I do not pretend to comprehend Holle's reasoning, nor why he thought this wing superior to any other, but there is not the slightest doubt that his claim that its lift was proportional to the cube of the indicated airspeed, instead of to its square, was absolute rubbish. Not even Holle could rewrite the laws of physics, and yet no less a person than aviation pioneer Robert Blackburn helped subscribe £30,000 to set up Holle's company.

Indeed Blackburn's own works, at Sherburn-in-Elmet, Yorkshire, converted a DH.6 to test the first Alula wing. This aircraft, G-EAWG, was flown on 2 January 1921 by Captain Clinch, who discovered

One of the men working on the unfinished Alula is wearing the newly designed uniform of the RAF!

that the flimsy wing-tips had almost no torsional strength, and that the ailerons were 'perfectly useless' (I did mention earlier that lack of lateral control figures in several stories in this book). After Clinch had twice almost killed himself, Holle added hinged slats on the leading edge, which did afford some lateral control. He also several times modified the wing, and added extra bracing struts underneath. But by this time Holle was blaming the DH.6 for his wing's non-performance, claiming that marvellous results would be achieved if only it could be mounted on a streamlined racer.

Accordingly Holle bought the little Martinsyde Semiquaver racer, which had already had an eventful career. Powered by a 300-hp Hispano-Suiza engine, it was shorn of its very short-span biplane wings and fitted with an aesthetically beautiful Alula wing. Completely unbraced, this wing was awesomely thin, and by waggling the tip you could send waves rippling inwards along the thin skin. The famed test pilot Frank Courtney, who had been hired by Holle and had flown the DH.6, noted that the racing wing 'wobbled in all directions', and declined to fly it. Holle was disgusted, and even more so when he found great difficulty in finding a replacement for Courtney. Eventually he got Reginald Kenworthy to take on the job. Courtney described Kenworthy as 'not noted for his technical judgement or reasonable caution'. On 12 October 1921 Kenworthy flew the Alula-winged Semiquaver at Northolt. Courtney described the flight as 'harrowing', though G-EAPX got back in one piece. Take-off speed was estimated at 110 mph, faster than the normal flight speed of most 1921 aircraft.

What Kenworthy may not have bothered to find out – though Courtney certainly would have done – was that the Alula wing was frighteningly weak structurally. Holle must have been one of those inventors to whom the idea and outward shape are everything, such trivial details as the stressing of the structure being relatively unimportant. The wing fitted to G-EAPX consisted of upper and lower skins of 0.125-inch mahogany veneer, on the inner surface of which were glued light spanwise and chordwise formers. There were no spars at all. Farnborough tested a similar wing and found its overall design factor – ignoring any extra factor of safety – was 1.75. Thus, in absolutely still air, with the aircraft flown with perfect smoothness and precision, the wing would have collapsed in a turn at a bank angle of about 50°. And, as I said earlier, the claims for enhanced efficiency were complete nonsense.

KOMTA

Russia may have been a pretty terrible place before the October 1917 Revolution, but the Soviet Union was certainly far worse immediately after it. For the first ten years civil war of one kind or another was still going on, and several of the earliest Soviet aircraft designs were specifically for use against their own people. But one or two had peaceful objectives, and the first of these was proposed in 1919 by the great Professor N.Ye. Zhukovskii, the 'father' of Russian and of Soviet aeroplane flight. He pointed out that the only large aeroplanes available were wartime IM reconnaissance-bombers designed by Sikorsky (who had legged it for France and then the USA). Not unreasonably, Zhukovskii suggested that the Soviet Union, being the largest country in the world, ought to build big transport aeroplanes.

The obvious thing to do was form a committee, and for this purpose almost everybody who was anybody in Soviet aviation was roped in. Called KOMTA, from the Russian for Commission for Heavy Aviation, it was chaired by Zhukovskii and included numerous aircraft designers. One member proposed a transport based on the IM bombers (I don't think he was sent to Siberia, but he was certainly outvoted). Then someone proposed a twin-engined triplane, having recently been impressed by pictures of the British Bristol Braemar and proposals for the Pullman and Tramp. Indeed, the original idea was to put the engine in the fuselage, as in the Tramp, but eventually they were tamely hung under the wings in the usual way.

With big committees it often takes ages to get agreement on anything, but KOMTA – perhaps because of its strong chairman – didn't waste time. Starting in February 1920, the configuration was broadly agreed by March, and in the summer a model was being tested in the first wind tunnel in the Soviet Union (at least two built earlier had been destroyed after the Revolution). The planned giant transport, called KOMTA or Komet (comet), actually came out a bit of a tiddler, with a span

They were very proud to be working on this great new transport aircraft for the Soviet Union.

of only just over 49 ft and a loaded weight of 7,826 lb. Two wartime Fiat A-12 engines were made available, each rated at 240 hp. They were picked, said historian Shavrov, for their reliability. With so much power in so small a machine the performance ought to have been sparkling. What nobody probably liked to mention was that they were creating a transport markedly inferior in capability to the 1916–17 versions of Sikorsky's old IM.

What nobody expected was that, in addition, they would make the proverbial pig's ear of it. Assembled at GAZ (state aircraft factory) No. 1 and flown in March 1922, KOMTA proved only just able to stagger into the sky if the control wheel was pushed forward with the strength of both pilots. What Shavrov calls 'major reconstruction' followed, in the course of which the engines were moved forward one metre (39.4 in)! In autumn 1923 the unfortunate A.M. Cheremukhin was told to begin a further series of tests. This time the centre of gravity was a bit nearer, but performance was abysmal, the ceiling being 600 m (1,968 ft) and the maximum speed with throttles 'firewalled' being 81 mph. Very soon the pride of the Soviet Union was parked at the entrance to the Serpukhov air-firing school, perhaps becoming the first gate guardian in history.

The youngest member of the KOMTA committee said he could have designed a better aircraft, a claim which he later proved repeatedly. His name was Tupolev.

The KOMTA was finished in winter and mounted on skis.

BESSON H.5

In the formative period before 1920 some designers appeared to think, 'Wings are good for aeroplanes, so we'll have lots of them.' Many of the pioneers produced aircraft that looked like Venetian blinds, one of them being the Englishman Horatio Phillips, who was a gifted and painstaking aerodynamicist. Even such practical engineers as Igor Sikorsky and Anthony Fokker stuck an extra set of wings on one of their aircraft, hastily taking them off again after flight tests. In 1916 the Oertz W 6 flying boat actually flew successfully with tandem sets of triplane wings, while the 1919 Johns Multiplane bomber had (consecutively from the nose) a biplane, a triplane, a biplane and finally a biplane tail!

By 1920 most designers recognised such configurations as aberrations, outside the mainstream of development. Thus one wonders why, in 1922, Maurice Besson chose to build the H.5 (*Hydravion* No. 5) with an arrangement which could be considered either as an odd double-biplane or as a staggered quadruplane. Besson always did his utmost to disprove the supposed Gallic love of beauty, almost all his designs having been unnecessarily ugly and ungainly, but the H.5 was the only one with a bizarre basic layout.

The H.5 had been intended as a long-range reconnaissance and bombing flying boat, but it was finally completed in 1922 as a passenger transport. The structure was almost entirely of wood, and Besson's considerable experience over the previous seven years resulted in a hull possessing excellent hydrodynamic qualities. The length was 22 m (a little over 72 ft), which was exceptional for 1922. The bulky fore-part housed the crew of five and twenty passengers (again, most unusual for the day), the latter having Celluloid windows all the way along the cabin. The aft part of the hull tapered gracefully to the triple-finned biplane tail.

It was the wing arrangement that was odd. Mounted above the passenger cabin were biplane wings of typical Besson rectangular outline, linked by straight X-form interplane struts. On the lower wing were mounted the left and right engine nacelles, each with two 260-hp Salmson 9Z water-cooled radial engines arranged as a tandem push/pull pair. So far, so good, and by later standards the area of this biplane cellule of 1,211 sq ft would have been ample for a flying boat with a maximum weight of 10 tonnes (22,046 lb). Besson obviously thought otherwise, and added a second, almost identical, biplane cellule immediately behind the first, but at a lower level. Thus, the upper wing of the aft cellule was positioned at a level halfway between those of the upper pair. The rear cellule carried the ailerons and stabilising floats. Its upper wing was cut away at the rear to clear the pusher propellers.

With a Nieuport XI Scout to give scale, the Besson H.5 looks like a nasty accident.

It all looked like a bad dream, or a nasty accident involving two biplanes. Yet, when tested at St Raphaël in July 1922, the H.5 was alleged to have had quite good flying qualities. Reading between the lines, however, there must have been another side to this coin. After flying less than three hours the aircraft suffered slight damage and was never repaired, and Besson switched from triplanes and double-biplanes to monoplanes.

BRISTOL 72 RACER AND 95 BAGSHOT

I have often written about the problem of lateral control, which was ignored by most would-be aviators prior to the Wright brothers. The Wrights solved the problem by arranging for the wings of their Flyers to warp (twist) under the command of the pilot. Later they fitted ailerons, auxiliary surfaces pivoted at the tips of the wings and driven in opposition to roll the aircraft to the left or right, or to hold the wings level. They patented the idea, which resulted in a protracted lawsuit with Curtiss, but in fact the first to use ailerons was the Frenchman Robert Esnault-Pelterie, in a glider of October 1904. Funny octagonal ailerons were a later addition to Alberto Santos-Dumont's tail-first *14-bis* in November 1906.

In those pioneer days there was almost no background of knowledge or experience. Each designer-pilot did what he thought best, and often discovered that he had made a mistake. Each learned from his friends or rivals, so that by 1910 there was an established corporate body of knowledge which, provided one did not embark on a wildly new configuration, ought to have guaranteed a more or less successful aeroplane. After World War I, when about 100,000 aeroplanes had been built, one might have expected the design of a successful aeroplane to be well on the way to becoming routine.

That it was not is shown by the fact that two aircraft built by the proud Bristol Aeroplane Co. in the 1920s suffered from the potentially lethal fault of aileron reversal. Aileron reversal means that, when you move the stick or turn the wheel or yoke to the left the aeroplane instead rolls to the right. It is difficult to imagine anything more disconcerting, and of course if it occurs at low altitude it is likely to be 'curtains'. One obvious cause is that the wires connecting the pilot's controls to the ailerons may be crossed. In olden days this had been a not uncommon occurrence, and perhaps hundreds of skilled and cautious pilots were killed by it. Then in 1947 the wires were incorrectly rigged in the prototype Avro Tudor 2 (see page 117), and one of those killed was A.V. Roe's chief designer and technical director, Roy Chadwick. The resulting publicity resulted in AP.970, *Manual of Design Requirements for Aircraft*, at last stipulating that all flying-control connections had to be so designed that control reversal was impossible. Precisely what one might have expected to be laid down in 1910!

The other common cause of aileron reversal is inadequate torsional stiffness in the wing structure – which the wing-warpers aimed at. Conventional ailerons do not actually form the tips but are hinged along the trailing edge. When deflected by the pilot, they push the wing up or down by the trailing edge, and this obviously has the effect of trying to twist the wing. If the structure is not stiff enough, any attempt to roll the aircraft will merely twist the wing. The outer part of the wing is thus converted into a giant aileron operating in the reverse sense to that intended, causing the aircraft to roll the wrong way. This is all obvious; it was fully understood by most of the pioneer designer-pilots of the pre-1910 era. Thus, when you design your wing, you calculate the maximum force imparted by the aileron, when fully deflected at the limiting IAS (indicated airspeed) of the aircraft, and make the wing stiff enough to resist this force without significant twist.

So what's the problem? Simply that an extraordinary number of times designers have got it wrong. I do not know how often. On perhaps 200 occasions test pilots have discovered aileron reversal on a maiden flight and managed to get back to report the matter, without the fact becoming public knowledge. Perhaps on a similar number of occasions, they have crashed on take-off without anyone being able to identify the cause. This 'chapter' is about two wing-twisting aircraft built at Bristol. I do not 'have it in' for Bristol; I have picked out the Types 72 and 95 merely as well-publicised examples by a major company. Indeed, they were created by different chief designers.

In 1921 Captain Frank Barnwell had left in a huff to seek a new career in Australia. His successor,

The Bristol 72 was virtually the smallest flying machine that could be bolted on the back of a Jupiter radial engine.

Wilfred Reid, designed the Type 72 Racer to set speed records with the company's new Jupiter engine. It was expected to reach 220 mph, but most of today's designers would cringe at its appearance. Because the long-stroke Jupiter radial was buried inside the nose the fuselage was like a portly barrel. At the rear were tiny tail surfaces, while on each side sprouted tiny wings. The main landing gear was retractable, the legs being pulled upwards by a hand crank. Altogether it looked a very 'hot little bus' (to use the language of 1922), but when Cyril Uwins made the first take-off in early July of that year he found something far worse: total aileron reversal.

When I was a boy we used to have fun, and a few bruises, seeing how good we were at riding our bikes with our arms crossed. That's probably easier than flying with aileron reversal! There was no excuse for this. The Type 72 had wings of short span but large chord, in some ways the simplest plan-form for good torsional stiffness. Tendency towards aileron reversal is roughly proportional to the square of the airspeed, yet Uwins got it (violently) as soon as he became airborne, at about 60 mph. The mind boggles at how the aircraft would have handled at the hoped-for 220 mph!

Nobody would have suspected that the Bristol 95 Bagshot (originally called the 'Bludgeon') was designed to be a fighter!

Reid added wires to brace the wings immediately in front of each aileron. On the next flight Uwins had at least some lateral control, but the giant spinner disintegrated. On the spinnerless third flight the extra drag was obvious, and so was the grossly over-powerful effect of the ailerons. On the next flight the stick had a cam at the bottom driving the ailerons via rollers, the idea being to give a progressive increase in surface deflection with stick angle. As soon as the aircraft became airborne the tension in the cables lifted the rollers completely off the cam, so this time Uwins had no lateral control at all. He was quite glad to have to fly the Racer only seven times ('Seven too many,' he told me).

With such a disastrous record one might have expected the importance of aileron control to be etched on the brain of every Bristol designer. But Barnwell had had no part in the story of the dreadful Racer. In 1923 he humbly came back to Bristol, saying, 'The biggest job I did "down under" was to redesign an Avro 504 tailskid.' One of the first things he did after returning was to design the neat little Type 91 Brownie, an ultra-light tandem-seat monoplane. It was made of such thin metal tube that the structure was badly bent by knocking out the ashes from a pipe against it! Seeing this, the Air Ministry made Barnwell himself fly a Brownie with a passenger, and loop it.

A little later Barnwell designed the Type 95 Bagshot. This was a rather cumbersome fighter, with two Jupiter engines mounted on the high monoplane wing. The span was 70 ft, but the Bagshot was an odd sort of fighter, which was not expected to need to manoeuvre! Instead it had two gunners, each able to aim a giant 37-mm cannon fed by clips of milk-bottle size shells. On the other hand, like any other aircraft, the Bagshot had to be able to fly properly. There was no problem with the wing. Barnwell just took the Brownie wing and scaled it up × 2, keeping the profile, aileron geometry and everything else the same. To make doubly sure, he added two large bracing struts on each side. Uwins made the first

flight on 15 July 1927, exploring handling at speeds from 60 to about 90 mph. On a later flight, nearing the estimated maximum of 125 mph, he encountered aileron reversal!

Of course, with the Bagshot it was possible to land reasonably safely, because the problem faded as airspeed decayed. But aileron reversal is still frightening, and potentially very dangerous. It is all very well to claim that in the late 1920s not enough was known about the stressing of metal-framed cantilever wings, whose fabric covering made almost no contribution to rigidity. In my opinion it is a straightforward application of the basic theory of trusses, and to ignore torsional stiffness would surely be unthinkable. How the same company could do it twice is hard to understand.

The Bagshot, J7767, was subjected to prolonged structural testing. The results (surely amazingly) appear to have defeated Barnwell, who decided that the only way to overcome the problem was to redesign the aircraft as a biplane! The Air Ministry then paid for two further years of testing, with the objective of trying to decide how cantilever wings could be made torsionally stiff. Nobody appears to have noticed that the first thing to do should have been to replace the fabric by stressed metal skin. We seemed still to believe that an aeroplane's structural strength had to reside wholly in an internal network of ribs, spars, frames and stringers, so when in 1928 Bristol were awarded a contract for a metal wing that would be torsionally stiff they decided it should have *seven* spars! This wing was eventually used on the Type 130 Bombay, last of the so-called RAF bomber/transports. But by the time the Bombay first flew, in 1935, Bristol had learned a bit about stressed-skin structures. The Type 142, much faster than the Bombay, had a two-spar wing, leading to Blenheims, Beauforts and Beaufighters, and also to a two-spar wing on the Type 170 Freighter, which flew in 1945 but can still be found hard at work in a few places, with no fatigue and no aileron reversal.

SIMPLEX-ARNOUX

It is perhaps understandable that when aircraft designers feel they are thrusting ahead into an unknown region they should try out unconventional configurations. This was very much the case after World War II, when the advent of jet engines opened up hitherto unattainable realms of speed and altitude. Many designers, especially in Britain, thought it would be a good idea to leave the tail off. The Vulcan began as a pure triangle and remained a tailless delta, but the Comet and Victor fortunately eventually grew tails.

In rather the same way, after World War I there was a rash of so-called tailless designs. One or two designers omitted the whole tail, but usually 'tailless' meant the omission of the horizontal surface. One designer bitten by the bug was René Arnoux. Seeking to design the fastest possible racing aeroplane, he thought it would be possible to reduce drag by leaving bits out. He left off the horizontal tail, and made the fuselage the shortest possible streamlined shape that could house a 300-hp Hispano-Suiza vee-8 engine and the cockpit. Through this tiny laminated-veneer structure he put the wing, with no dihedral and little taper. On the wing he put full-span hinged trailing-edge controls which – though the word

had not been coined – were in fact elevons. Arnoux was at pains to explain that these surfaces, operated in unison by moving the stick centrally forwards or backwards, would take the place of elevators.

Sitting in the cramped cockpit the unfortunate pilot, Georges Madon, had an outstandingly restricted view. His eyes were roughly level with the top of what must have appeared to be a huge wing, totally blocking off all view downwards. Directly in front of the windscreen was a huge Lamblin radiator, which effectively blocked off the view ahead, besides surrounding the pilot's head with hot air.

These shortcomings were trivial compared with the basic fact that the tiny racer, made by Simplex in 1922, was seriously lacking in control authority. Madon flew the Arnoux racer on 24 September 1922. He lost control and crashed. This was a time when such a happening was so common that only the most cursory attempt was made to discover the cause, and an open verdict was returned. Were this machine to be built today, I doubt if any pilot would be found to fly it (and, of course, certification authorities would hardly take it seriously).

To me the Simplex-Arnoux racer looked like an accident waiting to happen.

FARMAN JABIRU

As I related earlier, if an aeroplane looks wrong, then it almost certainly *is* wrong. I have no cast-iron evidence that there was very much actually wrong with the family of civil transports built by Farman and called by the generic name Jabiru (stork). But they all looked to some degree wrong, and the three-engined F.4X version was astonishingly ugly.

Since early in World War I the British-born Frères Farman had gained a reputation for austere design, with not the slightest concession to aesthetic appeal. The highly successful F.60 Goliath family of bombers and airliners had biplane wings of such purely rectangular form that it was said they were made by the kilometre and just cut off to length for each aircraft. In 1923 Goliaths were in full production, so it is not obvious why the brothers felt impelled to build the F.3X, the first Jabiru. It was entered in the 1923 *Grand Prix des Avions de Transport*, which laid down certain requirements for safety such as ability to fly after failure of an engine, and it won first prize.

Whereas the original Goliath airliner, the F.60, had been a long-span biplane, all the F.121 Jabirus were not only monoplanes but monoplanes of grotesquely short span. The wing was mounted at the top of a fuselage of unnatural depth; indeed most things about the Jabirus seemed unnatural. The chord of the wing was so enormous it was almost half the total length of the aircraft. Despite

this, the wing loading was almost twice that of the F.60, but that was because the old biplane had a huge wing area and hardly any weight. By modern standards even the Jabiru had an exceedingly low wing loading, but with such an inefficient wing the take-off and landing speeds must have been quite high. It is doubly strange that it was Breguet, Farman's arch-rival, who defined the formula for cruising efficiency, and thus for the achievement of long range on any given fuel capacity, showing that what was needed was high aspect ratio. I am sure that the aspect ratio of the Jabiru at 4.39, was lower than that of any other subsonic airliner.

Most Jabirus were of the F.3X type, usually powered by four 180-hp Hispano-Suiza vee-8 engines in tandem push/pull pairs. The nacelles were mounted on the ends of stub wings at the bottom of the strange fuselage, which reminded one of the head of a sperm whale. The reason for this depth was so that the pilot's cockpit above the leading edge did not project down into the passenger cabin. The main cabin at the back usually seated six. Next came a midships section with either one or two seats, and there were two more seats in the bay-window nose, with an all-round view ahead.

If one wonders why the Jabiru was designed in the first place, one is left speechless by the F.4X, which appeared in 1924. Surely among the ugliest aircraft ever built, the F.4X had the nose comple-

The grotesquely ugly F.4X version.

F-ESAR was a standard F.121 Jabiru.

tely removed. It was powered by three tractor Salmson radials of 300 hp each. Two were mounted on nacelles in-board of the tips of the stub wings. Their propellers almost touched, so the nose of the fuselage was cut right back behind them, under the leading edge. The third engine was mounted high on the centreline directly in front of the pilot, its propeller being ahead of the lower pair. This monstrosity was heavier than the F.3X, but the published performance was exactly the same, despite the appreciably greater power (900 hp instead of 720).

Four F.4X transports were delivered in 1925. According to John Stroud, 'They did very little flying, and two had been destroyed by mid-1925.' A further F.4X type aircraft, built in 1924, was powered by just two 400-hp Lorraine-Dietrich vee-12 water-cooled engines mounted on the stub wing. This appeared to have the nose cut back even

further under the wing than on the F.4X. At the top, instead of a third engine, was a bulge projecting ahead of the leading edge to contain the cockpit. This was the heaviest of the Jabirus yet, if the figures can be believed, it was 14 mph faster than the others, reaching about 120 mph. The F.170 had only one engine.

It says a lot for French salesmanship that quite a few Jabirus were built, two were exported to Denmark and two were actually made in Denmark under licence. This was in spite of the fact that almost every part of these aircraft would make any aerodynamicist, of 1925 as much as of today, either cringe or weep. After he had written about the Jabirus, John Stroud was intrigued to receive a request from a man in Stirling for a three-view drawing of the F.4X. John asked why he had picked such an ugly aircraft, to be told, 'It's so hideous I've grown to like it.' Masochist.

HAWKER DUIKER

Like many other firms which had done well out of the First World War, the Sopwith Aviation Company was faced immediately afterwards by, on the one hand, a sudden and seemingly complete absence of customers (nobody wanted military aircraft, the land was knee-deep in them) and, on the other, by gigantic bills for tax due on wartime profits. Sir Thomas Sopwith said – and these are as nearly as possible his own words – 'There wasn't any way we could go on like that, so we called in the Receiver. Then we started up a new swindle, and decided to call it after our pilot, Harry Hawker.'

The giant works at Richmond Road, Ham, was ignored, but the new firm, called H.G. Hawker Engineering (because it was uncertain that anyone would ask it to make aircraft), occupied part of the old former skating rink at Canbury Park Road, Kingston. It immediately began to make motor-cycles and cars, though only in small numbers. Before long Snipes were coming into the works for a meticulous overhaul in order to keep them in RAF service much longer than had been envisaged when they were designed. Captain Bertram Thomson was appointed chief designer, and by early 1922 there was an optimistic belief that the RAF would soon want new aircraft. The hope was not misplaced, and in April 1922 the postman brought to the struggling H.G Hawker company an Air Ministry specification, calling for a Corps Reconnaissance Aircraft, to work with front-line army units.

Captain Thomson got to work straightaway on what any sensible company might have called the H.1, or HR.1 (Hawker Recon) or even HT.1 (in honour of the designer). We British have, however, gone in for names which often makes overseas marketing unnecessarily difficult. Instead of H.1 this first-born became the Duiker, which rhymes with biker. It is an antelope and also another name for the cormorant. The resulting prototype, J6918, was flown by F.P. Raynham in July 1923. Apart from having a parasol monoplane wing, with the centre section omitted to improve view from the tandem cockpits, it was a traditional wooden aircraft with fabric covering. The engine was one of the first Bristol Jupiter radials, as an alternative to a Jaguar.

One might have expected so straightforward a machine to pose no problems to the test pilot, even if its performance was pedestrian. Fuel capacity was no less than 99 Imperial gallons giving an endurance of nearly four hours, but at the end of that time it had travelled barely 340 miles. The time to climb to 10,000 ft was 20 minutes 25 seconds. Tested at Martlesham, it was concluded that the design weight of 4,940 lb was unsafe; 240 lb was removed, which meant taking out *all* armament and military equipment. Even so, to quote Francis K. Mason's 'Putnam', 'Apart from displaying severe aileron flutter (which resulted in a tendency for the wing to part company with the rear cabane struts) the aircraft was directionally unstable throughout the speed range. Moreover, undamped pitching oscillations resulted when the throttle was closed.' So much was riding on this awful aeroplane – there being no other obvious business in prospect – that the infant Hawker firm spent almost a year trying to make it better.

Captain Thomson's next design, the Woodcock

Head-on view of the Duiker. The thin wheels and tyres would have given trouble on soft ground, but trouble was better there than in the air!

biplane fighter, likewise suffered from instability, wing flutter and other problems. Hawker had had enough, and in August 1923 appointed a new chief designer, George Carter. He went to Gloucestershire (later Gloster), and was replaced by the young Sydney Camm.

Designing aeroplanes has never been particularly easy. There are countless examples of ordinary-looking aircraft which have performed dramatically beyond prediction, and with beautiful hand-

ling as well. There are also countless examples of aeroplanes which outwardly appeared to be perfectly adequate, and yet which either fell far short of the design performance, or exhibited appalling flying qualities or, as in this case, both.

Mr Mason, in recording the troubles of the Duiker, considers this name to have been 'highly inappropriate'. I'm afraid I disagree. It comes from the Dutch, and means 'to dive into a bush or into the sea'.

POLIKARPOV I-1, IL-400

Nikolai N. Polikarpov was the most important aircraft designer in the first ten years of the Soviet Union, 1917–27. Throughout this time most of that vast country was racked by civil war, enforced collectivisation and other conflicts, but at GAZ

cowling and the fabric skin over the wing aft of the front spar and over the control surfaces. The engine installation was similar to that of the R-1, the pioneer reconnaissance aircraft derived from the DH.9a, with a flat frontal radiator. This fighter

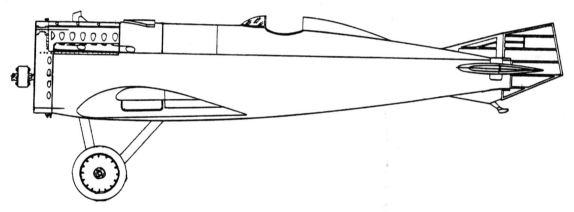

Few photographs exist of the original I-1 (IL-400).

No. 1 in Moscow, from 1918 onwards Polikarpov did manage to gather a small team. By 1922 his brigade was ready to consider an original design, having previously worked on derivatives of the DH.4/DH.9. The outstanding need was for a modern single-seat fighter.

In many respects the I-1 (*Istrebitel* = fighter) was an outstanding achievement. Among other things it was an unbraced (i.e. cantilever) low-wing monoplane, with an excellent overall appearance. The choice of a 400-hp Liberty, an engine made in the Soviet Union as the M-5, guaranteed adequate power, and suggested speed and possibly rate of climb superior to that of any foreign rival. Structure was of wood, apart from the metal

was also called the IL-400 (*Istrebitel Liberty* 400 hp).

K.K. Artseulov made the first flight on 23 August 1923. Perhaps the only critical comment an impartial observer might have made beforehand was that the nose appeared to be very short. Indeed most of the hefty engine was mounted directly on the wing. In fact, though it would have been easy to check, Polikarpov had got it wrong. The CG was at 52 per cent of the wing chord, whereas the centre of lift was, inevitably, at around 20 per cent. With such a massive moment arm tending to rotate the aircraft nose-up there was nothing Artseulov could do. The new fighter did rotate nose-up, stalled at a height of some 70 ft and fell back in a flat attitude.

Even the redesigned I-1 (IL-400B) seemed obviously to have its centre of gravity too far aft.

The aircraft was accordingly completely redesigned. The engine was moved forward, and to reduce drag a smaller radiator was put in a ventral tunnel. The reprofiled wing was all metal, with a corrugated covering of *Kolchug* aluminium alloy. Similar corrugated skin was used for the ailerons, tailplane, elevators and rudder. The cockpit was moved forward, and to improve view the wing trailing edges were cut away below the cockpit. The CG was planned to be at 24 per cent; in fact it was still nearer to 29 per cent, but that was manageable.

The new fighter was designated IL-400B. The first flight came on 27 March 1924. This time Artseulov – who had not been badly injured with the original machine – found no serious problems, though he said later he did not feel completely in control. Orders were placed for eight IL-400Bs, followed by a further twenty-five, but it was soon found that recovery from a spin could be very difficult. At least two pilots were killed, and the great M.M. Gromov made the USSR's first emergency parachute descent on 23 June 1927. Later that year A.I. Sharapov failed to recover from a flat spin, but survived by sheer luck. So this pioneer fighter never went into service with the newly formed Red Air Fleet.

FLYING BARRELS, MATTIONI AND STIPA

The entire history of aviation has been sprinkled with drawings, patents and sometimes actual hardware created by inventors who were convinced that they had a better answer to the problem of defying gravity. Occasionally the ideas flew, and this story tells of an idea which took to the sky as the result of work by two Italians working quite independently. As practised by them, the idea is nonsense.

Briefly, the notion was that aeroplanes would fly better if their propeller was put inside a giant, close-fitting tubular duct. In fact, putting a suitable propeller inside a *short, properly profiled* duct can produce results superior to blades threshing around in the open air. This is what drives Jumbo Jets. If you were to put a suitable multi-blade propeller inside a duct tapering to a convergent/divergent nozzle, then in theory, if you had enough power from an engine that did not degrade flow

through the duct, you might make a piston-engined aircraft supersonic.

Propellers in ducts are fertile ground for those who search the patent literature. In 1910 Bertrand suggested putting a propeller at each end of a tube with a diameter rather less than that of the propellers. In 1911 Jourdan built a flying machine with a propeller at the front of a duct having pronounced taper. What the Italians suggested was putting the propeller inside the duct. Merely putting a traditional piston-engined propeller inside a big tube simply adds weight and drag, loses thrust because of scrubbing and boundary-layer effects along the walls, and means that the payload and fuel have to go somewhere else. The only advantage, which the Italians did not mention, is that the aeroplane will be quieter.

The first of the flying-barrel merchants was

Luigi Stipa's creation had a strange kinship with today's wide-body turbofans.

Antonio Mattioni. Something in World War I gave him the idea that fuselages ought to be huge tubes, and he managed to find the resources to try to prove it. I do not know why he put the Gnome rotary engine and its attached propeller in the bottom of the duct, instead of on the central axis. The pilot sat in a tiny cabin underneath the duct, resting on the cross axle of the undercarriage. Mattioni's firstborn was flown successfully at a military base near Florence by a Major Vasco Magrini, on 22 December 1923. It is supposed to have flown several times since, giving the inventor confidence to build a second machine. This had the engine and propeller mounted centrally in the front of the duct, and tail surfaces behind the open rear end, but it never flew.

Even more surprising is that a professional engineer working in the Studies Department of the Italian Aviation Ministry should have become equally convinced that aeroplanes ought to be in the form of fat tubes. He was Dr Ing Luigi Stipa, and he succeeded in getting the Caproni company

to build to his outline design. This time the pilot, and passenger, had a more normal cockpit perched on top, which must have felt very strange nevertheless. The engine was a de Havilland Gipsy III of 120 hp, driving a normal two-blade propeller near the front of the duct. He went further than Mattioni and claimed to have profiled the fuselage (both the inside and outside of the duct) to give lift.

The Caproni-Stipa was flown in December 1932. It naturally found its way into the newspapers in many countries, but achieved nothing else. Like almost all unconventional aeroplanes it was markedly inferior to conventional two-seaters with the same engine.

As noted earlier, short, properly profiled ducts can enhance net thrust and can if necessary serve as a foundation for deflecting the slipstream with control vanes. When Bell built the odd X-22A VTOL in the 1960s they put each of the four tilting propellers in a duct of significant length, and today several aeroplanes are flying with ducted propellers.

WESTLAND DREADNOUGHT

In *Aeroplane Monthly* the great test pilot and historian Harald Penrose recalled, 'In May 1924 the big monoplane at last was ready, and looked magnificent, its design far ahead of the times . . .' There was just one snag: it wouldn't fly.

The big monoplane was the outcome of the dream of a Russian emigré named Woyevodski (or Voyevodski or Woyavodsky, there were as many spellings as there are of Shakespeare). Like Hugo Junkers he dreamed of a more efficient aeroplane, a cantilever monoplane with the thickened wing root blended imperceptibly into a flattened lifting fuselage. With plenty of internal volume all bracing could be inside, and to reduce drag further the undercarriage would retract. Most of Woyevodski's studies showed twin engines on the leading edge, a crew of two in tandem cockpits in a tiny projecting nose and a conventional tail.

His concept was merely for a shape, and was perfectly sound in principle. He did not concern himself overmuch with structure, but in 1920 the British Air Ministry decided that by ordering a company to build a Voyevodsky they could at one stroke create not only a modern monoplane but also take a quantum leap in structures. British industry was sadly behind the times structurally. Short Brothers had built the all-metal Silver Streak, but this was a braced biplane with an unstressed skin. The Air Ministry was eager to catch up with Junkers, Dornier and Rohrbach, all of whom were trying to continue to build advanced all-metal aircraft by setting up establishments outside defeated Germany.

Accordingly, contracts were signed with Westland and with Parnall Aircraft, but the latter were soon switched to an odd triplane with a traditional structure. Westland Aircraft were thus left to build what appeared to most people to be the aeroplane of the future. It was to be a long and difficult project. Months were spent working with the Aeronautical Research Council, National Physical Laboratory and Royal Aircraft Establishment getting the basic shape right. It came out as a single-engined machine, with a 450-hp Napier Lion on the nose, with a flat frontal radiator and driving a two-blade propeller, and the landing gears were fixed. It looked a very large aircraft for the single quite small engine, the span being almost 70 ft. Officially it was called the Dreadnought Postal Monoplane. I have no idea where the name came from, and the aircraft was not equipped to carry mail; indeed in some places it was described as an 'eight-seater'.

Though the Russian's idea was a more efficient shape, almost all the next three years of toil were devoted to the structural design. It was perhaps the worst form of all-metal construction, the underlying skeleton of the very large wing being of enormous complexity (there were six spars and numerous secondary members, all complicated trusses posing severe stressing problems) yet with the skin doing very little to bear the loads. The central portion, comprising the main fuselage which also formed the centre section of the wing, was covered in quite small panels of corrugated aluminium. The rest was covered in fabric. The wing profile was RAF (Royal Aircraft Factory) T64, but with one strange alteration. Ahead of the front spar the upper surface was curved down to meet the almost flat undersurface along a

Captain Keep performing cockpit checks before the Dreadnought's brief flight. The sharp profile of the wing leading edge is obvious.

sharp leading edge. Such a leading edge is seen today in the B-2 'Stealth bomber', because that gives minimum radar reflectivity. Today we know what we are doing; seventy years ago we did not. I have no idea why this important and possibly critical alteration was made to the established aerofoil.

As it was on Air Ministry account the Dreadnought bore Service roundels and serial J6986. It was to be flown by Captain Stuart Keep, Westland test pilot and son-in-law of Robert Bruce, the chief designer. The two men had often been briefly airborne together in the futuristic machine during high-speed taxi tests, but for the first proper flight, on 9 May 1924, Keep was alone. The take-off and initial climb appeared normal; then the climb grew steeper, despite Keep's attempts to prevent the nose from rising. At about 100 ft the machine stalled and dropped, right wing down, striking at a very steep attitude. Among other things the engine was pushed back into the cockpit; Keep survived but lost both legs.

No attempt was made to repair the Dreadnought. Indeed, the only subsequent action seems to have been to subject the wing and centre section to static testing; I do not know what that was expected to tell anyone. Penrose wondered if 'the wake from the wing root rendered the elevators ineffective, and the sharp-edged blunt wing section precipitated a stall.' Apart from wondering if the CG was too far aft, I can't offer any better explanation. The day was still, not turbulent, and Keep was an experienced and cool-headed pilot. Of course, the whole thing was marginal, in that 450 hp was hardly enough to get the Dreadnought off the ground and establish a positive rate of climb. Thus, in getting to 100 ft altitude the airspeed may well have decayed below the take-off value. But this is speculation. The one fact is that this aeroplane of the future, which Westland hoped would make them industry leaders, refused to stay in the air.

It had one good effect. Bruce decided the company could do with a wind tunnel.

SHORT S.1 COCKLE

In 1923 Oswald Short was eager to make a marine aircraft – a seaplane or flying boat – with an all-metal hull. His chance came when Lebbaeus Hordern, a big Australian, wanted a small seaplane for sporting and fishing around Botany Bay. Short and Francis Webber jointly designed for him a small single-seat flying boat, the S.1 Cockle. It was launched in September 1924.

The Cockle was an extremely neat design, with a strut-braced monoplane wing mounted on top of the nicely profiled hull. The cockpit was in the bows, and the two engines were mounted above the wing at about mid-chord, where it was hoped they would be out of the way of waves and spray. Shafts extended forward to propellers just ahead of the leading edge.

The intention had been to use two Bristol Cherub engines. These were small (1 litre, 61 cu in) flat-twins, rated at 32 hp. Among the Cherub's attractive features were roller-bearing big ends turning a one-piece crankshaft running in four ball-bearings. It was designed for the 1924 Air Ministry Light Aeroplane Trials, where it did extremely well, powering six of the seven prizewinners. In 1925 it powered eight of the ten prizewinners, and on both occasions it was the engine in all

the first awards. The only problem was that, though the reciprocating masses were almost perfectly balanced, the torque recoil was severe. Many of the early Cherubs were geared, to run faster and develop greater power, and these imparted such violent torque recoil that they broke their mountings.

For the Cockle, Oswald Short substituted two Blackburne vee-twin motorcycle engines. Such engines were used in a number of light aircraft in the early 1920s. Ostensibly rated at 30 hp at 4,500 rpm, the shafts in the Cockle installation limited rpm to 2,400, equivalent to only 16 hp. I think everyone must have known that this was totally inadequate. J. Lankester Parker, a test pilot of exceptional skill and experience, spent thirty-three minutes trying to get the little flying boat to unstick from the River Medway. The wing incidence was increased, but further attempts to get the Cockle to fly on 7 October 1924 were abandoned. Incidence was again increased, to a desperate 7°, and on 7 November Parker at last managed to get it into the air, buzzing around at very low level at 57 mph at full throttle. In his 'Putnam' on *Shorts Aircraft*, Chris Barnes writes 'Parker, himself a lightweight, could fly it only in a

Captain Lankester Parker on one of his runs trying to get the Cockle to rise from the River Medway.

minimum of clothing, and even wore plimsolls to save the weight of shoes, so it would have been of little use to a hefty Australian. Indeed, subsequent analysis of the first flight showed that the barometer was unusually high that day, the pressure altitude being 100 ft below sea level, which no doubt made all the difference in taking off.' A lovely story!

Makes one think of the first hovering tests of the Hawker P.1127, forerunner of the Harrier. The early BE.53 engine gave less than half the power of today's Pegasus, and everything, including radio, was removed from the aircraft. Pilot Bill Bedford was really worried about the extra weight of his leg in plaster (he had been crashed by a German chauffeur a few days earlier).

BEARDMORE INVERNESS

The development of the aeroplane is stuffed with irony and paradox. Time and again a new prototype incorporating radical and untried features has run into all kinds of problems caused by its ordinary parts, while the new features have given no trouble whatsoever. Again, aircraft which ought to have signalled a major advance have sometimes turned out to be simply terrible. Of the latter group, few could equal the Inverness.

To digress for a moment, at the start of the 1930s almost all aircraft were traditional biplanes or braced monoplanes, with a structure in the form of a skeleton of wood or metal, braced by wires and struts. The skin was fabric, unable to bear any

significant part of the loads. The result was aircraft with such poor performance that there was little incentive to streamline them by cowling the engine properly or retracting the landing gear. But by the end of that decade aircraft were almost all cantilever monoplanes, without wires or struts, flying at up to three times the speed of the biplanes. The key to this giant advance was all-metal stressed-skin construction, in which most of the major flight loads are carried by the skin of aluminium alloy.

This form of construction was pioneered by Germans. The best-known names are those of Dornier and Junkers, but the greatest of the early stressed-skin designers was Adolf Rohrbach. He played a key role in the design of the huge Dornier flying boats of World War I, and in 1920 produced the outstanding Zeppelin-Staaken E.4/20. This four-engined high-wing monoplane airliner was aerodynamically and structurally ten years ahead of its time. Too bad that, having watched it fly, the Allied Control Commission thought it might be turned into a formidable bomber and so ordered it to be broken up.

In 1922 Rohrbach formed his own company in Berlin, with an assembly factory in Denmark to avoid the Allied Control Commission's prohibition of the manufacture of powerful aircraft in Germany. He then produced a succession of efficient cantilever monoplane airliners and flying boats, though (that paradox again) they did not sell in large numbers, and his firm was soon taken over by the 'Weser' company.

In 1923 the British Air Ministry requested the Scottish shipbuilding and heavy engineering firm of William Beardmore to reopen its wartime air-craft department, take a Rohrbach licence and build a huge landplane. This eventually materialised as the Inflexible, and though it was incapable of serving any useful role it could at least fly, and made several public appearances. For reasons that are far from obvious, in 1924 the Air Ministry placed a further order for two flying boats, much smaller than the landplane but still pretty big (94-ft span, not counting the projecting aileron balances). One, N183, was actually made by Rohrbach, assembled at Copenhagen and flown to Felixstowe. The other, N184, was made by Beardmore. I am indebted to Philip Jarrett for researching the story, and much of what follows was first published in his article in *Aeroplane Monthly* for February 1990.

One of the small design team in Berlin was Kurt Tank, later to be famed for designing and also flight-testing a succession of Focke-Wulf aircraft, including the Fw 190. He asked what Britain intended to use the flying boats for, and was

Just before the first Inverness, Rohrbach had built the very similar RII. It was equipped with two large masts and sails, for use in the event of an emergency descent on the sea. The Inverness might have been better at sailing than flying!

informed they were merely to be tested at the MAEE (Marine Aircraft Experimental Establishment) at Felixstowe and then broken up. He was told, 'We have no intention of going any further ahead with the development of this type of aircraft. In the first place, we have no faith in the mono-plane, and secondly a plane built entirely of metal is much too heavy. Aeroplanes of the future must be safe, and must therefore be biplanes.' Tank was secretly pleased at the British backwardness.

N183 arrived in England on 18 September 1925. It was a high-wing boat with a simple tail, inboard stabilising floats and two tractor 450-hp Napier Lions carried as close together as possible high above the wing. So far, fine. It was in the execution of the design that the Inverness was less than impressive. First, it looked crude beyond belief. The wings and all tail surfaces were stark rectangles. The hull, stabilising floats and nacelles likewise all had a plain rectangular cross-section, the sides, top and bottom being skinned by flat sheets or sheets bent along single curvature. Even the planing bottom was flat, though there was a single diagonal step amidships. There was an open cockpit for two pilots side-by-side, and open rings in the bow and near the tail for mooring, and for observers (or even gunners). Most of the flight-control cables were run externally, the propellers were of carved wood, and the engines were cooled by a single enormous radiator mounted flat-on to the airflow above the hull.

It was clear at the start that, when the fuel tanks were filled and four men were aboard, the permissible useful load was negative! Thus the Inverness could never carry anything. The more Felixstowe examined N183, the worse it seemed. For example, vibration occurred in the attachment of the tail to the fuselage, and even after Beardmore stiffened it in accordance with Royal Aircraft Establishment proposals, slackness developed again. Despite the protective enamel coating, there was serious corrosion which continual retouching of the finish failed to prevent. There was also internal corrosion, attributed to the fact that little attention had been paid to keeping spray out, especially around the wing roots.

Detail design was described as 'unnecessarily heavy without being robust'; the metal wing covering did not remain taut, and the nose ribs tended to press through it. The hull threw up water (not just spray) into the propellers, in spite of their high position, and on two occasions the step collapsed on alighting. It was thought that the loading on the step was excessive and that a landing on a true level keel caused a shock which the bottom could not withstand. The consequent repairs increased weight, and the hull was not watertight. Porpoising occurred in a light swell.

The fuel system was complicated, and its accessibility was poor. Engine maintenance was complicated by the difficulty of removing the cowling, and access to the engine controls could only be gained by removing the wing boxes and, in some cases, the fuel tanks as well. It proved impossible to conduct fuel consumption tests because fuel pressure was too low for satisfactory engine running when the flowmeters were fitted. Compared with contemporary machines the Inverness had poor performance. Although manoeuvrability was good at top speed, it deteriorated rapidly, and the aircraft was described as 'dangerously unstable' at low speeds – despite its enormous dihedral. 'There is a feeling of lack of liveliness similar to that experienced when flying a normal aircraft close to its ceiling,' said the MAEE report.

Cruising speed was about 70 knots, but at this speed rudder control was almost non-existent; for a safe landing the throttles had to be opened and the water hit at nearer to 80 knots! For this reason, operations from anything but smooth water were considered dangerous. The pilot had 'badly placed controls', the seating was uncomfortable and the instruments difficult to read. The only way for the crew to communicate was to walk along the hull and shout in the recipient's ear.

The MAEE staff thought it worth trying to discover why the Inverness was so bad. Further investigation showed that the angle of the engines should be increased, while the angle of attack of the wings should be reduced. Part of the reason for the slow top speed of 95 knots was found to be that the efficiency of the propellers was an abysmal 66 per cent! It was also found that drag of the cockpits and radiator was excessive. Nobody was sorry when N183 was taken to Farnborough, inverted and the wing loaded with bags of lead shot to see how strong it was. The result was excellent; the strength of the long plank-like wing was the only good thing about the aircraft.

SCHNEIDER RACERS: MACCHI MC.67 AND 72, SAVOIA-MARCHETTI SM.65, PIAGGIO PC.7, BERNARD HV SERIES AND NIEUPORT-DELAGE 450 AND 650

At least until quite recent times, any aircraft designed for speed above all else was likely to be a bit of a handful to fly. This was certainly the case with the seaplanes designed to win the Schneider Trophy from about 1923 onwards. Earlier contestants had been fairly pedestrian aircraft, but from 1923 the competition hotted up. Engines grew ever larger and far more powerful, while wings if anything became smaller. These seaplanes included some of the most challenging aircraft to fly ever built. Several are grouped here, some because they were a handful, some because they were dangerous, some because they never even received their engine, and one because it proved unable to leave the water.

Jacques Schneider donated his magnificent trophy specifically to be competed for by seaplanes. The basic contest was a race round sufficient laps of a (usually triangular) course to total at least 150 nautical miles, but there was also a 'navigability contest' to ensure seaworthiness and eliminate impractical monstrosities. In fact, until long after the Schneider contests had become part of history, airfields were mere small grass or dirt fields, totally inadequate for 'hot ships' such as those built for the Schneider races, so the fastest aircraft were all seaplanes. Having said that, taking off and landing a Schneider racer called for the very highest degree of piloting skill.

By the mid-1920s biplane racers were swiftly becoming obsolete. The Schneider racers tended all to become low-wing monoplanes, with a single giant engine in the nose and a cramped cockpit over the trailing edge. All had metal structures, but they were not modern stressed-skin machines; instead they had wire bracing and often portions of fabric covering, especially over the control surfaces. Almost all had water-cooled engines, and to reduce drag the water was cooled in some form of flush radiators which often formed large

With the SM.65 Savoia-Marchetti tried to get two engines for the frontal area of one, whilst simultaneously solving the problem of propeller torque.

At rest, this was all one could see of the Piaggio Pc.7.

parts of the skin of the wings and floats. The lubricating oil was likewise cooled in surface radiators, often made up of a tight sheet of folded tubing along the fuselage or tops of the floats.

Obviously such craft tended to have small, light airframes and huge, heavy engines. Worse, the engines were designed to give the utmost power, often using strange fuels quite unrelated to ordinary aviation petrols. Not a great deal was known in the 1920s about the importance of anti-knock (octane) rating, or how it could be increased. Many of the racers used mixtures of methanol, benzole and even acetone, fed at such a rate that, at full throttle, the engine screaming its head off (sometimes literally), the speeding seaplane left a trail of smoke and droplets. Throttling back resulted in neat fuel pouring from the exhaust pipes, and often violent backfires.

The power of the engines was far greater than anything seen previously in aviation; indeed, never before had so much power been wrung from such relatively small engines. The torque applied to the propeller was tremendous, and this was accentuated by the fact that variable-pitch propellers (which would have been ideal for such an application) were not yet available. Thus, the propeller pitch had to be exceedingly coarse in order that propulsive thrust should still be forthcoming at maximum speed. In the foyer of the great Fairey

Aviation factory at Hayes (today demolished and replaced by a giant Mercedes-Benz parts warehouse) there used to be a Fairey-Reed propeller of the kind fitted to the Supermarine S.6 and S.6B, the seaplanes which finally won the trophy for Britain. It appeared to be almost feathered. With such machines, if you hamfistedly banged open the throttle on take-off you would merely carve a hole in the air and, in all probability, flip the seaplane on to its back. I was told that if, in a glide at 200 mph, you suddenly opened the throttle fully, without full opposite stick, the seaplane would rotate at least twice in opposition to the propeller! So with most Schneider racers you opened the throttle on take-off with extreme caution, gradually letting power come on as the speed built up, and using plenty of coarse aileron and rudder to try to keep straight and level. It was usual to put all the fuel in one float to help offset the enormous torque.

At full speed there was plenty of control power. The problems then were likely to be extreme heat, extreme discomfort, poor forward view, buffeting from the aircraft and by the violent eddies round the windscreen, and, as like as not, engine failure. Several Schneider pilots were killed by flying straight into the sea or a hillside, though often this was through no fault of the aircraft. Such high-speed flying at low level was very demanding, especially over a glassy sea whose distance was difficult to determine. But some of the Schneider seaplanes accomplished nothing for technical reasons.

The Supermarine S.4 (1925) was a beautiful little aircraft, but it crashed because of an in-flight emergency. There are strong grounds for believing that it experienced wing or aileron flutter. Reginald Mitchell made his future wings, such as those of the Spitfire, more torsionally rigid.

The Short Crusader (1927) was a neat monoplane powered by the first Bristol Mercury radial. This engine was ostensibly rated at 960 hp, but to ensure a streamlined nose the propeller was driven by a long shaft. This had a critical whirling mode at about 1,600 rpm, so pilots had to open the throttle as fast as possible between about 1,300 and 1,800 rpm, which was just one more thing to think about on take-off. The shaft never broke, but some idiot connected up the ailerons in reverse, so that the Crusader crashed on take-off (yet one more instance of the lateral-control problem).

The Italian Macchi M.39 (1926) was a straightforward racer which won the 1926 race, but another had to retire with a fractured oil pipe, the sort of thing that ought not to have happened by 1926. Another stalled and crashed fatally. At the 1927 race three M.52 seaplanes all dropped out with engine failure, to the frenzied distress of a vast crowd at Venice (Fiat effigies were burned in the streets). The M.67 (1929) had not a Fiat engine but a giant Isotta-Fraschini with eighteen cylinders. The white-hot exhaust from the centre bank of six cylinders was discharged through plain stubs on the left, so that it passed immediately past the pilot's left ear. The 1929 race was run round a left-hand course, so the scorching gas and smoke came straight into the cockpit on each turn. Lieutenant Cadringher made a heavy forced-landing after one lap and was dragged semi-conscious from the cockpit. His partner, Lieutenant Monti, was also forced down after one lap, but he had the added problem of a burst oil pipe and suffered severe oil burns. The third M.67 stalled and crashed.

For the 1931 race Macchi determined to do better. Designer Castoldi created a truly impress-

This is what the rest of it looked like.

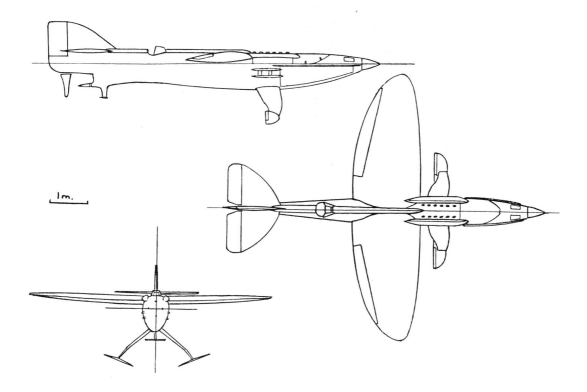

ive seaplane, the MC.72. Its gigantic Fiat AS.6 engine comprised two vee-12 engines bolted together one behind the other, fed by a single colossal supercharger. Each unit drove one half of a contra-rotating propeller, at last eliminating the severe torque problems. It was estimated to reach 450 mph, much faster than any rival. Five were built, serial numbers MM.177-81, to make sure of the 1931 race (which, if won by Britain, would end the series, because the trophy would be Britain's to keep). The first flew in good time, in June 1931. MM.177–180 were all destroyed, partly through flying into the ground or into Lake Garda, and partly because of catastrophic backfires in the engine's induction system, sometimes on the ground. These splendid machines suffered one tragedy after another, and it was not until mid-1932 that MM.181 began to come 'out of the wood'. On 10 April 1933 Francesco Agello set a speed record for piston-engined seaplanes at 682

On its first flight the Bernard HV.120 flew straight into the Etang de Berre, killing pilot Georges Bougault. The second HV.120 never overcame its engine and cooling problems.

kph, raising this on 23 October to 709.2 kph (440.68 mph), which still stands over sixty-three years later.

The Savoia-Marchetti SM.65 (1929) was another way of simultaneously packing in more power and overcoming the torque problem. A rather spidery-looking machine, its tail was carried on two metal tubes which looked dangerously slender. The nacelle housed the push/pull 1,050-hp Isotta-Fraschini Asso engines, cooled by surface radiators covering the wing. Sandwiched between them was a cockpit so cramped that Warrant Officer Dal Molin was the only racing-seaplane pilot small enough. Brave and experienced, Molin was killed on 18 January 1930 when the SM.65 crashed. The cause was variously surmised as loss of control or in-flight structural failure.

Perhaps the most radical of all the Schneider contenders was the Piaggio Pc.7 which, like the SM.65, was built for the 1929 race. Designer Giovanni Pegna had never shrunk from unconventional ideas, and in 1921 he had proposed a racing seaplane whose complete engine and propeller could be hinged upwards for the take-off and alighting. For the Pc.7 he proposed to use hydrofoils instead of floats.

Italians had been the greatest pioneers of hydrofoil boats, in which various forms of foil, or sea wing, lift a high-speed boat completely out of the water, thus reducing wavemaking and greatly increasing the possible speed. Pegna reasoned, correctly, that if the huge floats of a racing seaplane could be replaced by foils, drag and weight would be dramatically reduced, enabling the machine to fly faster.

Having ascertained that such a machine did not violate the strict rules of the Schneider races, Pegna designed the Pc.7 with great care. He made the airframe mainly of wood, sealed to be watertight. The 970-hp Isotta-Fraschini engine was cooled by surface radiators covering the elliptical wings, and its exhaust was piped to apertures on top of the fuselage. The engine was started with almost the entire machine submerged. The pilot then had to engage a clutch transmitting the drive from the rear of the engine via a long inclined shaft to a marine propeller under the tail. This was to drive the machine ever faster through the water, the foils lifting it ever higher until, at about 100 knots, the air propeller ought to be clear of the water. Then came the even trickier part: the drive had to be switched from the marine screw to the air propeller. Moreover, the clutches had to be disengaged and engaged at high speed and under full power, because the pilot could hardly close the throttle in the middle of the take-off run! The problems proved to be too difficult, and this technically exciting machine never managed to take off.

France was also a contender for the 1929 and 1931 contests. Their proposed seaplanes were the Bernard HV.40, 41, 42, 120 and 220, and the Nieuport-Delage 450, 650, 651 and 652. I have no idea how good or bad these aircraft might have been, though the HV.40 was described as 'unsatisfactory', the 41 was relegated to training, the three 42s had very brief careers as trainers, and the 120 crashed fatally on its only flight, a second example being rebuilt as a landplane. As for the NiD racers, the 450-01 suffered from the old torque problem and overturned on take-off, the 650-01 was destroyed in an emergency landing on the Seine, and the 650-02 was scrapped after two short flights. This abysmal record might have been rectified by the impressive HV.220 and NiD 651, both of which were to be powered by the supposedly fantastic Lorraine 12RCr Radium inverted vee-12, claimed to give 'more power than any other engine in the world' and advertised as 2,200 hp. This was an era when the Paris airshow was stuffed with marvellous aircraft which, on closer inspection, proved to be mock-ups. The so-called 'Radium' engine did get as far as running on the bench, but it never got anywhere near flying in either of the racers, so they accomplished nothing.

THE F.7/30 FIGHTERS: GLOSTER SS.37, HAWKER PV.3, BRISTOL 123 AND 133, VICKERS 151, SUPERMARINE 224, WESTLAND PV.4 AND BLACKBURN F.3

Between the world wars a succession of specifications or Official Requirements emanated from Britain's Air Ministry. A few were sent to anyone interested, but most were restricted to a closed clique of favoured firms. The result was usually either a revised specification or a prototype aircraft. Occasionally there would be two prototypes, deadly rivals for whatever production might ensue. But the F.7/30 specification (Fighter, seventh specification issued in 1930) resulted in not two deadly rivals but eight!

This was because F.7/30 encapsulated in a few words all that the RAF was looking for in a future fighter. It was naturally expected that it would result in a winning design being chosen in early 1932, leading to RAF squadrons receiving the new type in 1934 at the latest. It didn't turn out that way at all. The eventual winner began to reach the RAF in 1937,

by which time it was fair to describe it as obsolete. And in my opinion some of the rival prototypes ought to have resulted in the Air Ministry simply crossing those companies off their list of contractors.

F.7/30 was certainly among the most important British specifications of the entire inter-war period. Everyone involved wanted to see the best new fighter chosen at the earliest date, and worked under intense pressure towards this end. The requirements were anything but demanding. The armament of four Vickers machine-guns was double what had previously been accepted, but nothing to cause furrowed brows. Other air forces were already using guns of 12.7-mm (0.5-in) and 20- or 23-mm calibre. The speed of over 250 mph was again well within the state of the art. Britain had set a world record in 1931 at over 407 mph, and foreign fighter designers (such as Polikarpov in the

An observer might consider the Bristol 123 about as unconventional as a biplane could be, until he studied the Blackburn or Westland F.7/30 offerings.

The Bristol 133 was a cantilever monoplane with stressed-skin construction, retractable undercarriage, split flaps and an enclosed cockpit. Having said that, it was clumsy and unimpressive.

Soviet Union) were drawing 300-mph fighters. The US Army even had a big two-seat fighter which, having been designed years earlier, in 1932 reached 247 mph at 15,000 ft, so the RAF was if anything setting its sights rather low. The only other point worth mentioning is that RAF airfields were literally just fields, often a mere 1,200 ft across.

From near the end of the century we can see that the competing designers ought to have said to the RAF, 'You must rethink your airfields and, for fighters as well as for bombers, put down paved runways not less than 3,000 ft long.' They should then have designed clean cantilever monoplanes of all-metal stressed-skin construction, matched to the 1,000-hp engines that were obviously going to be available soon after 1935 (even if the prototype had to have an engine of lower power). What actually happened was that nearly all the designers said to themselves, 'I know nothing about modern stressed-skin design, and I do not propose to visit

such people as Northrop, Rohrbach, Junkers, Martin, Boeing or anyone else in order to find out. Instead I will mess about with traditional structural methods and see which configuration appears to be best.'

A further spanner in the works was that the Air Ministry stated that favourable consideration would be given to designs using the Rolls-Royce Goshawk engine. This was a derivative of the vee-12 Kestrel, cooled by water which was allowed to boil in the cylinder blocks. The steam was then condensed back to water in condensers which, unlike water radiators, could be made flush with the skin, for example along the leading edge of the wing. When the specification was issued it was not appreciated that this 21-litre engine of 690 hp was quickly going to become inadequate, and that by 1933 steam cooling was going to prove too difficult for combat aircraft. Among other things, despite endless effort on cunning valves and bypasses, in air combat the steam and water tended to swap places. Fortunately, Sir Henry Royce was persuaded to think again as early as 1932, so that in 1933 his small team at West Wittering designed what became the Merlin. All this was too late for the unfortunate F.7/30 aircraft. So let's have a look at what Britain's top fighter designers came up with.

The one which finally won was H.P. Folland's Gloster SS.37, later called the Gladiator. One thing this did have was a good engine, the Bristol poppet-valve Mercury, which gave 830 to 890 hp (depending on sub-type) even on 87-octane fuel. The rest of the aircraft was just like a World War I fighting scout, the only differences being Mr George Dowty's new internally sprung wheels, the addition of radio and two extra guns (initially Lewis, with 97-round drums) and, on the production aircraft, a sliding hood over the cockpit. The Gladiator was a very manoeuvrable and pleasant aircraft. Had World War II started in 1933 it would have been quite effective.

The other top designer of fighters, Sydney Camm at Hawker Aircraft, likewise stuck to the

devil he knew and came up with a traditional fabric-covered biplane. The PV.3 was the most likely of all contenders to win, because it stuck implicitly to the terms of the requirement, including use of a Goshawk with six condensers forming the leading edge of the upper wing. Descriptions of the PV.3 comment that, when it was fitted with 'ram's horn' flame-damping exhaust pipes for night flying, these tended to 'explode when hot'. The implication is that unburned mixture was getting past the exhaust valves, and that the exhaust manifolds were able to collect this in sufficient quantity to cause a dangerous explosion (with plain stubs there was nowhere for it to collect). I am surprised that, even in rich mixture, a Goshawk could have pumped so much unburned mixture overboard. In any case, by 1935 anyone could see that the PV.3 was an example of the previous fighter generation, not the next.

Bristol tried to get the best of both worlds by offering a choice of two, a traditional biplane and also a totally unrelated stressed-skin monoplane. The biplane, the Type 123, was traditional only in its method of construction. Every part of it

With great difficulty test pilot T.W. Campbell managed to bale out of the spinning Bristol 133, which ended up like this.

One might almost consider the Westland contender an ancestor of the Bell Airacobra.

abounded with new and usually difficult features. Moreover, it was easily the smallest of the F.7/30 contenders, having a span of 29 ft 6 in and length of 25 ft 2 in. The steam from the Goshawk was condensed along the leading edge of the thick lower wing and in a honeycomb-matrix radiator in the bottom of the fuselage. Had the 123 ever gone into service the maintenance problems of this cooling system, to say nothing of the engine and fuel system, would have been severe: and the spats over the fixed main gear would certainly have been removed.

Bristol's alternative was the Type 133, a clean stressed-skin monoplane. For some reason, aesthetically pleasing designs in the early 1930s seem to have been elusive, and the 133 was a travesty of what it might have been. Basic unattractive features included a wing completely without taper, a strangely cowled Mercury radial engine (but at least it *was* cowled) and a clumsy main landing gear which retracted backwards (pumped by the unfortunate pilot) into large 'bathtub' fairings under the lowest part of the sharply cranked wings. Originally the cockpit was open, but later

it was enclosed by a hood which made even short pilots crouch. As in the 123, the odd rudder had a triangular horn balance which virtually took the place of a fin, and this rudder was twice altered in shape. Another modification was to replace the original ailerons, which occupied the whole span of the wings outboard of the kink, by normal ailerons and split flaps, also hand-pumped. The wing guns, often described as Lewis, were in fact Vickers.

Barnwell designed the 123 and 133 to have the same wing area (247 sq ft, almost precisely the same as a Spitfire I), and by sheer chance they both came out to the same loaded weight of 4,738 lb. The biplane reached 235 mph and was a pretty obvious non-starter. The monoplane reached 260 mph, which was promising on 640 hp. It still would have stood no chance against 109Es, but on 8 March 1935 the Type 133 was destroyed after getting into an unrecoverable flat spin. Two sources say the landing gear was left down inadvertently, while two others say the purpose of the flight was to investigate spinning with the wheels extended.

The Vickers F.7/30 was merely the Type 151 Jockey of 1929 with a few minor changes. When this metal low-wing monoplane appeared in 1929 it had looked quite modern, and caused such headlines as '240 mph above the clouds'. As revised in 1931, with spatted wheels and a Jupiter engine with a Townend-ring cowl, it no longer looked competitive. Indeed Vickers were half-hearted in their promotion of it, and did not bother to add the required two extra guns. The ring cowl cannot have done much for the larger engine (it replaced a Mercury) because speed fell to only 218 mph. In any case, like the Bristol monoplane, the Vickers submission crashed in a flat spin.

Rex Pierson was bold to offer this monoplane, because in 1931 British official prejudice against monoplanes was still 100 per cent. Another bold designer was Reginald Mitchell of Supermarine. He spent most of his life with biplane flying boats that might make 100 mph with the taps wide open, but as a contrast he produced the string of racing seaplanes that won the Schneider Trophy three times in succession (1927–29–31). He went on record as saying that, despite official prejudice, he never even considered a biplane F.7/30.

His offering, the Type 224 (unofficially called the Spitfire), was a totally fresh design, though owing a little to such predecessors as the S.6B seaplane. An all-metal stressed-skin monoplane, it was a much better-looking job than the Bristol or Vickers monoplanes, yet it was still ungainly and so big that, with a 660-hp Goshawk III, it had no chance of having either the performance or agility needed to win in combat. The 224 took a long time to appear, and did not fly until 19 February 1934! By this time Mitchell had already recognised its uncompetitive nature and drawn a successor. The Type 224 reached a maximum speed of 228 mph, 17 mph below wind-tunnel prediction, and climbed to 15,000 ft in 9.5 minutes, compared with the tunnel estimate of 6.6 minutes. Much of the blame for the shortfall rests with the Air Ministry, who considered the original wing loading of 15 lb/sq ft to be too high, and made Mitchell enlarge the wing. With a span of 45 ft 10 in, the revised fighter would have been useless in combat. We can be deeply grateful that Mitchell had the courage to junk it in time to create the Type 300 Spitfire, which was, to put it mildly, somewhat better!

One of the most unorthodox F.7/30 contenders was the Westland PV.4 (better known by the specification). Arthur Davenport followed traditional fabric-covered biplane construction, used a Goshawk IIS with conventional water cooling and a heavy radiator under the fuselage, and stuck to an open cockpit and fuselage-mounted guns. Having thus far bowed to tradition, he then put the engine in the middle of the fuselage and the cockpit in the nose. The objective, as in many subsequent fighters (notably the Airacobra), was to put the biggest single mass on the centre of gravity, so that manoeuvrability would be as good as possible. Of course, it meant the addition of a long and heavy shaft to drive the propeller. All the references I can find state that the reduction gear was 'built into the engine', which is a funny way to do things because it more than doubles the weight of the shaft. More serious was the fact that the aft-mounted engine set fire to the rear fuselage (fortunately on the ground).

Westland took until mid-1934 to produce this obviously unattractive aircraft. Subsequently they added a cockpit hood, increased the height of the fin and rudder, and replaced the dangerous separate exhausts by long pipes which left the fabric in peace. They also drew attention to the superb view from the cockpit and several other attributes, omitting to state that the PV.4's performance would not have been especially impressive back in 1920! One source claims it could reach 185 mph (a dreadful figure anyway), but in fact the uncorrected figure was 147.7 mph at 13,000 ft. It also took 8 minutes to reach 10,000 feet. The Air Ministry found K2891 to be quite useful, as an instructional airframe at Halton.

This leaves just the Blackburn F.3. Though less unconventional than the Westland effort, this looked even stranger. Perhaps even the hidebound Air Ministry must have thought their specification was being interpreted too literally. Certainly, F.7/30 was one of the biggest single examples of the fact that aeroplanes built exactly to official requirements tend to be disasters. The F.3 was such a disaster that it never even flew. The Blackburn team, led by George Petty, tried so very hard to meet all the requirements that they overlooked the fact that they were creating something useless and probably dangerous, even on the ground.

Thanks to his experience with marine aircraft Petty was able to give the F.3 an all-Duralumin stressed-skin fuselage, but the wings were a typical biplane cellule braced by struts and wires and with fabric covering. Relative to this cellule the fuselage was mounted so high that the spars of the *upper*

Of all the F.7/30 contenders there is no doubt that the Blackburn was the worst. Equally without doubt, this was because its designers tried hardest to comply with the specification.

wing passed under the floor of the cockpit, while the lower wing passed 3 ft below the bottom of the fuselage. The two were joined by pairs of diagonal struts on each side, and in the gap under the fuselage was placed the honeycomb matrix steam/water radiator resembling a larger version of that on the Bristol 123. There were no surface condensers. The main landing gear again resembled that of the Bristol biplane, though with a larger track. To prevent too excessive a fuselage angle the tail was raised on a tall skid.

Taxi tests began on 20 July 1934. The steam-cooled Goshawk III gave endless trouble, and pilot A.M. Blake said he liked sitting so high with such a good view, but did not relish his chances in the event of the aircraft nosing over. His misgiving was well-founded, because, in between rectifying the cooling-system faults, it was found that the aircraft was dangerously unstable when running across the ground at any speed. It was feared that, long before reaching take-off

speed, the aircraft would swing uncontrollably, and the very high centre of gravity made it tend to tip forwards or sideways at the least provocation. The spats were soon removed to permit frequent changes to the landing gear, and the skid was replaced by a castoring tailwheel (which must have made things worse). I have no doubt that Blackburn very soon recognised that their fighter was never going to reach the speed at which it could take off. In order to cease the taxi trials they said that 'cracks and dents' were appearing in the fuselage. Like other F.7/30 contenders, this literal non-starter went to Halton as an instructional airframe (perhaps in how *not* to do it).

It was sheer luck that the RAF in 1939 had left the F.7/30 era far behind, even though squadrons were still converting to the Gladiator. But as a patriotic Briton I regret our inability to create eight competing fighter designs simultaneously today – or even *one* all-British fighter!

DORNIER DO 11 AND DO 13

Dornier Metallbauten GmbH was one of the three German firms that were the greatest pioneers of all-metal aircraft. Since 1915 they had not only concentrated on such aircraft, increasingly using alloys of aluminium, but they were particularly experienced with large machines. It is hardly surprising that, via the Dornier P and Y built in Switzerland, they should have been entrusted with the first bomber for the still-clandestine Luftwaffe. The prototype Dornier F first flew on 7 May 1932, the designation being changed a year later, under the '8-scheme' of the RLM (German Air Ministry) to Do 11.

It was a perfectly normal, unambitious twin-engined monoplane. The high-mounted wing car-ried on its leading edge two 650-hp Siemens Sh 22B radial engines, derived from the Bristol Jupiter. An unusual feature was that the main undercarriages were retractable, the top of each leg being pulled inwards along a track under the wing until the wheel rose into the nacelle. Actuation was electric, but this proved so useless that the task had to be performed by laborious hand-cranking. The pro-posed series version, the Do 11C, appeared in October 1933, and no fewer than 372 were ordered for delivery the following year.

They were to be delivered as civil freight aircraft either to a newly formed traffic inspection unit of the airline, DLH (Luft Hansa), or to a special

A production Do 11C, first of the still-clandestine Luftwaffe's bombers. Its crews called it Die Fliegender Sarg *(flying coffin).*

Even the further-refined Do 23 was an extremely unsatisfactory bomber, quickly withdrawn from operational use.

subsidiary of the DR, the German railways. In reality, of course, these units were merely a cover for military training operations, their night mail and cargo services providing an excellent training for future bomber crews. Bill Green, in *Warplanes of the Third Reich*, noted, 'What was not publicly revealed was that each Do 11 . . . was accompanied by crates which, labelled as spares, in fact contained an interchangeable fuselage nose section complete with bomb-aiming position and machine-gun mounting, dorsal and ventral machine-guns and mounts, and bomb racks.'

Fine. A logical and predictable bit of subterfuge which I am sure fooled nobody – except that Britain and France were no longer interested. Peopled by pacifists, we were far too busy being nice to *Herr* Hitler – never just Hitler in those days – and trying to suppress that warmonger Churchill to take any notice of a giant Luftwaffe bomber force being raised under our very noses. Actually this force was not at first very formidable. I doubt if any large and experienced aircraft manufacturer has ever been more incompetent in the design of a totally conventional and indeed pedestrian aircraft.

I cannot do better than quote Bill Green again:

. . . development of the Do 11 proceeded anything but smoothly, and Reichswehr and DLH pilots were highly critical of the flying characteristics of the bomber. Under certain conditions the wings of the Do 11C vibrated alarmingly, and the risk of a structural failure necessitated restricting the Do 11C to angles of bank no greater than 45 degrees. Poor stability had already necessitated redesign of the vertical tail surfaces. . . . A troublesome feature of the Do 11 from the outset had been its retractable undercarriage, and it had been found necessary to lock this permanently in the down position on all service aircraft. . . . Before the end of 1932 the company had begun work on a simplified version of the basic design, with 750-hp water-cooled BMW VI engines, a fixed spatted undercarriage and Junkers-type double-wing flaps. The prototype of this variant, the Do 13, flew for the first time on 13 January 1933. Initial trials with the Do 13 revealed structural weaknesses and dangerously unstable flying characteristics, coupled with the wing vibration already suffered by the Do 11. . . .

Despite this, orders were soon placed for 222 Do 13s. They suffered additionally from excessive radiator drag, and within a few weeks of initial deliveries in autumn 1934 several Do 13s had crashed as a result of in-flight structural failure. Eventually Dornier redesigned these awful bombers into the Do 23, which at least did not come apart in the air.

BOULTON PAUL P.64 AND P.71A

This is a difficult tale to assess. How do you rate three aircraft, a P.64 and two P.71As, which accomplished nothing because they all crashed? Were they inherently dangerous? There is no real evidence that they were, yet their track record could hardly have been worse.

In the years between the wars the carriage of mail, on British air routes at least, seemed to be more important than mere passengers. Air Ministry specification 21/28 called for a mailplane to carry a payload of 1,000 lb for 1,000 miles at 150 mph, and to be able to keep flying after failure of one engine. The winning design was the Boulton Paul P.64, a traditional biplane. Though the structure was metal, the skin was fabric and the airframe was braced and rigged by a multitude of wires. Two 555-hp Bristol Pegasus I radials – the very first production version of Jupiter to be called a Pegasus – drove fixed-pitch propellers. The main wheels were faired into the bottom wing by large spats.

The P.64 first flew in March 1933, by which time it looked somewhat dated in comparison with the Boeing 247 and DC-1. However, it was modern by British standards, and as it more than met the 1928 specification it was considered 'most efficient'. On the other hand, it had two small scrapes in its short life, and on 21 October 1933 was destroyed in a crash. There is some suggestion that directional stability might have been inadequate, though this had been improved by adding small auxiliary tail fins. It was certainly very prone to spinning.

Imperial Airways thus never even received their proposed fast mail carrier, but they did get two derived passenger versions. These were intended to be P.71s, direct passenger conversions of the P.64, with a longer rear fuselage making them look less stumpy. To cure the directional problem once and for all, the tail was redesigned with three fins and one rudder. In fact all these surfaces were very small, and none was in the full slipstream from an engine. The passenger cabin was skinned in corrugated metal. There were various other differences between the two types, but the chief one was that the airline had large stocks of old 490-hp Armstrong Siddeley Jaguar engines left over from its Argosy fleet, and it wished to save money by using these. The result was designated P.71A, and only two were built. Although they had been planned as fourteen-seaters, Imperial reflected the odd economic policies of the British operator in putting in just seven seats.

The two P.71As were delivered to Croydon in February 1935. The second aircraft, named *Britomart*, took off from Croydon for Haren Airport, Brussels, on 25 October 1935. It undershot badly on landing and was damaged beyond economic repair, the occupants being injured. The first, *Boadicea*, took off from Croydon on a freight service on 25 September 1936. It was never heard of again until, about a month later, a few pieces of wreckage and the pilot's body were washed up on the French coast. So, like so many airliners of sixty years ago, a tale of total disaster, but perhaps not really enough to pin all the blame on the design of the aircraft.

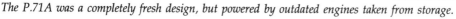

The P.71A was a completely fresh design, but powered by outdated engines taken from storage.

CAPELIS XC-12

The best that can be said of the Capelis is that it did succeed in flying.

In the United States, at least in bygone days, if you produced an unsuccessful aeroplane that was big and impressive there was a good chance it might star in the movies. One example from many is the S-29A, the first aircraft designed and built by Igor Sikorsky after his move to the USA. This ended its days as a 'German bomber', shot down in Howard Hughes's epic *Hell's Angels*. In most respects the solitary S-29A was a pretty sound design, like most of Igor's creations, but another big twin-engined machine, which appeared in at least eight films in the 1930s, was an example of that interesting species, the ambitious aeroplane created by amateurs.

In fact, the Capelis XC-12 was ostensibly the product of a serious company, the Safety Aircraft Corporation, of San Leandro, California. The trouble was, the actual design was carried out by people with plenty of good ideas but little knowledge and even less aeronautical experience. First flown in 1933, it was intended to carry eighteen passengers, though the cabin was never fully furnished. Basically, it was a modern cantilever stressed-skin monoplane, powered by two 525-hp Wright Cyclones. Its clean appearance was marred by the grotesquely forward-sloping windows around the cockpit, the biplane tail and the way the engines were fitted with short ring cowls and stuck far in front of tiny nacelles.

The XC-12 abounded in odd features. Linking

the landing gear to the throttles, so that whenever the throttles were closed the gear extended, was something that would not appeal to a modern certificating authority. This was done in the interests of safety, as was the even more remarkable decision to arrange for the pilot to be able to jettison the fuel tanks in emergency. Rubber vibration isolators were inserted in the main joints between the wing and fuselage. At the time the big oval passenger windows were also unusual, though in a pressurised fuselage (which of course the XC-12 wasn't) such a shape had everything to commend it, and was popular on the Viscount; later square windows were substituted. The maximum weight was said to have been 8,000 lb, but the true figure must have been double this.

So, what was wrong with the Capelis? I cannot do better than quote a delightful letter written in 1973 to *Air Enthusiast* by John H. Murphy, of Saginaw, Michigan:

The Capelis was probably just a promotional scheme – or maybe it was sincere. The airplane was designed by a Greek, built by Greeks, and the venture was promoted by a Greek – and every Greek restaurateur on the West Coast stuck a few bucks into it. The airplane was flown around for promotional purposes, and succeeded in breaking just about every law of common sense, the Aeronautics Bureau of the

Department of Commerce, and those of nature, including gravity.

With brilliant conception the aircraft was put together with Parker-Kalon self-tapping metal screws rather than old-fashioned rivets, and in flight these screws vibrated out by the bucketful. Replacing lost screws probably ran to 25 per cent of the fuel bill, and the canny promoters charged this up to sabotage by jealous rivals, and at one time hired detectives (Greek, no doubt) to bring these evil-doers to justice.

Somewhere there is an ex-American Airlines captain named Gus Whitke, a big fellow with a homely face, who was called 'The Greek' because of the humorous impersonations he could do. With a few snorts under his belt his treatment of the Capelis was truly great. A small bit

of it was on the toilet, which it seems opened at the bottom as on a Pullman car, but was subject to different velocities and conditions.

The venture failed before long, of course. As even Arrigo Balboni, the Flying Junk Man, didn't want it, the XC-12 became a Hollywood movie prop. It was constantly trundled tail-first between the studio's sound stages on Cahuenga Boulevard to the lusher areas of Griffith Park, where the Tarzan and Jungle Jim low-budget epics were being ground out. It served in every jungle crash scene for many years – and there were a lot of them then. In fact the Capelis probably logged more miles on Cahuenga than it did in the air.

And its performance? Lousy – the degree depending on how many screws were loose.

KALININ K-7

Vibration may be enjoyable in some circumstances, but where aircraft are concerned it can be sheer murder. Plenty of otherwise perfectly sound aeroplanes have come apart in the sky simply because the designers were unable to create a structure which did not resonate. And the biggest of these deadly resonators was the K-7.

To pursue the problem of resonance a little

further, most structures resonate only at one or two clearly defined frequencies. Sometimes the frequency is so clearly defined that it can be heard as a note, but that implies a frequency in the kilocycle (thousands of vibrations per second) range, which is generated by something small and rigid such as a tuning fork, a violin string or a turbine blade. For a wing or fuselage the resonant

The mock-up of Kalinin's monster K-7, with engines in front of the wheels.

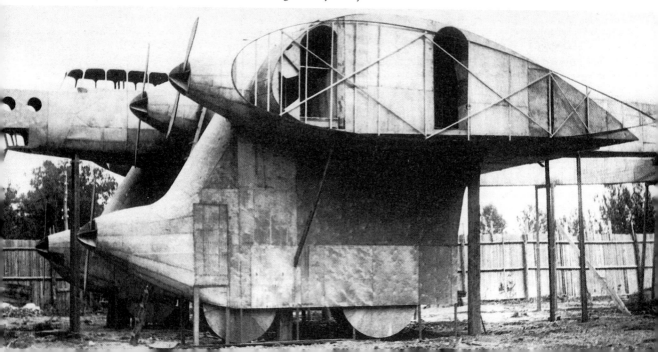

As built, the K-7 had six engines on the leading edge and one on the trailing edge.

frequency will be very much lower, perhaps as low as 3 Hz (three cycles per second), but the amplitude may be far greater, in the order of several inches. It does not take a very large amplitude for a resonant structure made of metal to fail by fatigue. Wood, and modern composites, do not fatigue in the same way, but they can just as easily be overstressed by forced vibrations.

The word 'forced' means that energy is put into the structure on each cycle. If it were not, the vibration would probably swiftly die away. Major sources of input energy are engines and propellers. Today's turbine engines generally output hardly any vibration, and what there is has frequencies much greater than major parts of the airframe – but, despite this, today's aircraft are painstakingly tested in powerful vibration rigs, able to apply any exact frequency at the rate of several hundred horsepower to see if anything responds. They are also tested in flight by firing explosive 'bonkers' at extremities. It was worse in the days of piston engines. Big piston engines and propellers generated far greater vibration, and it tended to be at frequencies more sympathetic to the airframe. For example, I once looked out of a parked Ambassador to see that the idling Centaurus was moving up/down and occasionally in circles with an amplitude of what looked like 6 inches; it threatened to tear itself loose. As soon as rpm increased, the problem vanished, but in cruising flight, at 2,450 or 2,500 rpm, the Ambassador's resonances were furnishings in the cabin, which buzzed loudly.

Sixty years ago there was no such thing as designing to avoid resonance, and no way of testing for it. Obviously, the bigger the structure, the lower the natural frequencies and the bigger the amplitudes. Poor Konstantin Alekseyevich Kalinin was no fool, and with the K-7 he tried his best to

get it right. Despite its brief designation, it was one of the biggest aircraft in the world.

The K-7 was perhaps the nearest thing to a real flying fortress – a battleship of the skies – ever built. A heavy bomber, it had a monoplane wing of almost perfect elliptical form (a Kalinin trademark) with a span of nearly 174 ft and an area of 4,887 sq ft (considerably greater than that of a B-52). On the wing were the strange number of seven 830-hp engines, six on the leading edge and one pusher on the centreline at the back. The pusher was possible because the twin-finned tail was carried by two huge booms more than 36 ft apart. Under the wings were what looked like two floats which were actually enormous gondolas housing the landing gears, gunners and the bombload of up to 41,887 lb. Each gondola was attached by a vertical rear strut, housing a ladder, and an inclined front strut, housing a staircase. Various cannon and machine-guns were located at the front and rear of the gondolas, in the fuselage nose and in the tail of each boom.

Altogether the K-7 looked like what it was, a real juggernaut of the skies. It was completed in the summer of 1933, and on 29 June the seven M-34F vee-12 engines were run for the first time installed. To everyone's consternation it was soon obvious that at particular engine speeds, including some likely to be encountered for prolonged periods, the booms and tail were resonating badly. The problem was quickly alleviated by opening or closing the throttles, but then it would appear again at a different engine speed. Today one could attack the problem with precision, and redesign the structure to have safe unforced natural frequencies. In 1933 nobody knew how to do this. The only solution appeared to be to 'beef up' the structure, and

A three-view of the K-7, the plan showing top and underside views.

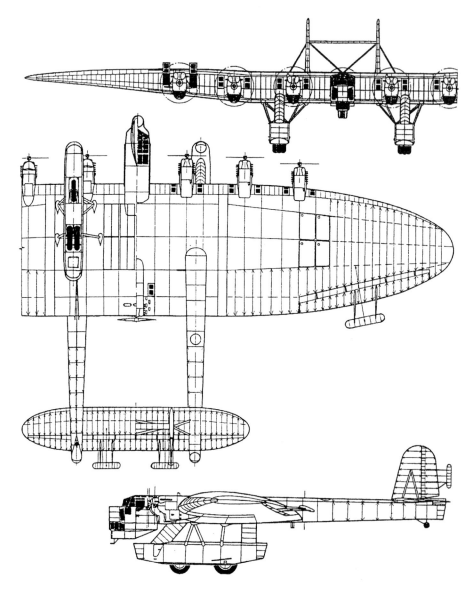

Kalinin ordered that steel angle sections should be bolted on along the booms until the movement appeared to have stopped. A few extra tons were nothing to the K-7.

Today we would recognise that this was not a cure but a botch. But the first flight, on 11 August 1933, was satisfactory, and soon the gigantic and very distinctive bomber was exciting the whole population of Kharkov. But on the ninth flight, on 21 November 1933, during full-power tests at about 100 m (328 ft) altitude, the deadly vibration suddenly struck, appearing to begin in the tail. Within seconds the right-hand boom had broken, the K-7 dived into the ground and burned, and the pilot, thirteen crew and a passenger were killed, five crew surviving. This put a blight on twin booms – and also on Kalinin, and may have been a factor in his arrest and execution on trumped-up 'conspiracy and spying' charges two years later.

WESTLAND PV.7

This high-wing monoplane was one of several designed to meet Air Ministry specification G.4/31 for a general-purpose aircraft able to carry out level or dive bombing or drop a torpedo. As it appeared in 1933, it was just another British aircraft from a company with no knowledge of stressed-skin construction. The wing therefore had to be braced by struts, and these were the Achilles heel in what was otherwise a sound – if obsolescent – aeroplane.

The PV.7 was a big machine, powered by a 722-hp Bristol Pegasus. The 60 ft 8 in wing passed through the top of the fuselage between the enclosed cockpits for the pilot and the radio operator/gunner. The left and right wings were braced by two large struts to the tips of triangular trusses on each side of the fuselage, the front truss also carrying the main landing leg. Auxiliary struts braced the main struts to the wing at their midpoint. The wings had no flaps, but slats, large

Dated 11 June 1934, an official works photo of the recently completed PV.7.

ailerons and, just inboard of the ailerons, powered airbrakes. Among the first on any British aircraft, these airbrakes took the form of metal panels pulled open by external levers and rods, one half hinging upwards and the other downwards.

Company chief test pilot Harald Penrose flew the PV.7 for the first time on 3 October 1933. After minor alterations he considered it a very satisfactory aircraft. He accompanied it to the Aeroplane & Armament Experimental Establishment official test field, which in those days was at Martlesham Heath, Suffolk, and in August 1934 was engaged there in overload diving trials. I cannot comprehend how the company appear never to have imagined that such tests might take place, nor to have designed the aircraft – a dive bomber – to meet this requirement. They sent a telegram to Martlesham instructing that the flight should be postponed, as they had belatedly discovered that the PV.7 might not meet the necessary strength requirements! But Penrose had already taken off, and, whilst the plane was diving through rough air, the port rear main bracing strut failed (according to one account, 'under an unexpected download'). In leaving the aircraft, the left wing also severed the tail unit. Despite the violent gyrations of the remainder of the aircraft Penrose managed to get out through the very small side door, and became an early member of the Caterpillar Club (the club restricted to those who have saved their lives by Irvin parachute).

To quote him for the second time, Dave Anderton once said, 'There's only one thing an airplane can do that's unforgivable and that's to come unglued.' I would add to that. In my opinion you *never* say, 'We didn't think you'd put it to

that test.' There is no such thing as 'an unexpected download'. And you don't send telegrams warning your pilot he has an unsafe aeroplane, especially if he has already taken off.

To round off the story, G.4/31 resulted in a typical host of competing prototypes (what a contrast with today's RAF, which, because we have so little industry, tends to buy things from the USA or Brazil). Most were biplanes, including the winning Vickers Type 253. Against intense competition Vickers-Armstrongs won a contract for 150. But designers Rex Pierson and Barnes Wallis were convinced that the Type 253 – *because* it met the official G.4/31 specification – was obsolete before it could go into production. They quickly schemed a monoplane (the Wellesley) which, with a similar Pegasus engine, carried double the load required, had twice the range and was 70 mph faster than the biplane. The company director in charge of aviation, Sir Robert McClean, was utterly unlike his contemporaries in the industry. He repeatedly told the Air Ministry they were years behind the times; without him the Spitfire would never have been allowed to happen. At the same time, in 1934, he wrote to the Air Ministry about G.4/31, 'I suggest to you that it might be better to reduce these orders in numbers, and in their place go into production of the monoplane as soon as tooling can be completed. Meantime, and until you can decide whether we shall be allowed to switch over from the biplane to the monoplane, I do not wish to proceed with work on the biplane because, in my view, it is not a modern machine.'

With factories desperate for work, it takes real courage to write a letter like that.

ISACCO-4

In the period between the world wars several aircraft designers in Italy and France, all avowed Communists, decided that their duty lay in emigrating to the Soviet Union. I don't know how many of them regretted it, but almost to a man they fell foul of Stalin's terror in the mid-1930s and found themselves behind bars. One such was Italian Vittorio Isacco. During the late 1920s he worried away at the problem of designing a helicopter, and at last, in 1932, he was able to start building it. The unfortunate constructors were ZOK NII GVF, the civil bureau of special construction. Isacco had as consultant Professor B.N. Yuriev, who had been trying to build a helicopter since 1912. Clearly, he didn't know much about the subject either.

Isacco's machine was finally finished in 1935. It was enormous. The four-bladed rotor had a diameter of just over 80 ft. Small by comparison, the fuselage had a 300-hp Wright Whirlwind J-6 on the nose, driving a four-blade propeller. Above the rigid rotor hub towered a mast from which bracing cables extended down to support the massive blades when at rest. The cables were certainly needed, because not only did each blade have a servo control surface carried on struts behind the trailing edge at the tip but, also at the tip, each blade carried a 120-hp de Havilland Gipsy III engine, driving a four-blade propeller! Isacco was by no means the only designer to try this arrangement, but his must surely have been the only helicopter ever built to have five four-blade propellers!

Isacco left documents outlining a succession of problems, some fundamental to the basic arrangements and the rest more immediate difficulties with the hardware. He realised that, though this form of tip drive meant that the only torque imparted to the fuselage was that due to friction in the main hub bearing, it was still essential to be able to control the direction in which the fuselage was pointing. This was one reason for having the propulsion engine blowing slipstream over the rudder. In translational flight the aerodynamics of the tip propellers was complex. Isacco thought centrifugal force along the spinning blades would help feed petrol, but appeared to overlook what it might do to the flow of lubricating oil inside each of the tip-mounted engines. Moreover, his calculations were found to contain errors, which held up the work until 1935. Then ground testing started.

Anyone with much imagination will see that it must have been hilarious. Have you ever started a Gipsy? You have to open a little access door to prime the carburettor, shut the door and lock it, and then go through the rigmarole of 'switches off . . . suck in . . . contact'. At which point the propeller has to be swung as hard as possible by hand, the helper then getting clear the moment the engine fires. How do you do all this four times at once when you are 12 ft up on a ladder?

But that was only part of the problem. The most serious difficulty was that as soon as the mighty rotor really started going round it suffered severe blade flutter, which caused one of the engines to come completely adrift and go sailing off into the sunset, leaving the off-balance machine almost coming apart.

One of the last reports on this programme states that Isacco eventually concluded that the basic concept was not practical. But he didn't really deserve to be arrested in 1936 and sent off to one of Stalin's special (i.e. prison) design bureaux. Or did he?

One of the few known photographs of the Isacco. As there appear to be only three blade-tip engines, this might have been taken after the test run.

HANDLEY PAGE HEREFORD

Students of RAF bombers will know that the HP.53 Hereford was simply an HP.52 Hampden with different engines. So I will begin by outlining the deficiencies of the Hampden.

Designed to the same B.9/32 specification as the Wellington, the Hampden had exactly the same engine (two 1,000-hp Bristol Pegasus) but otherwise it could hardly have been more different. It was smaller than the Vickers-Armstrongs bomber in overall dimensions, and the usable volume inside the fuselage was perhaps only about one-quarter as great. This is because the Hampden was deliberately made as narrow as possible. The pilot sat in solitary state in a cockpit rather like that of a fighter. The navigator/bomb aimer was in the nose, the radio operator above the trailing edge and the lower rear gunner under the trailing edge.

The Handley Page designers, under George Volkert, deliberately ignored the newly perfected power-driven turrets, pointing out the penalty these imposed in reduced speed and bomb load. Instead they arranged for the pilot to have a fixed gun firing ahead, and the other three crew each to have a single gun aimed by hand. Thus, the Hampden had the same sort of defensive armament as the contemporary German Dornier, Heinkel and Junkers bombers. Everything seemed fine. The guns covered all the blind spots, and in any case the Hampden was very fast and exceptionally manoeuvrable. Its makers described it as 'a fighting bomber' (even, on some occasions, as 'a fighter bomber'). They appear to have thought that, if war came, the pilot would chase other aircraft and shoot them down with his fixed gun.

When war did come it was not quite like that. In his classic book *Enemy Coast Ahead* Guy Gibson described how single Lewis or Vickers K guns were completely inadequate (and of course the pilot's gun was useless, and generally removed). Bypassing official channels, Gibson himself got the aft upper and lower positions modified to fire twin Vickers K (gas-operated) guns, plus beam guns fired by the radio operator. This was at least an improvement, but there remained several grave deficiencies. The most serious was probably the fact that the interior was cramped and generally uncomfortable. This was especially true of the lower rear gun position. The worst aspect of this lack of room was that it made it very difficult for the two rear crew-members to change places, and impossible for either of them to communicate with the rest of the crew except by intercom. It is part of Bomber Command folklore that on one occasion a navigator changed places with a critically wounded pilot and brought the aircraft back, but it is difficult to see how he did this.

As for the Hereford – made by a new company in Belfast, Short & Harland – this had 955-hp Napier Dagger engines. Turning at up to 4,200 rpm their shrieking noise drove crews crazy. Worse, the noise was often absent, for their unreliability was notorious. Cooling was excessive in the air and inadequate on the ground, and ground crews hated checking 192 valves and changing 96 plugs per aircraft. Herefords flew just one combat mission; then they were junked.

Dated 27 July 1940, a Short & Harland picture of newly completed Herefords awaiting collection.

BREWSTER SB2A BUCCANEER/BERMUDA

In today's stringent climate it is hard to imagine the RAF having to receive 750 useless aircraft it didn't want!

Aircraft design is a funny business. While many seemingly outrageous devices have from the start handled beautifully, countless pedestrian machines have made it into this book. The story of the Brewster B.340, called the SB2A Buccaneer by the US Navy, the A-34 by the US Army and the Bermuda by the RAF, was told in *Aeroplane Monthly* for November and December 1989 and January 1990. That being so, this will be quite brief; this aircraft hardly merits much attention.

Brewster were proud of their long history; they

had been making high-quality carriages since 1810. In 1932 they formed Brewster Aeronautical, and proceeded to turn out a succession of Navy prototypes characterised by a slightly tapered dihedralled wing mounted in the mid position on a tubby fuselage with a big radial engine on the front. One was the SBA dive bomber, flown in 1936. From this, designer Dayton Brown developed the Model 340, flown as the XSB2A in June 1941.

Superficially it seemed just what the Allies needed. Having taken on board the lesson of the Ju 87

'Stuka', everyone wanted a really powerful dive bomber, able to put a 1,000-lb bomb accurately on a Japanese warship or any other target. Powered by a 1,600-hp Wright R-2600 14-cylinder Cyclone, the Brewster dive bomber had a capacious internal bomb bay and effective split dive flaps along the trailing edge, and certainly looked the part.

In June 1940 the French had placed a letter of intent, which Brewster somehow turned into a contract despite the capitulation of that country. A month after the prototype flew, a remarkably large order for 162 Model 340-17s was placed by the Dutch government in exile (for the Netherlands East Indies). By this time, July 1941, the prototype was suffering severe problems, of which the most dangerous was aileron overbalance. Almost equally lethal was asymmetric operation of the dive flaps. Other problems included severe buffeting, caused by the dive flaps and also by the mock-up dorsal turret. Before long the turret was abandoned and replaced by a traditional rear cockpit with gun(s) aimed by hand.

The French contract was naturally taken over by Great Britain, which in November 1940 signed for no fewer than 750 model 340-14 aircraft to be named Bermuda. From then on, the list of modifications grew daily. Brewster said it was all the fault of the British, and even screwed an extra $4 million out of the British Purchasing Commission 'for these delays which they caused us'. This was, of course, a time when Britain grabbed any warplane it could get hold of, but there are limits . . .

Eventually Brewster completed 1,052 production aircraft in six versions. Not one got into front-line use, and the vast majority were simply scrapped by the RAF, US Navy, USAAF and RCAF. Remarkably, the Fleet Air Arm managed to avoid becoming involved. The basic problem was endemic poor stability, especially in roll and yaw, compounded in some conditions by rudder reversal. Lateral control, in the prototype dangerous at high speeds, was modified until it was virtually non-existent at low speeds. One can muse on the fact that, compared with this aircraft, the US Navy preferred the terrible SB2C!

In the mid-1950s I was privileged to meet a few times with Chris Clarkson, who had been chief test pilot for the British Air Commission in Washington, and retired to an apartment in New York. Asked if he could give an overall opinion of wartime US aircraft, he replied, 'On the whole, they were outstanding. Of course, there were exceptions . . . the Seamew, Helldiver and certainly the Bermuda'. Writing to *Aeroplane Monthly* from Connecticut in March 1990 he declared, '. . . it ranked high on my list of nastiest – and in some respects most dangerous – aircraft I ever flew.'

Let's wrap it up by quoting from the company magazine *Brewster Builder* for July 1943: 'Bermudas are over there by the hundreds, and everybody who has flown them is enthusiastic. The squadrons are located in North Ireland, Scotland, England and South Wales. They would rather fly the Bermuda than any other plane . . .'

Breda Ba 88 Lince

Throughout most of aviation's history there seems often to have been a fairly narrow margin between brilliant success and abysmal failure. For example, the Spitfire's strange wing construction, with a difficult elliptical plan form, and just a single spar assembled from a mass of square tubes which fitted inside each other like a set of Russian dolls, could easily have led to the design being rejected in favour of something simpler. And the something simpler might have been the fixed-gear Martin-Baker MB2, which as far as structure, accessibility and maintenance were concerned was streets ahead of the Spit. (Thinks: we picked the right one, despite its faults.)

In the same way, in 1936 Junkers built the prototype Ju 88. The third Ju 88 set world re-

cords, and subsequently almost 15,000 of these versatile aircraft were built. I have the highest opinion of Ju 88s. They were true war-winners, and it was not the fault of *die drei-finger 88* that Germany actually lost the war.

At about the same time, the Breda company in Italy was busy designing a different '88' in vaguely the same class. The Ba 88 Lince (Lynx) was designed as a multi-role attack aircraft, urgently needed to replace existing types which were obviously obsolescent. Again, the prototype set records. Flown by the company's chief test pilot, Furio Niclot, it went round the 621-mile (1,000-km) circuit at an average of 325.6 mph; over a 62.1-mile circuit, in about a 30° bank all the way, it averaged 344.24 mph.

Italian dictator Benito Mussolini would have declaimed that this line of Ba 88s was an impressive display of Fascist airpower.

Clearly, the Lince was an aircraft of great potential. One of the minuses was not obvious. Instead of having the very latest stressed-skin structure, like the Ju 88 (which was designed with the help of two experienced American stressmen, incidentally), the Italian machine had a traditional structure of welded chrome-molybdenum steel tube, on to which was added a light secondary metal structure to create the streamlined outer form. Though quite small and compact, the Italian 88 had two engines which in the prototype were 900-hp Gnome-Rhône K14 Mistral Majors. The big engine nacelles were slung under the wing, which was mounted mid-high to leave room for a bomb bay under it. Main and tail wheels were fully retractable, the crew of two sat in tandem, and there was a single fin.

Mussolini was convinced this 88 was a world-beater, and he urged its production with all speed. Accordingly, the definitive armed version went into production not only with Breda but also at Meridionali (IMAM). The production model was powered by 1,000-hp Piaggio radials, and had an armament of three 0.5-in nose guns, a single 0.303-in in the rear cockpit and various internal or recessed bomb loads. The prototype had exhibited several undesirable and even dangerous characteristics. In particular, directional stability and control were always poor, especially at low speeds, and loss of an engine was likely to be quickly lethal. Addition of armament resulted in far more than the expected fall-off in performance, to the extent that the production aircraft did not even meet the Regia Aeronautica's requirements. Stability and control were slightly improved by fitting a twin-finned tail, but once service acceptance pilots got their hands on the 88 it was immediately apparent that it was very far from being a good aircraft. In battle trim, maximum level speed was *one half* that promised by the manufacturer, and rate of climb less than one half!

Of course, all this was discovered when production was in full swing. If an aeroplane has a great reputation, can you simply issue it to front-line aircrews and hope they will continue to have high morale? I don't believe this for a moment, and I think all the *Gruppi* and *Stormi* that were unlucky enough to get the Lince very soon learned its true worth. A few did see action, notably over French airfields in Corsica in the first days after Italy's entry into the war in June 1940, when Mussolini thought the conflict was already won. But the war was not actually over. The Regia Aeronautica had to take on the RAF in Cyrenaica (Libya), and that meant fitting sand filters to the engine inlets. It is on record that, when fitted, the record-breaking Linces 'could not gain sufficient altitude nor maintain formation'. By November 1940 new Linces were delivered straight to the scrapyard. Those in service were used as decoys parked around Italian airfields.

BLOCH 150

There is absolutely nothing automatic or stereotyped about aircraft design. One might think that, at any given point in time, two design teams given similar requirements, adopting similar configurations and using broadly the same type of engine, might be expected to create almost identical aircraft. In fact the historical record shows that the opposite is usually the case. Some of the aircraft will be winners, and the others inferior or even disasters.

Today the arrogantly French firm of Dassault has a high reputation in the world of fighters, but it was not always so. I was privileged to have several friendly discussions with Marcel Dassault, whose original name was Marcel Bloch. Once we got on to the subject of the Bloch 151 and 152, which saw hectic combat in that terrible spring of 1940. They could have been instrumental in beating the Luftwaffe. Instead, said Marcel, 'It was never the superior aircraft we were all seeking; we were always trying to rectify faults, which is difficult when all the emphasis is on production.' The mass-produced 151 and 152 would not rate inclusion here; they were abysmal in some ways but quite good in others. But the original prototype, the Bloch 150, almost surpasses belief in the ineptitude of its design.

There is some uncertainty over how the project started. In September 1934 the French Service Technique issued an important specification for a new single-seat fighter. Several authoritative accounts state that Avions Marcel Bloch decided to participate, entering the Type 150 design. Others claim that – for some unexplained reason – Bloch did not compete, yet instructed Maurice Roussel to design the Type 150 as a company-funded venture. The only reason for building the prototype as a private venture would have been if it deliberately contravened the STAé requirements, for example by incorporating some radical new idea. On the contrary, the Bloch 150 could hardly have been more pedestrian.

Readers will know by now the saying, 'If it is right, it looks right' or 'If it looks right, it is right.' Whichever saying you prefer, the 150 certainly looked wrong. Simply described, the Type 150 sounds fine: an all-metal stressed-skin cantilever low-wing monoplane fighter, powered by a large fully cowled radial engine, with inward-retracting main landing gears and split flaps driven hydraulically. Construction took place at the Courbevoie (Paris) factory between September 1935 and spring 1936, when the parts were trucked to Villacoublay for assembly and flight test. The Bloch 150 was completed in early July 1936, and it was hardly a thing of grace or beauty.

The fuselage was skinned with sheet wrapped around between the numerous frames. The cockpit was right up at the front, immediately behind the engine. It had a sliding hood, and small rear windows on each side to give a very limited view diagonally backwards, leaving a blind arc of about 60° (as was the case in many mid-1930s fighters). The wing was made in four sections, joined at the centreline under the fuselage and at a point well outboard where the flaps met the ailerons. The engine was a Gnome-Rhône 14K rated at 850 hp for take-off. The intended armament was two 20-mm Hispano-Suiza 404 cannon, mounted at the extremities of the inboard wings. Each inboard wing housed a 200-litre (44-gallon) fuel tank, immediately aft of the bay for the landing gear.

So what were the problems? Basically, the Bloch 150 was just ungainly. The most obvious oddity was that the main landing gears looked half the size they should have been. The belly appeared almost to be touching the ground, the ground angle was barely 5°, and propeller ground clearance was also close to zero. The change in wing taper at the inboard/outboard joint suggested that something had been found to be very wrong with the position of the CG, the outer wings being almost swept back. According to all published reports, the CG was nearly in line with the main wheels, instead of being well to the rear. This would cause the aircraft to nose over on the slightest application of the brakes, which, combined with the inadequate ground clearance, would bode ill for the propeller. It would also make controlled taxiing almost impossible. Another shortcoming was that the engine, one of the Mistral Major family derived from the British Jupiter but with fourteen two-valve cylinders, had a direct drive to the primitive fixed-pitch three-blade propeller. There were countless points of detail design which simply looked crude.

Like most French warplanes of the 1930s, the Bloch 150 was hardly a thing of beauty.

The marvel is that this truly dreadful prototype should have been transformed into fighters which, if still mediocre, were at least better than some others in French service, such as the MS.406. How this was done is even today the subject of some argument. For many years it was 'common knowledge' that the Bloch 150 made its first attempted take-off on 17 July 1936 (some authors say 7 July) and that it simply refused to leave the ground. Today Dassault profess not to have any records of the occasion (and I cannot blame them). Writing in *Air International* Pierre Leyvastre tells a different story. He says that, on 17 July, while the 150 was taxiing out for the first flight, the tailwheel was damaged. The prototype was thereupon dismantled, trucked back to the factory and not flown for a further ten months!

Such a sequence of events makes no sense whatever. Bearing in mind that the tailwheel carried almost no load, it is hard to comprehend what damage it could have suffered. Even if the whole unit had been torn out, or if it had deformed the rear fuselage, repairs could obviously have been effected on the spot (Villacoublay was exceedingly well equipped with workshops). The multiple errors in the 150 design must have been obvious to everyone, and it would have been logical to use the ten months in rectifying as many as possible. Instead, nothing was done, and there is some

indication that Bloch had abandoned the fighter as a lost cause. The turmoil caused by the nationalisation of most of the French industry need not have interrupted work, had any importance been attached to it.

Indeed, the real puzzle is why, having done nothing for ten months to try to turn this pathetic aircraft into the semblance of a fighter, it was then restored to alleged airworthiness at Villacoublay, to make its maiden flight on 4 May 1937. The futility of trying to do anything with the 150 by this time should have been obvious. It was not only an aircraft of 1934 vintage, but possibly the worst fighter prototype ever designed at that time. When one recalls that the Bf 109 flew in May 1935 and the Spitfire in March 1936, the start of flight trials of the Bloch 150 in May 1937 appears to be a sick joke. It had no chance of reaching even 300 mph, had empty tubes where the cannon were to be installed, and was impossible even to taxi properly. How it flew is not recorded, but some indication is provided by the fact that the first flight was logged as five minutes and the aircraft was again dismantled and returned to Courbevoie to be rebuilt. Among other things it was given a new wing, and the main landing gears were greatly lengthened and angled forwards rather like those of the Fw 190.

What followed were very brief periods of test

flying, punctuated by much longer periods back at Courbevoie for numerous modifications. By spring 1938 it was gradually becoming apparent that Nazi Germany really did constitute a serious menace, and that France needed all the fighters she could get. Even at this late date the Bloch could only manage 298 mph at its best height, but was still thought to offer some potential. Unfortunately, from the viewpoints of mass production and maintenance, it could hardly have been worse, so a team led by Lucien Servanty totally redesigned the 150 to produce the 151, which was far easier to manufacture. This did not look very different, but hardly any parts of the structure were common. A single large tank was housed under the cockpit, the completely different wings being bolted on each side. Even then over 240 further modifications were necessary, many of them being incorporated during production at Châteauroux–Déols and Bordeaux–Mérignac as well as at Courbevoie.

The No. 4 Bloch 151, the first to be delivered, reached the Armée de l'Air on 7 March 1939. Marcel Dassault told me the objective was 200 per month, which could have been reached but for Communist saboteurs who made sure that nearly every aircraft was lacking its guns, or gunsight, or propeller, or some other vital component. Frantic efforts after the start of World War II brought the production total up to (it is believed) 699, of which some 450 were of the 152 model with a slightly different engine. These equipped seven *Groupes de Chasse*, where their chief asset was the ability to absorb battle damage. In almost every other respect – stability, agility, performance in the horizontal or vertical planes, trim changes, engine power and quantity of ammunition – they were still abysmal. I once asked a former MB.152 pilot the chief thing he would have done to tackle a 109E on even terms, and after a pause he replied, 'Fly a different type of aircraft!'

De Havilland DH.91 Albatross

It is self-evident how narrow is the margin between 'best' and 'worst' in aircraft design. The de Havilland Aircraft Co. had an impressive history of diverse aircraft which, for various reasons, were truly great. They also had many also-rans. Among the latter were a remarkable number of post-World War II types which combined potential greatness with a tendency to come apart in the air, which is a fairly worrying habit. In the 1930s the firm had a good line of staple products made by the traditional methods they knew well. With the DH.88 Comet they pushed slightly ahead into fresh fields, and almost came unstuck. With the DH.91 Albatross they went a good deal further.

It is surely ironic that the Albatross was one of the most aesthetically beautiful aircraft ever to fly. It has figured in numerous books as the very epitome of modern, streamlined design. Yet I have no hesitation in including it in these pages. It was a major project by a highly professional team, yet – well, the proof of the pudding is not in its appearance but in the eating.

According to legend, Geoffrey de Havilland himself was the moving spirit behind the ninety-first type to bear his initials. Although the DH.88 Comet had won the speed race to Melbourne in October 1934, the aircraft coming second was a Douglas DC-2. This commercial transport, entered by KLM, carried a full payload and won the handicap race by miles. It seemed obvious that aircraft of this class, with clean stressed-skin structures, flaps, retractable landing gear, properly cowled engines and variable-pitch propellers would quickly sweep away the obsolete and primitive airliners which were all the British industry had to offer. De Havilland's company made repeated attempts to get the Air Ministry to comprehend this. This took more than a year. At last, in January 1936, the company was awarded a contract for 'two transatlantic mail carriers', to carry 1,000 lb of mailbags for 2,500 miles against a 40-mph headwind. The design was to be capable of later being developed to carry passengers, in 1936 a rather secondary matter.

Design went ahead fast, the main team being led by Arthur Hagg, most of whose aircraft were aesthetic delights. He mounted a wing of 9.1 aspect ratio under a fuselage of breathtaking perfection of form. Though unpressurised, this had a perfectly circular cross-section, and the smooth profile variation from nose to tail was broken only by the pilots' windscreens. So great was the wish to minimise drag that the main landing gears, each with a single large wheel, had single legs retracting inwards into the wings. Even more remarkably, the air-cooled engines were

On 27 August 1938 a Hatfield shopkeeper infuriated de Havilland by sending this photograph to a newspaper. In the 1960s it was issued by Hawker Siddeley, stamped 'may be published without payment of any fee'!

enclosed tightly in sealed cowlings, the cooling air being rammed in through small inlets in the leading edge of the wing, ducted to the outer sides of the cylinder blocks and allowed to escape through a hinged door under the cowling. The engines were Gipsy 12 inverted vee-12s, rated at 525 hp for take-off but, with massive supercharger casings and gearboxes, inordinately heavy at around 1,130 lb. As it used standard Gipsy cylinders it was hoped to be reliable, but this proved to be a pious hope.

The Albatross was packed with pious hopes. The cowlings were aluminium and the flight-control surfaces steel tube or light alloy with fabric covering, but everything else was wood. The wing and fixed tail were made in a conventional way, the inner structure being covered with two layers of ply laths. The fuselage and flaps were quite different. The flaps had internal structure, but were covered in a ply/balsa sandwich skin. The fuselage was ply/balsa sandwich with nothing inside it! In other words it was a pure monocoque, the entire structure comprising the outer shell of stress-bearing cedar ply glued on each side of balsa almost an inch thick. This lent itself well to a perfect shape, with an absolutely smooth outer skin, with no fatigue problems and, said de Havilland, simple to repair without special skills or facilities.

The two mailplanes had been allotted serials K8618/19, but the first carried Class-B registration E.2 when it made its maiden flight on 20 May 1937. The landing gear failed to retract fully, but otherwise the only real problem was poor yaw control, especially in the climb. The tail was thereupon completely redesigned, with a much larger horizontal surface carrying unbraced fins and rudders (actually reduced in size) on the tips. This removed the only flaw in the aircraft's appearance. While this was being done, in July 1937, Imperial Airways placed an order for five of the passenger version. For these the fuselage was redesigned, with the aft flight-deck windows omitted, a crew door added at the front, a row of six wide passenger windows added on each side much lower down than the few small windows of the mail carriers, and the main door moved aft. As in the mailplane all fuel was low in the fuselage, but capacity was reduced from 1,320 gallons to only 440.

All seemed set fair for a successful programme, but de Havilland were rapidly moving into an era in which their proud belief in their own infallibility was to lead them into repeated troubles with almost every subsequent design. On top of this, their inexperience with many aspects of modern design – or you could lay part of the blame on their suppliers – led to the Albatross suffering a succession of embarrassments. Thus, on 31 March 1938, the electric actuation of the first aircraft's landing gear malfunctioned and defeated all the efforts of the test crew to lower the wheels. E.2 had to be belly-landed on Hatfield's grass. On 27 August 1938 the second mailplane, engaged in take-off tests, broke its back as it landed and came to rest with the rear half on the grass and the rest pointing up at the sky. A local shopkeeper infuriated DH by taking a photo and selling it to a newspaper.

On 8 November 1938 the first of the passenger liners was delivered, becoming the flagship of the outwardly beautiful F-class. The cockpit was nice enough, but Imperial captains soon suffered from the disconcerting tendency to swing on landing, something they had not encountered with the sedate biplanes. Passengers likewise found the interior cramped; after stooping to enter through the door, 3 ft 3 in high, the taper of the fuselage meant that the interior was very constricted except further forward. In-flight noise and vibration were worse than they were used to (DH had hoped to set a high standard) and the flexure of the wing and fuselage resulted in a sickening ride in any but very still air. A further point is that the rudders were, to quote one experienced pilot, H.A. 'Tony' Taylor, 'almost rigidly heavy'. He dismissed this, saying you hardly needed them; but if you swung on take-off or on landing you needed all the rudder you could get.

Throughout their careers, first with Imperial, and then with BOAC and the RAF, the Albatrosses suffered a mixture of faults, failures and plain bad luck. On an early flight to Paris a skid on wet grass damaged the landing gear. A little later the same thing happened at Croydon, but on this occasion one wheel hit the edge of the paved apron. The leg folded, the spars broke and the aircraft keeled over; then the other gear collapsed and the other wing also failed. Four months later, on 17 May 1939, one leg obstinately refused to lower; by chance a DH engineer was on board, and he knew how to spend some twenty-five minutes winding the leg down by hand. This soon became a standard, and often needed, procedure. On one occasion gear operation was being demonstrated with a machine on trestles. With too many people in the cockpit and nobody in the back the Albatross tipped up, its tail jamming the hangar doors.

In October 1940 *Fingal* was being ferried to storage at Bramcote when a single fractured fuel pipe stopped all four engines. She made a successful forced landing, though her pride was hurt by her elegant nose having penetrated the side of a cottage and coming to rest directly over the lavatory. Nobody can blame *Faraday* and flagship *Frobisher* for being burned by a pyromaniac (a disgruntled workman). The former was repaired, and began flying mail to Iceland. On 11 August 1941 she swung on landing at Reykjavik, collided with a Battle and was written off. On 7 April 1942 the same thing happened in the same place to *Franklin* (some people thought there was asymmetric brake failure).

BOAC and de Havilland inspectors repeatedly sent in glowing reports of how the structure would last 'at least another ten years'. They were over-confident and, because there was almost nowhere where they could inspect the structure, ignorant. On 4 August 1942 *Fiona* lost a large wing-root fairing. This had the effect of exposing some of the underlying structure, and it was obvious that the formers to which the fairing had been glued and pinned had rotted. This ought to have alerted everyone, but the three remaining aircraft rashly continued to fly occasionally and to handle commercial services. On 16 July 1943 *Fortuna* flew with fifteen people aboard from Hendon to Rineanna (Shannon). When flap was selected for the landing there was a loud bang, the aircraft slewed, sank rapidly and crashed into a field. Miraculously, nobody was killed. The flaps had simply torn free from the rotten rear spar. This at last made people take notice; *Falcon* and the repaired *Fiona* were fully inspected and, soon afterwards, broken up. A case of beauty being literally skin-deep. And the DC-2s and DC-3s just carried on, and still do.

DE HAVILLAND DH.93 DON AND AIRSPEED AS.45 CAMBRIDGE

In the late 1930s new types of aircraft were being designed all over the world at the rate of dozens per week. Britain contributed her fair share, with over 100 types in the final four years of the decade. Of that impressive total, fewer than thirty went into production – but then that compares with five for the whole of the 1980s, three of which were merely improved versions. Obviously, most of the late-1930s designs should never have been started, and two form the subject of this article.

At this time the technology of aeroplanes was advancing with unprecedented rapidity. The power of engines for fighters and bombers had already doubled from 500 horsepower to 1,000, and it was now doubling again, to 2,000 hp. Fighter armament of four 20-mm cannon was being requested, whereas the fighters actually in RAF service prior to 1938 had two small machine-guns. Any chief designer told to produce a new fighter wondered if it would be obsolete before first flight. But there were some classes of aircraft posing fewer problems.

One was the advanced trainer. Here there was no demand for the ultimate in performance or armament, merely good handling (with characteristics as far as possible reproducing those of operational types), well-designed cockpits for instructor and pupil, good all-round view and a tough airframe that could withstand years of possible mistreatment. Where single-engined aircraft were concerned Britain had just one success: the Miles Master, which began life – in the teeth of opposition from an outraged Air Ministry – with a Rolls-Royce Kestrel and, running short of these at No. 900, went on with the Bristol Mercury and Pratt & Whitney Twin Wasp Junior, production reaching 3,227, plus 1,724 of the Mercury-engined Martinet tug version. They were excellent aircraft, and most enjoyable to fly. The other advanced trainer was the Harvard. The fact that North American Aviation and their licensees produced 21,342 of the family speaks for itself.

In the days when Britain had lots of aircraft manufacturers it was perhaps inevitable that each should have been compartmentalised in the minds of officials. For example, after World War II they were prepared to let Saunders-Roe, who made flying boats, build a prototype flying boat that

Dated July 1937, this Air Ministry photograph shows the prototype Don in its original form, with Class-B registration and a dummy turret.

was a jet fighter, but they were outraged when the same firm wished to respond to a requirement for a supersonic landplane fighter. In the same way, when Phillips & Powis (later called Miles Aircraft) built the E.9 Kestrel, first flown in May 1937, the officials were anything but pleased. This maker of wooden light aircraft near Reading had absolutely no business to build not only an advanced trainer but an advanced trainer that nudged 300 mph! Everything possible was done to prevent Service pilots from flying it, in case they found it to be as delightful to fly as Tommy Rose's demonstrations suggested.

After all, this upstart firm had to be told that de Havilland were within days of flying the trainer that the Air Ministry really wanted, to specification T.6/36. The prototype DH.93 Don duly took the air at Hatfield in June 1937, and looked quite attractive. Part of the attraction lay in its clean nose, housing a DH Gipsy King inverted-vee-12 engine. As noted in the DH.91 Albatross story (see page 86), de Havilland and Frank Halford had schemed a beautiful low-drag installation in which this air-cooled engine was completely encased in a streamlined cowling. The air was rammed in through inlets in the leading edge of the wing, and ducted forward to pass downwards and inwards past the cylinders to emerge through an aft-facing exit underneath. Exactly the same installation was adopted for the DH.93, but the engine itself was bulky, massive and a very expensive way to get 500 hp. The Master I used reconditioned Kestrel engines rated at 715 hp which were lighter, much more reliable and cost one-fifth as much.

Specification T.6/36 had called for 'a three-seat general-purpose trainer'. In front sat the instructor and pupil side-by-side. For years there had been a debate over the basic question of whether the instructor should sit behind the pupil or beside him. It continues in 1996. Sixty years ago there were lots of DH Moths, including the first Tigers with tandem cockpits, but some instructors preferred the cosy side-by-side arrangement seen, for example, in Blackburn's B.2. T.6/36 had specified the latter arrangement, and as a young ATC cadet I actually sampled it at Hatfield in 1942, where an unwanted Don was parked between Mosquito II DD667 and Mosquito IV DK291 (which are remembered because they were secret and very exciting). The cockpit appeared cluttered, several controls such as the petrol selector were difficult to reach, and with two big men in flying clothing

the width appeared inadequate.

The Don was not just a pilot trainer, because in the port wing was a gun, fixed to fire ahead. The gun was intended to be a Browning and the sight a reflector type on an arm able to swing across for either pilot, but the prototype (L2387) had an ancient Vickers and a simple bead sight in front of each man on the top of the cowling. Behind was a station for a trainee radio operator, and further back again was a mock-up dorsal turret. Later the turret was actually fitted; it was a primitive, manually operated Armstrong Whitworth with a single Lewis gun, of the type fitted to the AW.29 light bomber. As if all this were not enough, in the floor was a prone bomb-aiming position, and under the wings were racks for eight practice bombs. One aircraft even did tests with a reverse-pitch propeller used as a brake in steep dive-bombing.

Altogether it was a quart in a pint pot, and the result was predictably overweight. An abiding memory of the interior was the massive structure of the bulkheads which had to incorporate overhead arches to protect the crew should the aircraft overturn on the ground. This could well have been needed, as directional stability on the ground was non-existent and the track of the backwards-retracting landing gear very narrow. DH used Tiger experience in adding long strakes ahead of the tailplane, but after much discussion spinning was prohibited, a bad shortcoming in a trainer. It was also found necessary to add auxiliary fins under the tailplane.

Suffice to say the contract for 250 was cut back to fifty, of which twenty were delivered without engines. The other thirty were redesigned as simply three-seat communications aircraft, almost all of them doing little or no flying. I once asked a pilot who had just arrived in one (at Halton) for his opinion, and he replied, 'Not a patch on the Proctor,' which of course seated four and cruised at about the same speed on much less than half the power.

Another British advanced trainer, which arrived after the war had started, did even worse. Why the Air Ministry ordered it is a mystery, because it was never intended to do anything that was not already being done perfectly well by the Master and Harvard. Specification T.4/39 called for 'an advanced two-seat trainer powered by a Bristol Mercury engine'. At least it did not want radio training, gunnery and bomb-aiming thrown in, though the requirement did stipulate the ability to carry a fixed

A factory photograph, apparently with the background carefully erased, of the first AS.45.

gun and light series bomb carriers, aimed in dives by the pilot.

I know of only one tender to this specification, by Airspeed (1934) Ltd, at Portsmouth Airport. They received a contract for two prototypes, T2449 and T2453, designated AS.45 and named Cambridge as a partner to the same firm's Oxford. The first was flown by George Errington on 19 February 1941. By this time Airspeed were a mature team led by Arthur E. Hagg. He had a reputation for brilliant and usually elegant design, notable creations including the DH.4, DH.88 Comet racer, the Albatross and later the AS.57 Ambassador airliner. Strangely, the AS.45 was large, heavy and utterly pedestrian. Perhaps it was done while Hagg was on holiday?

Most of it was wood, though the front end was metal tube with detachable metal panels. On the nose was a Bristol Mercury VIII supercharged radial rated at 730 hp, driving a constant-speed DH or Rotol propeller. A tank in each wing provided a total of 130 gallons, which compared with 85 for a Spitfire. Dowty provided the inwards-

retracting landing gear, whose balloon tyres looked grotesquely large. Slotted flaps were fitted, plus a split flap under the fuselage serving as an airbrake, while the outer wings incorporated fixed slots. To reduce ground angle, and thus prevent excessive swing, the vertical tail looked as if it had been moved down relative to the fuselage, though appearances were deceptive; in normal flight almost the entire tail, horizontal as well as vertical, was actually above the propeller slipstream.

The cockpits were in tandem, and remarkably clumsy. Access, described in the official Boscombe Down assessment as 'most awkward' and 'particularly difficult', was by two car-type doors on each side. These doors were triangular, tapering almost to a point at the bottom, and, as they were 'badly placed relative to the seats' and the roof 'made it necessary to crouch' it was just about possible to get in provided that the seat-type parachute did not have to come as well. The canopy contained twenty-one panes of Perspex set in a metal framework, two of the bulkheads being massive crash arches. The pupil in front had a direct-vision panel, described as 'hopelessly inadequate' and serving only to 'obstruct the general view in that direction'. The Perspex panes on each side could be slid downwards, with the aid of a mechanism that was 'unnecessarily complicated', but they went down only halfway, which made it impossible for a pilot to put his head out.

All these were pinpricks compared with the deficiencies in the way the aircraft flew. The control columns were of typical British design for that period, with a spade-grip at the top of the upper part of the column, pivoted for lateral movement to the lower half which moved fore and aft only. The odd feature was that small lateral movements caused only very slight movement of the ailerons. The bigger the demand, the greater the proportional aileron deflection, which is just what most pilots would hate. As a result the ailerons were 'ineffective' with small demands and 'impos-

sibly heavy' for large ones. Airspeed, the RAE and Boscombe devoted prolonged efforts to investigating AS.45 lateral control, which even then remained unsatisfactory. As for the elevators, these were also sluggish and ineffective until cruising speed was reached. At lower speeds there was 'a feeling of insecurity' because there was no response to small control movements and only a very slow response to large ones.

Anyone interested in reading more about the AS.45 is referred to the late Don Middleton's book on Airspeed aircraft, and to a comprehensive article by Philip Jarrett in *Aeroplane Monthly* for April 1991. Fortunately for the citizens of Cambridge the AS.45 never hit the headlines; today's media would have made a story out of it. All in contrast to the Airspeed Oxford, of which 8,586 were built.

LWS Zubr

This is a tale of changed missions, repeated modification and, finally, repeated and increasingly desperate rectification of faults. And one has only to look at a photo of the result to feel that something went wrong.

The unfortunate chief designer, Zbysław Ciolkosz, worked for PZL, Poland's principal aircraft constructor. In early 1933 he schemed the PZL.30 passenger transport, a high-wing design powered by two 450-hp Pratt & Whitney Wasp Junior engines. LOT, the national airline, said (rightly) that the DC-2 was much better, so Ciolkosz turned his design into the PZL.30/I, a bomber and combat-proficiency crew trainer. This was the version actually built, but it did not fly until March 1936. The stage was set.

In 1935 the LWS (loosely, Lublin aircraft works) had been established, with Ciolkosz as chief engineer. He brought the bomber project with him, and it became the LWS.4 Zubr (bison). He was instructed to bring it up to full service standard quickly, and a preliminary order was placed for sixteen. Romania opened negotiations for twenty-four.

Aerodynamically this aircraft was a mess. The nose looked home-made, the fuselage was made up of severe straight lines, and two turrets did not help. The pilot's cockpit was offset on the left side,

and the sides and bottom of the fuselage contained numerous windows. Structurally the design could fairly be called a disaster. Odd bits were variously light-alloy stressed skin, welded steel tube with fabric covering, aluminium with fabric covering or all wood! Even that might not have been too bad had not the percentage structure weight been 43.3. In other words almost half the maximum loaded weight was accounted for by structure. A typical figure for a mid-1930s bomber was 29 per cent.

The bomb load was said to be 2,205 lb, but I am sure this could not actually have been carried. Obviously underpowered, this extremely uninspired machine nevertheless handled quite nicely, and its transport ancestry meant that there was plenty of room, so the service trials were judged generally favourable. In any case, by 1937 Poland could see the menace of Hitler's Germany all too clearly, and her need for bombers was overwhelming. The only alternative was the PZL.37 Łoś. The latter was a superb aircraft, but fell foul of influential fools in Warsaw who were convinced it was far too advanced in conception, and who doubted the need for a long-range bomber in any case. All these factors conspired to increase the importance of high-rate production of the Zubr.

The chief problem was the inadequate power, so

it was decided to switch to the 680-hp Pegasus VIII, licence-built by PZL/Skoda. The thoroughly proven British engine, used in Polish Ju 52/3ms, DC-2s and 3s, and the rival Łoś bomber, suited these aircraft perfectly. The LWS aircraft, in contrast, had been designed for a much smaller engine. Ciolkosz redesigned the engine mounts, and also revised the main landing gears so that they retracted not inwards but backwards into the nacelles. Obviously he should have carried out a thoroughgoing restressing of the whole aircraft, to clear it for what were inevitably going to be much greater weights and increased stresses, but so great was the pressure to get the bomber into production that this crucial step was almost completely omitted!

The prototype LWS.4 began its flight-test programme in July 1937. Within a week cracks and fissures began to appear in the ply skin of the all-wood wings. These were examined, and doubler sheets of ply were glued on the inside and, in some cases where the interior was inaccessible, on the outside. This process of gluing on extra bits of wood whenever a crack appeared extended to the second aircraft. In September 1937 the original prototype, with the Romanian acceptance mission on board, came unglued and disintegrated. Romania cancelled, and even the Polish LWS.4 programme was temporarily halted.

A prolonged investigation resulted. This showed up an almost unbelievable list of deficiencies; indeed, one could truly describe this bomber as an accident waiting to happen. The list included gross errors in the assumptions made in stressing the wing, mistakes in the arithmetic, and a considerable disparity between the theoretical and actual strength of the glue. Even without any strengthening of the structure, the change to bigger engines had eaten into the already almost non-existent payload. The projected LWS.5 seaplane version appeared to be unable to carry a full load of fuel or bombs, and certainly not both together.

Ciolkosz kept trying, and in early 1938 flew the prototype LWS.6. This had a twin-finned tail, which seemed irrelevant, but it also had a redesigned wing which was said to meet all requirements. The panic restressing had added nearly one tonne to the already grossly overweight structure, and as the original tail was fractionally lighter this was fitted to the remaining fourteen production bombers. These were delivered to the IIIrd Wing; this was called a training unit, because the aircraft could not take off if any bombs were put on board. They had many other deficiencies, such as electric motors insufficiently powerful to raise the landing gears, so these were locked in the down position.

By 1939 the indefatigable Ciolkosz was furiously designing a completely new wing of steel tube and fabric structure, which was expected to eliminate breakage and reduce weight. Then came the terrible German assault of 1 September 1939. This was Poland's hour of need, when every bomber had to be thrown into action. But not the Zubrs; they were unfit for front-line service.

The prototype Zubr, before it began cracking.

ROMANO R.110

Between the two world wars the 130-plus companies of the French aircraft industry produced well over 1,000 distinct types of aircraft. They included an exceptionally high proportion of disasters and errors, but one of the firms with a fair record was that of Etienne Romano. I have included his R.110 not because it was a bad aircraft, but as an example of a ridiculous specification.

A stressed-skin low-wing monoplane, first flown on 30 March 1938, it had a span of just over 42 ft, weight of 7,550 lb and speed of about 290 mph on two 450-hp Renault inverted-vee-12 engines. The fuselage looked lumpy and unstreamlined because, amidships behind the pilot's cockpit, there was a large humped cabin on top with glazed areas looking out to front and rear. It was planned to mount fixed guns in the nose and a pivoted gun in the upper rear cockpit.

So what was it for? Believe it or not, it was built to meet an Armée de l'Air specification for an *Avion de Direction*, an aerial command post. The pilot and rear gunner were merely secondary. The crucial member of the crew was the third man, who was also the captain of the aircraft. Styled a *Commandant de Manoeuvres*, it was his task to control the *escadrille* (squadron) of single-seat fighters to which each R.110 would be assigned. He would, by radio, steer them towards the enemy and then, battle having been joined, warn them of possible unseen enemy forces, offer helpful guidance on how to proceed and carry out any other command duties such as escorting damaged fighters back to base or checking on the position of downed pilots.

The only trouble is that, as any fighter pilot will see at once, the whole idea was nonsensical. Even an aircraft with a performance higher than that of the fighters would not be able to stay with all parts of an aerial battle. An aircraft considerably slower than the fighters, and with less than 40 per cent of their rate of climb, would never get into a position to be useful. If it did, it would be highly vulnerable.

Everyone who has been in a dogfight knows how, possibly within a few seconds, all the aircraft seem to have disappeared. Only with a fire-walled throttle plus luck can enemy aircraft be found again and brought within firing parameters. Aircraft built like a light transport would have no way of controlling the battle, if only for the reasons that it could not stay with the battle, nor could it identify individual friendly fighters to pass messages from a distance. Eventually better understanding must have got through to the procurement officials, because the idea was dropped.

It might be added that a modern equivalent is the E-3 Sentry. This is a totally different ball-game, and it really can control aerial operations.

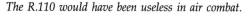

The R.110 would have been useless in air combat.

SARO LERWICK

A Lerwick I of unfortunate 209 Squadron.

We have seen that the margin between a good design and a very bad one is often slender, and a matter of unexpected details. The Lerwick (rhymes with derrick) was a patrol flying boat which ought to have been an important type with RAF Coastal Command in World War II. Instead it was profoundly unpopular, and made almost no contribution to the war effort. Such a result may appear surprising, because the Saunders-Roe design team under Henry Knowler was exceptionally experienced. One of their earlier productions, the Saro London, was an old-style biplane boat which was popular with everyone. Sadly, aircraft such as the London were made swiftly obsolescent by the advent of clean stressed-skin monoplanes, hence Air Ministry specification R.1/36 of 1936.

This merely called for a high-performance GR (general reconnaissance) flying boat with a crew of six, two of the most powerful engines, power-driven gun turrets in the nose, mid-upper and tail positions, and able to carry four 500-lb or eight 250-lb bombs. The Air Ministry were quite excited at the prospect of achieving really high performance in a flying boat for Coastal Command.

Indeed, Blackburn proffered a remarkable aircraft, the B.20, with a slim fuselage fitted with a retractable planing bottom. Powered by two Vulture engines, it was good for 306 mph. Like so many Blackburn aircraft it had problems; in this case the one that has been recorded for posterity is unsatisfactory aileron control (what, lateral control *again*?). On 7 April 1940 something unsurvivable happened in the air; only two of the test crew parachuted to safety, the pilot being killed. The B.20 was thereupon abandoned, so I suppose this constitutes yet another Blackburn entry in this book. Saunders-Roe, on the other hand, turned in a wholly conventional design. Not having a retractable planing bottom, the hull had to be very deep in order to put the 13 ft 6 in DH propellers clear of waves and spray. As the hull was also rather short, the A.36 Lerwick gained the RAF name of Flying Pig, but this was also for other reasons.

The Isle of Wight firm built the prototype A.36 in 1938. At the same time they completed the prototype of a larger patrol flying boat, the A.33. Designed to the earlier specification R.2/33, it was a fine-looking parasol monoplane powered by four Bristol Perseus sleeve-valve engines. An unusual feature for Britain was that it was stabilised on the water by sponsons, instead of floats under the outer wings. Of course, an accurate model of the A.33 had been exhaustively tested in a towing tank to prove that its hydrodynamic behaviour would not give rise to any problems. Everything went well and, as aircraft were urgently needed for the expanding RAF, eleven A.33s were ordered off the drawing board, with serial numbers L2147-57. As soon as the first got out into the Solent it was found to porpoise (pitch nose-up/down) very badly. In fact, when the final fast run was made prior to attempting the first flight, with Knowler himself on board, the porpoising was so severe that the boat crashed and was wrecked. The A.33 programme was abandoned; fortunately its rival was the Short Sunderland, without which Coastal Command would have been in some trouble.

After such a catastrophic experience with the A.33, Saunders-Roe were doubly determined to do well with the A.36. Tank testing was more prolonged than usual, towing detailed models through water with every possible arrangement of simulated waves. The new twin-engined boat had its wing as high above the sea as on the parasol A.33, but Knowler decided to revert to traditional outboard stabilising floats. The planing bottom was of a very modern form, the section downstream of the step being continued in a gentle curve all the way back to the tail. Unlike most flying boats the hull did not have an upswept rear portion, so the tail turret was only just above the water. The wing had a rectangular centre section, carrying the 1,375-hp Bristol Hercules sleeve-valve engines with the bomb bays in their nacelles, and outer panels which tapered to pointed tips. Anyone seeing the boat for the first time would probably have considered that the wing and tail were considerably smaller than one might have expected.

By the time the A.36 Lerwick flew, in early November 1938, the need for RAF aircraft was even more urgent, and an order was placed for twenty-one (L7248-68), again straight off the drawing board. Knowler fervently hoped that this time he had got it right, and the twenty-one were obviously intended to be the first of many. But right from the start L7248 behaved badly on the water. Knowler said, 'It bore no relation whatever to the way the tank model had behaved.' It pitched, swerved and tried to dig in its tip floats, and in addition it was found that the elevators were dangerously overbalanced. Numerous modifications were made before L7248 appeared fit to reach take-off speed. Once it was in the air a speed of 235 mph was soon recorded; this was believed to be faster than any other flying boat in 1938, but, more to the point, stability and control in the air were totally unacceptable.

More prolonged changes were made, including increasing the incidence of the wings and engines (but not the floats), adding auxiliary tail fins, increasing the chord of the rudder, redesigning the horizontal tail and finally removing the auxiliary fins but adding area at the top of the rudder. Perhaps most vital of all, the planing bottom was repeatedly modified to overcome the instability on the water. Even when everything Saunders-Roe could think of had been done, handling both on the water and in the air remained unpleasant. The clean stall was described as 'vicious', and with the slotted flaps lowered any stall resulted in total loss of control and the likelihood of structural damage.

With the proviso that stalling was prohibited, and that the aircraft was 'flown with kid gloves', the Lerwick I was at last cleared for service in summer 1939, and on 9 June of that year L7250 was delivered to 240 Squadron. Eventually all twenty-one were built, but there were certainly not to be any more. The main user was 209 Squadron, which on 22 April 1940 actually became wholly equipped with the unpopular boat. By February 1941 they had lost six (none through enemy action, so far as is known), and with enormous relief began re-equipping with Catalinas on 23 March 1941. Even the engines gave trouble, mainly from crankshaft failures, and when No. 209 re-equipped every aircrew had made an open-sea forced landing. Of course, none of the Lerwick's problems was publicised at the time, but the official announcement of April 1942 that the type was obsolete told its own story.

BLACKBURN ROC

This was yet another of the aircraft designed by Blackburn Aircraft which, though competently executed, was flawed from the very start by the basic conception. The B.25 Roc was named after a giant mythical bird, said to be able to carry off an elephant. Blackburn's Roc might indeed have been able to accomplish this feat; on the other hand it certainly could not accomplish its design mission, which was to shoot down other aircraft.

It was, in fact, a fighter version of the B.24 Skua, which appeared in February 1937 and caused gasps of astonishment. Until then Britain's Fleet Air Arm, like the RAF, had been equipped exclusively with fabric-covered biplanes held together by struts and wires. The Skua was a clean stressed-skin monoplane, with retractable landing gear, flaps, a variable-pitch propeller and enclosed cockpits. A dive bomber, it looked as modern as the hour,

though with only 890 hp available from a Bristol Perseus sleeve-valve engine its performance was not exactly sparkling, maximum speed without a bomb being 225 mph.

The Roc was a two-seat fighter based on the same airframe. Apart from having dihedral on the wings (to avoid the Skua's odd turned-up tips), it differed mainly in that the centre fuselage was widened to accommodate a Boulton Paul four-gun turret, of the same type as that fitted to the Defiant, a few feet behind the pilot's cockpit. As the turret was rotated, it automatically raised or lowered hinged fairings, one in front of the turret (not mentioned in most descriptions) and the other behind. Service experience with the Defiant in May 1940 was to demonstrate, in the most painful manner, that the basic concept of a turret fighter was unsound. Such aircraft were inevitably heavier

The ill-fated prototype of the ridiculous Roc seaplane version.

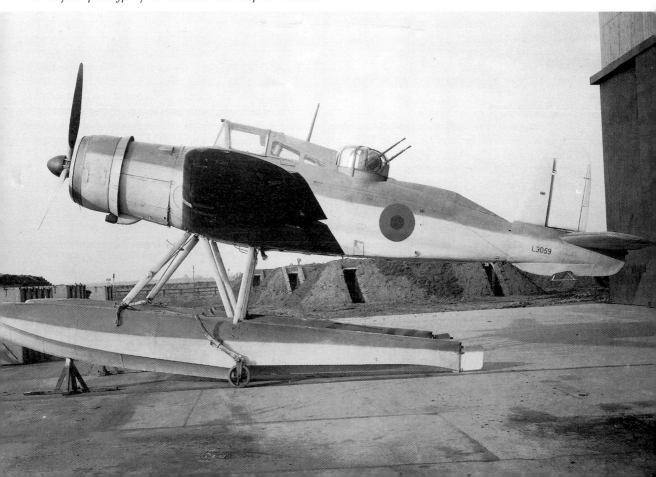

and more clumsy than single-seaters, slower and less agile, and also deficient in firepower. But in the case of the Roc not only did it have half the horsepower needed, but the whole concept was beyond belief.

It was built in two forms, a landplane for use from aircraft carriers, and a twin-float seaplane. The former first flew on 23 December 1938. The seaplane version followed in November 1939, proving so directionally unstable that on 10 December it crashed immediately after take-off. From the outset the capabilities of both versions were known pretty accurately, and one can only wonder why such an aircraft was built. The concept of a fighter raking enemy aircraft in a broadside in straight and level flight cannot have been seriously entertained for an instant. Fighters have to win in close manoeuvring combat, but the Roc could neither manoeuvre nor, in such combat, bring its guns to bear. The landplane had a ceiling of 18,000 ft, flat-out maximum speed of 223 mph at 10,000 ft, maximum speed at sea level of 194 mph and cruising speed of 135 mph. The seaplane was roughly 25 mph slower, and could not climb above 14,600 ft!

During the Battle of Britain many Hurricane pilots found that they could not catch Ju 88 bombers, let alone 109s. The notion of a fighter unable to exceed 170 mph might perhaps have caused someone to question the sanity of the procurement process. But 136 Rocs were delivered, and a few did see useful service. They were parked at Gosport and used as static machine-gun posts.

BLACKBURN BOTHA

Blackburn Aircraft appear in this book with distressing frequency. One must bear in mind that this company tended to build aircraft to meet particularly difficult official requirements. Their management were often only too keenly aware of the deficiencies of their creations, and powerless to rectify them. In the case of the B.26 Botha the underlying shortcoming was inadequate engine power. To this could be added all manner of other problems, so that this aircraft accomplished very little except burn a lot of fuel and also, tragically, aircrew.

It was designed as a three-seater to carry a torpedo or equivalent bomb load. In 1936 a revised specification called for a crew of four and a broader range of operating requirements. The prototype first flew on 28 December 1938, though it remained secret. Published articles suggest that it was not until it went to Martlesham Heath three months later that it was found to have inadequate elevator control; one wonders what the company test pilot had been doing during those three months. A stressed-skin aircraft, the Botha had a slim fuselage (but with a very draggy mid-upper turret), a high wing with a rectangular centre section and short, sharply tapered outer panels, underslung nacelles for two Bristol Perseus sleeve-valve engines, and a typical Blackburn tail with the vertical surface ahead of the horizontal. At first glance one instinctively felt that the outer panels were too sharply tapered and that the aircraft needed more span. Another odd feature was that the glazing on the nose was asymmetric, the navigator having a prone bomb-aiming position on the right. The pilot's 'greenhouse' was symmetric, though he sat on the left.

The Botha I was powered by Perseus X engines rated at 880 hp. In 1940 production switched to the Perseus Mk XA, rated at 930 hp. This was extremely welcome, because power had been inadequate to the point of being dangerous in some situations. With gear and flaps down you needed take-off power from both engines. There was no such thing as a single-engined overshoot. Even with both engines, extreme care was needed before the pilot dared to raise the flaps. And I was startled to learn from Michael Bowyer's *Aircraft for the Few* (PSL) that 'L6104 was rated extremely draughty, and when Blackburn made alterations the top speed increased by 18 mph!' The more I think about this, the more remarkable it seems; whoever heard of gaps *that* bad?

The standard 'Putnam' on Blackburn Aircraft notes that the 'engines and nacelles cut off all sideways and rearwards visibility' but then offers the opinion that the cockpit had 'a well-planned instrument and control layout'. This must have originated in some company advertising copy. For a pilot's opinion, try ATA ferry pilot Hugh Bergel, who flew many Bothas. In one of his authoritative books (*Fly and Deliver*, Airlife) he writes:

On the way to his seat the pilot passed a board

The Botha prototype. Taxpayers paid for 580 of these deservedly unpopular aircraft, but fortunately it was possible to cancel a further 676.

covered with taps and dials which controlled a peculiar fuel system. It was not difficult to set these taps so that all fuel tanks were turned OFF. Alas, this in no way stopped the pilot (who was then out of reach and sight of this panel) from starting, warming and running-up the engines, taxiing out and taking off. But eleven minutes further on a little collector tank which had no taps or gauge and which fed both engines would run dry and both engines stopped at once. Some pilots survived this.

It might be thought that only ATA pilots, who ferried it solo and so could not get at the taps in flight, thought ill of the B****. Not so. Service pilots too hated it, perhaps because it was said that when fully laden with crew and warlike stores it could lift only enough fuel for 50 miles' flying. I was nearly lynched when I delivered one to an aerodrome whose CO had that very morning grounded a whole squadron, as being too dangerous to operate.

Another very experienced ferry pilot was H.A. 'Tony' Taylor. He was one of the nicest people; he wrote under the pseudonym 'Indicator' in the pre-war *Aeroplane* and later was a colleague of mine on *Flight International*. He described the cockpit layout as 'prospectively dangerous' and also noted that in flying through rain you couldn't see through the windscreens. He continued [in *Air International*]:

There were marked changes in trim and elevator effectiveness with variations in power and configuration. The trimmers, which consisted of a small wheel for the rudder and a bigger one for the elevator, both on the same axis, were on the pilot's left. Controls for the undercarriage, flaps, gills and, of course, the powerplants, were operated by the right hand – so it was necessary to change hands whenever these controls were used, and retrimming was consequently required. For this reason we tended to fly the Botha on the elevator trimmer. . . . The layout was dangerous in the event of sudden engine failure. The right hand would then be busy with the powerplant controls, so the left hand could not be freed to operate the small rudder trim wheel, which, moving in an unnatural sense, had to be turned quickly and in the correct direction.

All these dangers were merely unnecessary extras. The underlying lack of power (and, in my opinion, span) made the idea of carrying bombs or torpedoes absurd. Surely the official who wanted a Botha to undertake tropical trials must have been joking? Bothas did equip one squadron, No. 608 (North Riding) AAF Squadron, flying North Sea patrols from August to December 1940. No bombs were carried. Of 580 Bothas delivered, several hundred equipped bombing, gunnery, navigation and radio schools in 1941–43, at least 120 being destroyed in crashes. Hundreds more languished at Maintenance Units until, in August 1943, the type was declared obsolete. Blackburn's plea to produce instead the Hercules-engined Botha II was rejected. Pity, it might have been almost adequate.

SILVANSKII'S IS

Occasionally one finds an aeroplane whose creators were so amateurish that the product seems like a sick joke. But I know of only one such aircraft that was intended to be a high-performance fighter.

Perhaps remarkably, in Stalin's terror-ridden Soviet Union of 1938 it was possible for private individuals to obtain state funds and facilities to build aeroplanes. One who did so was A.V. Silvanskii, who was already working in one of the GAZ state aircraft factory offices. In 1937 he teamed up with V.D. Yarovitskii and Yu.B. Sturtsel – who ought to have known better – to design a single-seat fighter. It had a low-mounted metal wing, a 1,000-hp M-88 fourteen-cylinder radial engine bolted to the front of a steel-tube fuselage, sliding canopy, tailskid and planned armament of two heavy machine-guns. Its designation was simply IS, from *Istrebitel* (fighter) Silvanskii.

By 1938 the prototype aircraft was in the erection shop. Then snags began to occur. On the first retraction test (yes, they did remember to put the IS on trestles) the gears came up all right, but it was found that the legs were too long, so the wheels came up beyond their recesses in the wing roots. The legs were therefore shortened until they were the right length, but then it was found that the wheel bays were too shallow, so that the legs and part of the wheel still stuck out into the slipstream. Then they put the propeller on its shaft and found

that, partly because of the shortened legs, it fouled the ground as soon as the tail was raised into the flying attitude. Not to worry – Silvanskii got a hacksaw, cut about 4 in off each blade and filed the sawed edges smooth again!

We are told there were other problems as well. For example, the aileron hinges were not all exactly in line, so it was very difficult to move the ailerons. The GAZ manager was, of course, aware of all that was happening, and refused permission for the IS to be flown on his premises. Undeterred, Silvanskii managed to get the LII (State Flight Research Institute) to agree to provide a test pilot and begin the test-flight programme. Probably in early 1939, Silvanskii's creation was brought to Moscow and the pilot briefed, even though calculations (revealed later) showed that the aircraft would probably never take off. In fact, perhaps because of very high mid-winter air density, the LII pilot did manage to get airborne. In stark terror, with the throttle absolutely wide open, he managed to creep round a circuit, always on the point of stalling, until he finally got the IS back on terra firma, landing still at full power. Visibly shaken, he pronounced the fighter incapable of flight.

The unfortunate design bureau of Silvanskii was bankrupted. The Ministry of Aviation Industry issued a nationwide decree informing everyone of the episode and banning Silvanskii from designing anything else.

Silvanskii's full-scale mock-up.

Avro Manchester and Heinkel He 177

These two heavy bombers, closely parallel in timing, were basically satisfactory aircraft fitted with a pair of extremely troublesome engines. Both were eventually redesigned with four engines, with very different results in England and Germany.

The British aircraft flew first. The Avro Type 679 Manchester was built to specification P.13/36, and emerged as a very 'hot' aircraft indeed. It began life at 45,000 lb and when actually put into service weighed 56,000 lb, yet it was designed with a span of only 80 ft 2 in and a wing area of 992 sq ft. The wing loading of 56.5 lb/sq ft was almost three times that for the Whitley I and five times as high as that of the Heyford, which was a standard RAF bomber when the Avro 679 was designed. One explanation for the high wing loading was that P.13/36 stipulated the use of a catapult for overload take-offs. The bomber thus had to be made extremely strong, and other parts had to be further stressed for dive bombing. Of course, the catapult was never used operationally, and the Manchester was never employed as a dive bomber, but it remained with all its inbuilt strength for both. Indeed, designer Roy Chadwick, explaining that this was his first stressed-skin design, admitted that he had made the skins thicker and heavier than necessary.

The prototype Manchester flew on 25 July 1939. It flew all right, but inevitably needed a long take-off run even at light weight. It also had a very poor rate of climb, and obviously needed more fin area. It was also apparent that the Rolls-Royce Vulture engines were not giving their advertised 1,750 hp. These twenty-four-cylinder X-type engines had four Peregrine cylinder blocks on one crankcase. A.V. Roe knew it to be an untried engine, but it was assembled from proven parts, and in any case Rolls-Royce's great reputation allayed any fears of prolonged trouble.

The second Manchester had a third fin, and later the span was increased to 90 ft 1 in. The extra fin still proved inadequate, and much experimentation was needed before a larger shape was found for the central fin, to make the aircraft directionally stable in normal flight and (just) capable of controlled flight with one engine idling. After a great deal of further development the Manchester was cleared for production. Deliveries to 207 Squadron began on 1 November 1940, and it was clear that in many respects the Avro bomber was outstanding, and markedly superior to the rival Stirling and Halifax.

It was equally clear that the Vulture engine was a disaster. Engines failed for various reasons. One of the two coolant pumps might cavitate, so that no liquid would reach one or even two cylinder blocks, which would burn out, seize or catch fire. Equally serious was a rare basic design fault which led to rapid fatigue failure of the big ends. Even when the engine did work, giving up to 1,845 hp, ground crews found extreme difficulty trying to check the ninety-six valve tappets and change the forty-eight plugs on each engine. The morale of Manchester crews was abysmal. No. 97 Squadron was grounded so often they were called 'the 97th Foot' as if they were an infantry regiment!

From the twenty-first Manchester onwards the tail was again redesigned: the tailplane was greatly increased in span, from 20ft to 33ft; it carried much taller fins and rudders; and the central fin was eliminated. This absolutely transformed the aircraft's handling and stability, leaving just the engines as a problem. It is part of British history that by again extending the span, to 102 ft, and fitting four Rolls-Royce Merlin engines, the Manchester II emerged in 1941 as an outstanding aircraft in all respects. Renamed Lancaster, 7,377 were built. Early Lancasters had been started as Manchesters, with little windows along the fuselage. Production was switched over at the 159th aircraft by Avro and the 44th by Metropolitan-Vickers.

In sharpest contrast, the Germans persisted with the dangerously faulty He 177, and switched to the much better four-engined versions only towards the end of the war, when it was far too late. The entire history of the He 177 is one of a large, highly competent and well-equipped company striving ceaselessly to rectify a succession of serious problems. While all this was going on, large numbers of 177s were put into service and flown with skill and courage on operations which seldom bore the

A crew of No. 83 Squadron (the Air Ministry caption says 'about to set out on a daylight raid') with their Manchester IA. (Overleaf)

RAF aeroplane TS439 was a captured He 177A-5.

slightest resemblance to those for which the aircraft had been designed. The 177 was officially named *Greif* (Griffon), but the English word 'grief' might have been more appropriate.

Like the Manchester, the Heinkel bomber was conceived as a very advanced aircraft, with two of the most powerful engines, a high wing loading and the ability to undertake dive bombing. The project began in the summer of 1938, and could quite quickly have led to a formidable aircraft. With a take-off weight of 59,520 lb, the combination of speed, range and bomb load should have been greater than that of any other bomber of the day, the estimated speed of 342 mph being faster than almost all contemporary fighters. The 177 was indeed developed to have impressive combinations of speed, range and weapon load, but until very late in its career it was a deeply flawed aircraft, said to be more dangerous to its crews than to its enemies.

From the outset, chief designer Siegfried Günter strove for maximum aerodynamic efficiency and minimum drag. Thus, he designed the wing with the impressively high aspect ratio of 9.86, and he was determined to pack the required 4,000–5,000 hp into just two nacelles. If possible, he wished to use either air-cooled engines or liquid-cooled engines with zero-drag surface evaporative radiators. Unfortunately, no engine of the necessary power was available. Hindsight is easy, but if only Günter had taken the simple route and fitted four separate engines, the He 177 would have been a much better bomber, much sooner.

Instead, the Heinkel company collaborated with Daimler-Benz in developing the DB 606, a massive engine consisting of two DB 601s driving a common reduction gearbox and propeller. The maximum output was 2,700 hp. This engine was tested in the single-engined He 119 prototypes, which showed that surface radiators were inadequate. There seemed to be no reason to believe that any particular difficulties would be encountered, and the He 177 V1 (first prototype) began its flight-test programme on 19 November 1939. Test pilot Carl Francke was generally quite pleased, report-

ing only a few minor problems such as slight torsional vibration of the long propeller shafts.

Little did they know what was to come. Over the next five years various types of He 177 suffered from eight very serious groups of problems, and several hundred minor ones. Most of the structural and aerodynamic difficulties were sorted out fairly rapidly, though at least twelve aircraft suffered more or less catastrophic structural failure in flight. A few aircraft (possibly no more than three) crashed because one propeller had suffered a hard-over pitch runaway. Not fewer than eighteen were destroyed by uncontrolled swing on take-off or, more rarely, on landing. There were many other difficulties, but by far the most dangerous and protracted was the tendency of the DB 606, and of the 2,950-hp DB 610 which succeeded it in later He 177 versions, to catch fire. Not for nothing was the 177 known throughout the Luftwaffe as the *Luftwaffenfeuerzeug* (Luftwaffe's lighter).

Much of the story is spelt out in the Motorbuch book on the 177 by Griehl and Dressel. I once discussed this aircraft with Ernst Heinkel. He said that, when writing his autobiography *Mein sturmische Leben* (My stormy life), he had got his staff to go through wartime records and list modifications to eradicate faults in the He 177, ignoring all other engineering changes. With far from complete records the total had exceeded 1,300. He added that, when the problem of engine fires was at last really tackled in January 1943 (incidentally discovering records of fifty-six of these fires), the DB 610 installation still needed a very large number of engineering changes to make it acceptably safe.

Throughout all the trauma Heinkel and Arado delivered 1,146 production aircraft. Moreover, in many respects they were truly outstanding machines. Like the Manchester, the 177 was dogged to the end by its unfortunate powerplants. Not until 1943 did Heinkel begin issuing shoals of drawings of He 177B, He 274 and He 277 projects, 177B being another designation for the 277. All had four separate engines, and there is no reason to doubt that they would have been safe and reliable aircraft, but there was no time left.

MESSERSCHMITT ME 210

During World War II we in Britain loved to frighten ourselves with rumours of all sorts of terrifying new warplanes that were said to be entering service with the Luftwaffe. The Fw 187, Fw 198, He 113, Me 115, He 118 and Do 29 were typical examples of awesome aircraft which either never went into production or else never existed at all. On the other hand the Me 210 certainly did exist. It was planned as the next-generation successor to the Bf 110, and was regarded by everyone from Goering downwards as probably the most important new type of aircraft in the entire Third Reich.

Of course, Goering had always regarded his *Zerstörer* (destroyer) crews as the *crème de la crème* of all the German armed forces. The *Zerstörers* were the big twin-engined fighters, and Goering loved the mental image of these long-range aircraft cutting a swathe wherever they went, wiping out aerial opposition so that his bombers would not be molested. In the Battle of Britain this idea came unstuck, because the Bf 110 could be shot down with relative ease by a Hurricane or Spitfire. This threw added emphasis and urgency on the development of the Me 210.

From the start the 210 was planned to have not only a higher performance and greater agility than the Bf 110, but also enhanced versatility. It was to be a long-range heavy fighter, dive bomber, reconnaissance aircraft and low-level attack bomber.

The Me 210 V2 flew somewhat better with a single-fin tail, until the tail came off.

The requirement was issued in early 1938. Arado responded with the Ar 240, but the standing of Bayerische Flugzeugwerke (renamed Messerschmitt AG from July 1938) was so high that it was taken for granted that the Me 210 would be accepted for production. Thus, the original prototype contract included long-lead items for production, and an option on the first 1,000 production aircraft.

The Me 210 was very much like a Bf 110, with twin fins, but with a deep and blunt nose terminating behind the propellers, main landing gears whose wheels turned 90° to lie flat in the rear of the nacelle (as in the Ju 88) and remotely controlled defensive guns in powered blisters on each side of the rear fuselage. The last feature was not ready in time for the first prototype, but it was a fine-looking machine, with no hint of what lay in store.

World War II had just started when Hermann Wurster took the first Me 210 into the air for the first time on 5 September 1939. According to Bill Green's *Warplanes of the Third Reich*, 'This initial flight was considered to be successful only in as much as its pilot succeeded in landing the prototype in the condition in which it left the ground.' Few modern aircraft have ever exhibited such appalling flight characteristics. With so strong a design and engineering staff, one might have expected the 210 to be put right in a matter of weeks, if not days. It was confidently expected that this would, in fact, be the case. Huge production lines for the new type were established at both the Augsburg and Regensburg factories, and it was arranged that in early 1941 the MIAG factory at Brunswick would also change over from the 110 to the 210. What actually happened was almost beyond belief. It was as if a jinx hung over the 210. Every test flight unearthed fresh problems, and every modification left a wholly unstable and in many ways dangerous aircraft.

As early as 23 September 1939 the original twin-finned tail was replaced by a large single-finned tail, but the improvement was hardly noticeable. There is simply no room here to catalogue the long list of undesirable and dangerous flight characteristics, and the wonder is that no aircraft was actually lost until the second prototype's tail broke up on 5 September 1940. The original plan was to go straight into production in 1940, using the first fifteen off the line as *Versuchs* (experimental test) machines. In fact by May 1941 a total of sixteen such aircraft had been delivered, but the expected flood of production machines could not follow on behind. In eighteen months of increasingly desperate work, the Me 210 had been developed from being almost unflyable to being merely dangerously unpredictable. As might be expected in such circumstances, no two aircraft were alike. Most were assigned particular tasks, such as the development of de-icing, landing gear or dive bombing. Such considerations were side issues, because the basic handling remained totally unacceptable.

With the Bf 110 already fast being phased out of production, Messerschmitt had no choice but to start delivering Me 210A-0 pre-production (service test) aircraft. By the beginning of 1942 there were ninety-four A-0s, which instead of being used for Luftwaffe conversion and indoctrination merely helped try to get the aircraft right. Things were bad enough with the highly skilled Messerschmitt test pilots. Even with five aircraft converted by Blohm und Voss as dual trainers, the Luftwaffe evaluation pilots, all with hundreds of hours on the Bf 110, had crash after crash. By 1942 the production lines switched to true series versions, the A-1 *Zerstörer* and A-2 dive bomber, sixty-four of the former being delivered in January 1942 alone. Amidst acrimonious scenes it was finally agreed that Me 210 production had to be halted, and the old Bf 110 restored to production; this was put into effect at the end of January 1942.

By this time deliveries totalled sixteen prototypes, ninety-four A-0s and ninety A-1s, with 370 A-1 and A-2 aircraft on the assembly lines. Among the consequences were that Willy Messerschmitt was forced by Luftwaffe chief Erhard Milch to resign his position as chairman and managing director; numerous Luftwaffe pilots and backseaters were killed; Messerschmitt AG lost DM30 million; and the Luftwaffe lost an estimated 600 aircraft through non-production.

Of course, almost as soon as the traumatic decision was taken to go back to the Bf 110, solutions to the 210's worst problems began to be found. The chief modification was greatly to increase the length and depth of the rear fuselage. Eventually, more 210s were built, together with well over 1,000 further refined Me 410s powered by the 1,850-hp DB 603 engine. The 410 was really quite a formidable aircraft in each of its several roles, but throughout the Luftwaffe both it and its manufacturer had to live down the dreadful reputation gained by its predecessor.

CURTISS SO3C SEAMEW

At the start of World War II the various divisions of the mighty Curtiss-Wright Corporation added up to the largest manufacturers of aircraft in the world. Unlike most US planemakers, Curtiss had mass-production contracts with both the Army and the Navy, as well as substantial (though declining) civil business. But at the end of that conflict the once giant firm was facing extinction as a manufacturer of aircraft, and the primary cause was that its numerous fresh designs were nearly all failures.

Such was the wartime need for aircraft that some of the failures were built in large numbers. A prominent example was the SB2C ('Son of a Bitch Second Class') Helldiver. No fewer than 7,200 of these were built in various versions, though all suffered from severe faults, notably in stability and control. Despite this, the SB2Cs did fly valuable combat missions. In contrast, another Curtiss creation, the SO3C, never flew any, even though several hundred were built. I believe the total actually constructed to have been 439, though various authorities insist on such figures as 459, 795 and 800. Whatever the total was, it was that number too many. The SO3C should undoubtedly have been drowned at birth.

It was first ordered by the US Navy on 9 May 1938 to replace the popular and reliable SOC (Scout Observation Curtiss) Seagull biplanes on the catapults of surface warships. Orders were also placed for the rival Vought SO2U, and for the OS2U Kingfisher. Like its rivals, the SO3C was a mid-wing monoplane, with a cockpit for a pilot well forward of the wing and a cockpit for an observer behind the wing, each normally having the big sliding canopy open. These aircraft were produced either with fixed tail-wheel landing gear or as a central-float seaplane, and in most versions they were stressed for catapulting. The Curtiss was all stressed skin.

The prototype XSO3C-1 made its first flight on 6 October 1939. It looked nice enough, if a bit stumpy, and was tested first with spatted wheels and then with floats. Like the rival SO2U, it was powered by the Ranger V-770 inverted-vee-12 air-cooled engine of 600 hp. From the outset it was clear that handling was terrible. Stability and control problems were serious enough to make the aircraft dangerous, and they resisted early efforts at rectification. Palliatives included adding a large ventral tail fin, enlarging all the vertical tail surfaces and tilting up the newly squared-off wing-tips.

On the one hand, the basic design was developed through numerous sub-types, introducing various armament provisions, equipment and other features. The proposed Ryan-built SOR-1 was to have bitten the bullet and, instead of the cocked-up tips, to have had proper wing dihedral. On the other hand, the basic flying qualities of the SO3C were so unpleasant that nobody wanted to go near one. In the case of the landplane, these qualities were accentuated by the tall main gears which combined a very narrow track with an almost ridiculously steep nose-up ground angle, which made take-offs, landing and even taxying very challenging.

At first the US Navy called the SO3C the Seagull, like its popular predecessor, but eventually adopted the British name of Seamew. Britain's Fleet Air Arm were allocated 250 Seamew I aircraft, plus a further thirty Queen Seamew radio-controlled target drones. Anyone who was familiar with the SO3C would say that a radio-controlled target was an ideal application. Sadly, a few piloted Seamews actually reached Britain, where they briefly trained TAGs (Telegraphist Air Gunners) at Worthy Down. Many SO3Cs were built with a fixed '30-calibre' gun, and a '50-calibre' aimed from the rear cockpit, but in service they were almost always stripped of combat gear and used as hacks.

High-ranking US Navy officers assured me that some warships managed to keep their old SOC biplanes, successfully resisting all attempts at replacing them with the SO3C. Others, eager to get the highly satisfactory OS2U Kingfisher, 'put their SO3Cs on the catapults and fired them off without a pilot'! I should have mentioned that the big Ranger was notoriously unreliable. I was familiar with the six-inline Rangers, which had no very bad reputation, but apparently the twelve-cylinder had a habit of simply stopping, for no obvious reason. Writing in *Aeroplane Monthly*, Warren H. Goodman recalled such an occasion, over a layer of California ground fog, which resulted in an emergency bale-out and broken ankle. Goodman

An unusual view of an SO3C landplane of the US Navy.

continued, 'Later in the war I met a flight-school classmate who had been acceptance-testing SO3Cs as they were delivered to the Fleet in Hawaii. He had three crashes, all because of engine failure, and turned in his wings rather than go on flying SO3Cs. . . .'

As for a British view, try Lieutenant-Commander William Menzies:

'I do not know if I was the first Royal Navy pilot to fly this thing, but I was the first of my squadron to do so, taking delivery at Roosevelt Field, Long Island, and flying them to Yarmouth, Nova Scotia. . . . I have forgotten how many Seamews were ferried to Yarmouth, and how many we broke in the process, but we finally had had enough and refused to fly them any more. . . . I had thought that someone had done a high-pressure sales job and sold us the rubbish that had been refused by the US Navy. Now that I know that both navies were suffering simultaneously, I feel better about the ten years that the Seamew took off my life expectation.'

DE HAVILLAND TK.5

The great de Havilland Enterprise was one of only three or four in the history of aviation to produce aeroplanes, engines and propellers (and guided missiles, for that matter). Not least of its branches was the DH Technical School, where many future leaders of the industry were trained. In 1934, when most of the company was still based at Stag Lane, in North London, the school designed and built a light aeroplane. In the class of the Moth, and powered by one of the new inverted Gipsy engines, it must have been a surprisingly pedestrian design because, though considerably smaller than a Moth, its empty weight was greater. The drawings were produced mainly by a Dutch student, and for some reason he labelled them in his own language, so instead of becoming the Technical School No. 1 it became the *Tekniese Kollege* 1, or TK.1.

A year later the TK.2 followed. This was a clean low-wing monoplane, though as originally built it looked rather amateurish, because the rear cockpit was replaced by a long-range tank and this resulted in an ungainly top line to the fuselage. During its twelve-year life the TK.2 was repeatedly altered, and after 1938 it looked beautiful. It also had a fine performance for a 140-hp Gipsy engine, winning races at speeds nudging 190 mph. In 1937 came the

The TK.5 had as much chance of flying as the car in the background, which happened to be called a Flying Standard!

TK.4, a tiny racer which was dwarfed by its Gipsy Major engine. It completed the 1937 King's Cup at over 230 mph, but like so many short-bodied racers was probably a rather tricky beast. It soon crashed, killing the DH chief test pilot, who had done most of the flying on both it and, in 1937, the TK.2.

Last of the TK family was the TK.5 of 1939. Again powered by a 140-hp Gipsy Major, it was a pusher canard. On the extreme nose was a rather small foreplane, carrying an elevator on each side. Halfway back was the enclosed cockpit. Right at the rear was the engine, driving a pusher propeller. The engine was mounted on the wing, which curved gracefully back and carried a fin and rudder near its tip. The spatted main wheels of the tricycle landing gears were mounted on the front spar of the wing. Few photos exist of this odd machine, and I have never seen one showing it painted and with the registration G-AFTK. In late 1939 the new chief test pilot, the brilliant Geoffrey de Havilland Jr, opened up for the first take-off. The TK.5 refused to fly. According to the school's students at the time, the faster it went across the Hatfield aerodrome, the more firmly did it seem glued to the ground.

Thus, the TK.5 joined the rather select group of modern aircraft which simply did not fly. Assuming there was nothing wildly wrong with the incidence of the fixed foreplane, I can only conclude that the CG was too far in front of the wing and main wheels for the small and ineffectual elevators. Doubtless the nose could have been raised if it had been given large all-moving foreplanes, but I was told by C.T. Wilkins, a senior Hatfield designer, that the company management did not approve of the TK.5 and were apprehensive that it might prove dangerous. In fact, it proved 100 per cent safe!

CAPRONI-CAMPINI N.1

The diminutive Count Gianni Caproni created almost as many companies as he did successful aircraft, and in addition these companies must have built more than 100 aeroplanes that were one-offs. Occasionally he received a contract to build the design of an inventor, as in the case of Luigi Stipa mentioned earlier (see page 53). Another example was the Caproni-Campini. It could hardly have been less deserving of its worldwide fame as 'the world's first jet aeroplane', although this is what it was thought to be at the time.

Signor Secondo Campini patented several designs of aeroplane in which a conventional piston engine drove some form of compressor to blow air out of a propulsive nozzle. His CC.1 design, the first to be published in a 1936 patent, was ambitiously described as 'intended for operation at either subsonic or supersonic speeds', and the patent drawings showed a jagged sharp-edged fuselage as if Mach 1 was within its capability. This was utter nonsense, because the source of power was an air-cooled radial piston-engine, intended to drive two centrifugal compressors in series to blow air out of the jet pipe. Downstream of the compressors the air had to navigate a 'rectifier radiator', which was partly a heat exchanger and partly a flow straightener. Then fuel could be added and burned, the heated jet escaping through a nozzle whose area was controlled by a central bullet. There was no provision for varying the area or profile of the inlet, nor the profile of the nozzle. Fortunately this assemblage of errors was never built.

Campini's next design, the CC.2, was built, however, the maker's designation being N.1. A ponderous all-metal machine, it had a wing of 52-ft span mounted completely beneath the tubular fuselage so as not to interfere with the duct profile. The fuselage comprised, in order: a plain pitot inlet, a large central cone fairing, a three-stage axial fan with hydraulically variable-incidence blades, a large peripheral coolant radiator and tank, a 900-hp Isotta-Fraschini vee-12 piston engine, a giant central obstruction containing the tandem cockpits, a large open space followed by a ring of vaporising fuel burners, and finally a propulsive nozzle with a very large central bullet slid in or out by a hydraulic jack upstream of the burners. Design and construction took ten years.

The N.1 was quite remarkably clumsy. Despite its great size the fuel capacity was extremely limited, as shown by the empty weight of 8,024 lb and maximum loaded weight of 9,250 lb. Mario de Bernadi, a famous Schneider-trophy pilot, made the first flight on 28 August 1940. On 30 November 1941 he, with Ing Pedace in the rear

The Italians are proud of the Caproni-Campini, and put it in the Milan aeronautical museum.

cockpit, flew the N.1 from Milan Taliedo to Guidonia. Despite a cruising speed of 130 mph, the distance of 168 miles was too far for a single hop and they had to refuel at Pisa! With maximum fuel flow to the burners the top speed was increased from 205 to 230 mph, at a cost in fuel burn of four times that of the piston engine alone. At full power the maximum speed at the ceiling of 13,000 ft was only 196 mph, this height taking fifty-three minutes to reach!

Almost everything that could go wrong with this pathetic aeroplane did. A simple list of all its flights and what happened on them almost stretches credulity; one is left thinking, 'There's nothing else left to fail.' The official figure for cruising speed was 207 kph (129 mph), and the staff at the Guidonia test centre did not disguise their contempt. Yet predictably, the flight from Taliedo to Guidonia was followed by fantastic publicity all over the world. The N.1 was hailed as 'the first really successful jet-propelled aeroplane ever to fly'. In fact, had Caproni merely made a normal two-seater with the same piston engine it would have weighed half as much, burned one third as much fuel and cruised between two and three times as fast.

JUNKERS JU 322 *MAMMUT*

When the RAF demonstrated in the Battle of Britain that it would not be possible for the Germans to carry out an invasion of southern England from the sky unopposed, Adolf Hitler decided, on 12 October 1940, to forget about the prickly island for the time being. All effort was henceforth devoted to planning the attack on the Soviet Union, due in the summer of 1941. This gigantic campaign in the East was not expected to take very long. Then the successful invasion of Britain was to take place, after much more careful planning than in 1940. In particular, it was recognised that whereas in 1940 the British army had left almost all its weapons behind in France, by 1942 it would largely have re-equipped. Accordingly, the Luftwaffe had to find a way of flying in such heavy equipment as a PzKW IV tank (19.7 tons), an 88-mm dual-purpose gun and its twelve-seat tug, or artillery of 105- and 155-mm calibre. As each load would only have to be brought once, on a one-way trip, the answer appeared to be large numbers of gliders, much bigger than any previously built.

Contracts were placed with Messerschmitt for the Me 321 (later named *Gigant*) and Junkers for the Ju 322 (later named *Mammut*). Rather surprisingly, Messerschmitt, which had extensive experience of wood construction, was told to use steel tube and fabric, while Junkers, whose experience was entirely with all-metal structures, was told to build the *Mammut* out of wood. Messerschmitt made a competent job of the Me 321, and both it and the six-engined Me 323 derivative proved enormously useful to the Luftwaffe and to the German army. There were still reservations, however.

One was that these aircraft were extremely vulnerable, and in such theatres as Tunisia in early 1943 and the Eastern Front from late 1943 they hardly dared to venture out in daylight. A further fundamental drawback was that, while a giant glider was excellent for a single overwhelming assault, it was extremely ill-suited to transport duties over a period of months or years. Each time a *Gigant* landed on its skids it presented a large obstruction on the airfield until it could somehow be jacked up, put on its unwieldy four-wheel trolley and towed out. The problem was compounded by the fact that the Luftwaffe had

no suitable tug. Highly dangerous arrangements had to be resorted to, notably the *Troika-Schlepp*, in which each glider was towed by three Bf 110s which had to pull at full power whilst avoiding each other. Eventually the He 111Z was produced, a purpose-designed tug consisting of two He 111 bombers linked by a common centre wing with a fifth engine.

Junkers never even got as far as experiencing the nail-biting take-offs by *Troika-Schlepp*. After an initial study designated EF 94, work went ahead under high pressure on the definitive Ju 322. True to the original objectives of Hugo Junkers (who had died in 1935), the configuration adopted was that of an almost all-wing aircraft. Many companies have considered such a layout sensible, especially when the load is not passengers but cargo or bombs. Within fourteen days the company had submitted its Ju 322 proposal. Almost the whole aircraft comprised a huge wooden wing, the biggest in terms of area ever built up to that time, with a span of 203 ft 5 in. The cargo was carried in the capacious rectangular centre section, with two large removable sections of leading edge to permit loading and unloading. On top, to the left of centre, was the enclosed pilot's cockpit. On each side were bolted the colossal tapered outer wings, with steel half-hoops under the tips to prevent damage from dragging along the ground. At the rear was a relatively modest rear fuselage and tail. Three defensive guns were to be carried, two in cockpits ahead of the leading edge and the third on top of the rear fuselage. The monster glider was to take off from a jettisonable trolley and land on four large sprung skids.

Leaving aside the absence of suitable towing aircraft, Junkers were surrounded by problems. The initial command had been to design the glider, build a prototype, and stockpile material for 100 more. A week after the design was submitted, Junkers were instructed to build not 100 but 200. This was of academic interest, because it was quickly discovered that timber of the necessary quality was unobtainable. The inevitable consequence was that Junkers had to go into frantic production with any timber they could get. Tests on a front spar resulted in failure at 50 per cent of the design load! This was put down to defective gluing and sap rot. A second spar was tested, only to fail at 60 per cent. Procurement chief Ernst Udet, a good judge of aircraft, hardly helped by expressing the opinion that, should a *Mammut* ever get into the air, it would prove unstable.

Not least of the problems concerned the take-off trolley. Never in the history of aviation have so many people worked on so many jettisonable take-off trolleys as in Nazi Germany in World War II. Those for the *Mammut* were the biggest. Some designs had thirty-two wheels. The final form had only eight wheels, but was still a huge steel-tube structure weighing 17,637 lb. After hoping to let the glider just rise off the trolley, the fear of it being pulled off at below flying speed and run down by the trolley forced Junkers to devise a locking system which the pilot could release as the *Mammut* climbed away. This, of course, demanded that the tug lift the trolley as well, and also raised the danger of the trolley bouncing and striking the glider.

A minor problem was that, instead of using hinged leading-edge sections as ramps, separate ramps had to be brought up and attached while the glider was on its trolley. The first time a PzKW IV was driven on board it tipped smartly forward as it entered the glider and smashed through the floor. Redesigning the floor, with other problems, reduced the available payload from 44,092 lb to only 26,455 lb.

At last the first *Mammut* was hooked up on a 400-ft cable behind a Ju 90. A path three miles long had been cleared through a forest off the end of the Merseburg runway. All was ready in early April 1941. At full power the four-engined transport was still on the ground only a few hundred feet from the end of the runway, and the swathe cut through the forest helped. The glider naturally gained flying speed first. The huge trolley fortunately disintegrated when it was dropped to the ground. The glider, on the other hand, weather-cocked violently, the vertical tail proving totally ineffective. Worse, the pull of the high glider forced the tug into a dangerous nose-down attitude. The glider pilot cast off just in time for the tug to recover to level flight with its wheels skimming the ground. Once free, the *Mammut* stopped its mad yawing and made a nice landing on the last bit of open ground. Thousands of man-hours were then expended sawing up ninety-eight almost complete *Mammuts* and parts for 102 more into blocks suitable for firewood.

Not of the best quality, this is the only photo of the Ju 322 known to me.

BLACKBURN FIREBRAND

At the end of World War II many aircraft were downgraded from the Secret category. One such was the Firebrand. It looked quite an impressive torpedo fighter (a fighter able to carry a torpedo). Teenagers often daydream, and one night in 1945 as I 'climbed into my pit' at University College, Durham, I pretended I was climbing into a Firebrand, which I then imagined I was flying. Had I known a bit more about the Firebrand I'd have pretended something else!

To begin with, its development timescale was a disgrace. This was partly the fault of the manufacturer and partly because – as still happens in Britain, when we occasionally try to do anything – the customer prevaricated, failed to take decisions, changed his mind and generally made certain that progress would be slow and halting. Thus, although the Firebrand was originally designed to a Fleet Fighter specification of March 1939, it missed the war completely!

I do not propose to relate the entire pathetic saga of how the Firebrand spent the entire conflict fiddling about with Sabre-engined Mks I (first flown on 27 February 1942) and II, and then developed into the Centaurus-engined Mks III and IV. After all this time one might have expected all the bugs to be well and truly ironed out, and the handling qualities of the basic aircraft to be immaculate. Today our computers are so powerful that we can usually make a new type handle almost flawlessly from the start. This was not so fifty and more years ago, but, after flying dozens of different prototypes and pre-production versions for several years any competent team might have been expected at least to have made the aircraft safe to fly. The B.45 Firebrand TF.III at last began to reach the Fleet Air Arm, non-operationally, in the final weeks of the war. It suffered from the same directional instability and take-off swing as the earlier marks, though twenty-seven production Mk IIIs were delivered. They were followed by 102 B.46 Firebrand TF.IV aircraft, with a much larger vertical tail and many other changes. These began to reach RNAS Anthorn from 4 June 1945.

The Anthorn pilots quickly discovered that, far from the faults having been rectified, some of the Mk IV's handling qualities were highly dangerous.

The trouble affected stability about all three axes, and in particular the lethality of stalling. Several pilots were killed in 1944–45, and the result was not a high-priority programme to make the Firebrand safe to fly, but instead a massive behind-the-scenes political row in which powerful forces did their utmost to discredit any pilot who dared to criticise the Firebrand. Much of the evidence has been lost, but a lot remains, such as these 1945 notes from a very senior officer:

15 September ATA pilot arriving from Brough told us that, following another fatality, the Mks III and IV should not be flown with fuel in the auxiliary tank. Reported to Admiral (Air) and requested instructions.

18 September Reply received from Admiral (Air) that there is no restriction regarding use of auxiliary tank. Lt G.R. Clarke took up Mk IV EK610 with auxiliary tank full, met with an accident and was killed. Spun in under full throttle.

20 September Anthorn reported to Admiral (A) that, since accident suggested unsatisfactory flying characteristics, similar to those which caused the decision of the MAP overseer at Blackburn, it was intended to ground all Firebrands at Anthorn pending AIB investigation.

27 September Articles appeared in all daily newspapers announcing release of Firebrand from Secret List. Statements eulogising the aircraft were at variance with certain facts which, as CASWO.63 showed, were known and officially accepted.

28 September AIB completed preliminary investigation. Anthorn reported intention to resume flying subject to: no clean stalling; not more than 25 gal in auxiliary tank; no instrument flying; no climbing at low speeds, and tail to be well raised before and during take-off. Restrictions recommended to all units holding Mk III and IV aircraft, since reports in Press convey to inexperienced pilots a misleading impression of handling qualities.

1 October Chief of Staff at Lee informed CO that it was not within his competence to ground a type of aircraft, that it was evident

The second prototype TF.III, with Centaurus engine, teardrop canopy and big vertical tail. To counter swing on take-off the fin was offset 6°, which brought more troubles than it solved.

Flying Commander was insufficiently experienced on Firebrand, and that advice he had given was bad advice. After discussion Chief of Staff admitted grounding was probably right but that reason should not have been lack of confidence in the aircraft but lack of confidence in the knowledge of the aircraft possessed by the pilots.

23 October Message received from Admiralty: Following restrictions are imposed on flying all Firebrand aircraft: stalling, flaps and undercarriage up, is not to be carried out intentionally; no fuel is to be carried in the auxiliary tank; aircraft should not be climbed at speeds below 160 kt IAS; take-off, flaps up, should never be made in a tail-down attitude.

19 November Message from Admiralty: Further to my signal 231820, care should be taken when cruising in bad weather to observe the lower cruising speed limits quoted in Mk III Pilots Notes; failure to do so may lead to an involuntary stall, as natural stall warning is slight. Deliberate stalling is still prohibited.

At the subsequent enquiry at Culham on 31 December 1945 the Firebrand was found, *after six years*, to be 'unacceptable for naval service'. Bringing the facts into the open at last ended an outrageous situation in which the Fleet Air Arm's investigations were not of the Firebrand but of the pilots who dared to criticise it. One of the most senior officers involved recorded, 'One cannot but be left with the uncomfortable suspicion that . . . there has been criminal negligence or inefficiency or both. . . . I must ask you to forgive me for quoting something you said yourself. You told me that the whole of the flying business is as dirty as horse-racing. . . .'

Following further important modifications the Mks 5 and 5A did see first-line service in 1948–53. By this time the Firebrand's bad reputation was well known, and perhaps no longer deserved.

BRISTOL BUCKINGHAM

At the beginning of World War II many manufacturers were trying to develop new twin-engined bombers. In California North American Aviation were working to turn the NA.40 into the NA.62, which became the famed B-25 Mitchell. At Weybridge, Surrey, Vickers-Armstrongs were trying to develop the successor to the Wellington, the Warwick, which was simply the same thing on a bigger scale. At Bristol a team was working on a proposed Type 162 'Beau bomber' or Beaumont, a sort of Beaufighter bomber to replace the underpowered Beaufort.

Nothing could better highlight the difference between the American and British ways of doing things – in the field of defence procurement at that time – than these three programmes. The American aircraft was allowed to develop rapidly, the Army Air Force merely keeping a close eye on the decisions, so that before the end of the war a total of 9,816 had served on every Allied front. In contrast, the British bombers progressed in an interminable series of meetings which produced a marvellous amount of talk and paper, but no squadrons. When they were finally in production they were so obviously outclassed as bombers that they were pressed into service as transports, burning roughly ten times as much fuel per passenger-mile or ton-mile as a Dakota.

There is a further difference between the two British aircraft. The Warwick was in itself a perfectly adequate machine which suffered mainly from a lack of sufficiently powerful engines. When the Bristol Centaurus became available, a fine eighteen-cylinder sleeve-valve radial in the 2,500–2,700-horsepower class, it got a new lease of life, and the GR.V version went into front-line service with Coastal Command. In contrast, the Bristol bomber's life was a seemingly endless succession of modifications to try to rectify faults or to adapt it to meet the current week's ever-changing Operational Requirements. Can you believe that, throughout the crucial years of World War II, dozens of officials were happy to attend meetings oblivious of the fact that the surest way to make a proposed aeroplane both costly and eventually obsolescent is to show a steadfast determination never to come to any firm decisions.

There simply is no room to relate the harrowing tale in detail. Part of the trouble was that, in traditional British manner, the customer did not know what he wanted. The original specification, B.7/40, overtaken by B.2/41, called vaguely for a tactical bomber able to make dive attacks or strafe ground targets. Later it was thought nice to add torpedo bombing, and over the months and years the picture moved away from close support of troops and envisaged a bigger aircraft to hit ships and major land targets. The anti-warship role suggested the need for heavy forward-firing armament, and this meant a 'solid' nose, which in turn demanded the addition of a large ventral gondola for the bomb-aimer, who was also supposed in some way to aim the lower rear gun. The gondola had high drag, significantly reducing speed and therefore range. Nobody thought of leaving the bomb-aimer in a comfortable streamlined glazed nose and just adding 'package guns' on the outside, as was done with the B-25. Moreover, while the American aircraft's guns were 'fifty-caliber', the British bomber had puny 0.303s.

Design change followed design change, and the wonder is that, having suffered 228 modifications in 1942 alone, the Bristol prototype did at last fly on 4 February 1943. By this time it was named Buckingham, and was the subject of large orders. Still official requirements vacillated, while the war went ahead with Beaufighters being made to carry torpedoes, Mitchells equipping the squadrons as a useful medium-level bomber and the peerless Mosquito carrying 4,000-pounders to Berlin at 400 mph. Once the horizontal and vertical tails had been considerably enlarged the Buckingham flew with acceptable stability, though of course the one thing that never fails to happen is that weight increases and performance keeps getting worse.

Soon it was obvious that the Buckingham was going to be not only obsolescent but also too late for the European war. Urgent work therefore went ahead to tropicalise it for the campaign against Japan, though this reduced speed still further. There was also a suggestion that it might serve in Italy, but when a production example was made available to 2 Group, for operational crews to evaluate, the response was devastating. The

Group's AOC, Sir Basil Embry, encapsulated a plethora of damning crew opinions in a damning report, which among a host of other things commented, 'No one with medium or light bomber experience could have been consulted in its design.'

The upshot was that, just as (years late) production aircraft were coming off the line in large numbers, nobody wanted the Buckinghams and everyone wondered what to do with them. The initial block of 400 (beyond the four prototypes) was cut to 119, reflecting the number already on the assembly line. Of these fifty-four were delivered as bombers, almost all going after acceptance test straight into storage at No. 5 or No. 19 Maintenance Unit. The other sixty-five were fitted out as luxurious 'courier transports' for four passengers, who rode on 5,000 horsepower, except that probably two aircraft would have fulfilled the need.

Two Buckinghams were completed as the prototypes of the Type 166 Buckmaster, a dual-control trainer. As Bristol had made 150 sets of Buckingham parts that were never assembled into aircraft, these were used to make 110 Buckmasters, which like the Buckinghams were scattered around Operational Conversion Units and anywhere else they could be got rid of. Meanwhile, Bristol's marketing enthusiasm had long since been transferred to the Type 164 Brigand, a derived torpedo-bomber with a completely new slim fuselage seating three in a compact cockpit amidships.

In 1948–50 Bristol delivered 147 Brigands. These actually got into front-line squadron service, usually replacing torpedo-carrying Beaufighters. After a while these settled down into service, only to run into a spate of wheels-up landings once they got into the Malayan operations from 1950. It was eventually discovered that the rubber seals in the hydraulic jacks had not been designed for service in the tropics, making the jacks useless and simultaneously allowing particles of semi-vulcanised rubber to jam the selector valves.

Worse was to come. Once the Brigands started strafing ground targets with long bursts of cannon fire, one aircraft after another either went straight on into the ground or caught fire. Eventually tests were done, for example by firing long bursts from the four 20-mm cannon at the butts. It was found that gun gas was building up in the exceptionally long blast tubes, which eventually caused an explosion. This in turn damaged the undercarriage selector valves and pipes, spraying highly inflammable DTD.585 hydraulic oil around the fuselage, which further firing ignited. Thus the Brigand became one of the few aircraft able to shoot itself down.

KV303 was the third production Buckingham I, the production series being preceded by four prototypes. Despite this, much remained to be done to make the aircraft acceptable.

Blohm und Voss BV 40

The BV 40 V1, first prototype of the only fighter to be designed without an engine.

Once Nazi Germany began really to be hurt by Allied bombing, in 1942-43, ways of shooting down the Allied 'heavies' began to proliferate. In addition to an unbelievable amount of *flak* (triple-A) of all calibres up to 88, 105 and 128 mm, and conventional fighters, several unconventional ideas were explored with all possible haste. These included a wide range of early SAMs (surface-to-air missiles), one of which was piloted (Bachem Ba 349). Another unusual fighter was a short-duration rocket (Messerschmitt Me 163B). The last and biggest panic programme of all was the Heinkel He 162A *Volksjäger*, which in an incredibly short time resulted in hundreds of brilliant little jet fighters. They were part of the *Salamander* programme, which then introduced an element of unreality by suggesting that the 162s should be flown by thousands of almost untrained Hitler Youth. It was highly dangerous to anyone not a trained fighter pilot. Having said that, the 162 was a superb last-ditch fighter, and has no place in this book. Had thousands appeared in 1943 they would have posed quite a problem.

The BV 40, a totally different animal, was perhaps the most unexpected fighter in history.

Blohm und Voss often built pedestrian aircraft, but even these always incorporated unconventional features which were the hallmark of technical director Richard Vogt, such as a tubular main wing spar which also served as the fuel tank. In 1943 Vogt studied the problem of shooting down the B-17s and B-24s of the US 8th AF. The massed firepower of the bombers was making serious inroads into the Luftwaffe's dwindling supply of fighter pilots. Vogt came to the conclusion that the only answer was to make the fighters smaller, and so more difficult to hit. Conventional baby fighters with small engines were one possibility, but Vogt hit on a much less obvious solution. Eliminating the engine could result in a fighter glider with an extremely small frontal area. Refining the idea, he sketched a 'fighter' which had a bizarre kinship with crude primary training gliders. Having no pretensions at soaring, it had stubby rectangular wings and a bluff unstreamlined fuselage. Where it differed was that the pilot lay prone on his stomach, the part ahead of his ankles being in a cockpit with heavy armour against fire from any direction, the front windscreen having a thickness of 120 mm (nearly 5 in).

Vogt proposed that the glider should be made as simple as possible from non-strategic materials and by non-skilled labour. The glider fighters would be mounted on a two-wheeled dolly and towed off behind a Bf 109 or Fw 190, the pilot jettisoning the dolly as soon as he rose from the ground. Calculations suggested that each fighter could, in fact, tow two gliders and still reach 23,000 ft in under seventeen minutes. Casting off, the glider would (it was thought) be very unlikely even to be seen by the bomber crews before it had opened fire with heavy cannon. Vogt initially thought of fitting one 30-mm MK 108 cannon plus, for a second firing pass, an explosive charge towed on a long cable. Eventually it was agreed there would seldom be an opportunity for a second pass through the bombers, so the armament was settled as two MK 108 cannon tucked under the wing roots.

Authorised as the BV 40, orders were placed for nineteen prototypes, with the intention to follow with the first 200 BV 40A series aircraft for the inventory. The idea was that, having cast off at a height greater than that of the bombers, the gliders – hopefully a swarm of them – would be able to reach speeds of the order of 560 mph in steep diving attacks. Alternatively, head-on attacks would be made at about 250 mph. After the firing pass, each glider would dive for the ground, extending a skid and then lowering flaps to assist in making an accurate landing.

The first prototype made its first flight behind a Bf 110 in late May 1944, remaining on tow. On the second test, on 2 June, the pilot cast off. Testing rudder response, he was startled to find that, at 87 mph, the glider 'fell out of the sky'. The machine was wrecked, but the pilot survived. Both the second and fourth BV 40s met with accidents, though this does not necessarily mean the thing was dangerous to fly. On the other hand it was certainly extremely tiring if the flight lasted longer than a few minutes, especially because the pilot's chin rested on a small padded pillar. Suffice to say, in autumn 1944, just as the whole Luftwaffe procurement was switched over to defensive fighters, the basic unsuitability of the concept resulted in the whole programme being abandoned. For one thing, the Luftwaffe was knee-deep in fighters; what it lacked was combat-ready pilots.

JUNKERS JU 287

I have always been intrigued by the Ju 287. It was not the first aircraft ever built with an FSW (forward-swept wing), but it was the first to have such a wing as a means to improved performance and handling at high subsonic Mach numbers. What puzzles me is that it is easy to demonstrate that, when the Ju 287 was designed, such a wing was structurally impossible, unless it was forever to be restricted to quite low airspeeds, far below 500 mph. A further puzzle is why this pure research

aircraft was made into such a cumbersome monster.

It was in 1943 that Siegfried Kneymeyer, Luftwaffe head of technical air armament, recommended the urgent development of jet bombers both larger and faster than the Ar 234. Dipl-Ing Hans Wocke at Junkers was already studying how best to design such an aircraft. Quite a lot was already known about sweptback wings, and several great research institutes, including the Hermann

Here ready to take off on the power of four turbojets plus three large rockets, the Ju 287 V1 had five fixed wheels, a wing structurally unsafe at high speed, and a camera in a cubic box carried on struts in front of the fin!

Goering at Volkenrode, the LFA, DVL and University of Göttingen, all had swept models in tunnels. Nothing like this was going on anywhere else in the world. This research confirmed the manifold advantages of sweepback in enabling wings either to be made thicker or to fly at higher Mach numbers, but they also confirmed the predicted low-speed problems of tip stall, pitch-up and loss of lateral control. Later further difficulties, such as Dutch roll, were encountered. Wocke simply said, 'OK, so why not sweep the wing forward?'

An FSW is today recognised as having, at least in theory, fourteen distinct advantages. Indeed, the wonder is that, its practicability having been demonstrated by the Grumman X-29, nobody is yet using the FSW. Back in World War II the main advantage was that such a wing tends to stall first at the root, which leaves the tip working powerfully and with good lateral control. Among many other gains can be reduced leading-edge angle, increased aspect ratio, reduced wing-bending moment and a fundamental transfer of lift from the upper surface to the underside, which reduces the strength of high-subsonic shockwaves.

Of course, there are also drawbacks. A minor one is that if an FSW aircraft is yawed, as for example by applying rudder, then the wing rotated forward increases effective sweep and loses lift, while the wing going aft reduces sweep (perhaps meeting the air like an unswept wing) and thus gains lift, rolling the aircraft strongly. But there is an even more basic problem. A little thought will show than an FSW is aeroelastically unstable. If such an aircraft pulls g, as in a turn or dive pull-out, the wings flex upwards. Unlike the conventional swept wing, the FSW bends upwards at the tips in such a way that, unless the structural designers are extremely clever, the incidence will increase from root to tip, because the wing twists as well as bends. This will increase the load on the tip still further, so that in a fraction of a second either the aircraft has departed violently into a loop or the wings have come off.

One can get an immediate picture of the problem by imagining a sheet of some flexible material – cardboard, plastic or ply – held out of a speeding vehicle. Held from the leading edge there is no problem, though a very flimsy sheet may suffer high-frequency flutter like a flag in a breeze. But if the sheet is held from the trailing edge, as in an FSW, it will instantly rotate violently nose-up or nose-down, and either break or wrench itself free. Thus, until recently, no practical FSW could be made.

Of course, an FSW could always be made for speeds of about 300 knots or less, but at such speeds there is no point; a normal 'straight' wing is better. What made the high-subsonic or supersonic FSW practical was the development of modern composite structures using plies (thin sheets) of graphite fibres bonded by epoxy resin adhesive. By tailoring the directions of successive plies it is now possible to make an FSW which, when it bends upwards under severe flight loads, does so either without any twist, or else with negative twist such that the angle of incidence of the outer section actually decreases. Then the wing will remain aeroelastically safe, even when pulling 9g at high airspeed.

In World War II none of this was possible. In my view a high-speed FSW jet bomber was incapable of fulfilment, and this must surely have been confirmed by tunnel testing of aeroelastically representative model wings. After such testing, I would have expected the idea to be dropped. If it was necessary to persist with FSW technology, the next move would have been to make one or a series of small research aircraft, powered by a single BMW 003A or Jumo 004B turbojet, able to be fitted with various test wings. Amazingly, Junkers instead built the Ju 287 V1. The designation Ju 287 was that of the proposed FSW bomber, and the V1 (experimental No. 1) was seen as a sort of prototype. In fact it was just a large lash-up, roughly the same size as the eventual bomber but made up of bits of other aircraft. The objective was to test the FSW at low speeds. Surely it would have been far better to build a high-speed testbed so that a scaled wing could be tested at *all* speeds?

The Ju 287 VI used a fuselage based on that of an He 177, a tail from a Ju 388, main wheels from a Ju 352, and two nose wheels from captured B-24 Liberators! To avoid cutting into the wing the main gears were fixed and spatted, though the wing box was cut open to receive the legs and bracing struts. The fixed nose gears were also spatted, and mounted side by side under the He 177 type cockpit. Four Jumo 004B turbojets were used, two on the sides of the nose and two under the trailing edge of the wing, where under high g loads they twisted the wing the wrong way.

This ungainly contraption first flew on 16 August 1944. Bill Green says it was once dived to 404 mph; they were pushing their luck. It certainly showed that at low speeds an FSW aircraft could fly well, but that was never questioned. Even at speeds around 300 knots it was found that wing deflection was causing serous problems. Junkers decided with the Ju 287 V2 – which may have been completed by the Russians – to use six Jumo 004Bs in triple clusters hung *ahead* of the wing, to try to stop it twisting. But with traditional metal wings the whole idea was an impossibility, unless the wing was almost solid!

GENERAL AIRCRAFT GAL.56

In his book *Wings of the Weird and Wonderful* (Airlife) Captain Eric M. Brown begins his reflections on this experimental glider with 'Often I have been asked which is the worst aircraft I have ever flown – well, this is it.' As many people would consider him to be the world's most experienced test pilot, the GAL.56 can fairly be called the worst of the bad.

During World War II there was a general belief among aerodynamicists that the arrival of jet propulsion ought to mean a radical rethink of the shape and configuration of aeroplanes. This was manifest in most of the large jet aircraft planned in Britain at the time. For example, the Vulcan and Victor bombers, and the Comet airliner, all began as tailless designs. Fortunately, the Victor and Comet were eventually given tails, and the Vulcan filled in the gaps to become a delta.

Not unreasonably, many research aircraft were ordered to explore these configurations, and General Aircraft received a contract for three GAL.56 gliders with a short central nacelle seating a pilot and observer, and fitted with fins and rudders on the tips of the wings. The first, TS507, had a sweep angle of 28°, and was called Medium V; TS510 was the Medium U, and TS513 was the Maximum V. A

From this angle one of the clumsy main wheels of the first GAL.56 hides the equally clumsy long tailwheel. Experimental gliders and tugs had the underside striped black and yellow.

powered version, the GAL.61, was ordered as TS515 to be built as soon as the best configuration had been decided.

Chief designer F.F. Crocombe had been responsible for numerous prior designs, the most recent, the GAL.55, having been a perfectly normal training glider. Even this was found to display many undesirable, if not dangerous, characteristics. Three were ordered, two were built and one was flown at Beaulieu as little as possible. As for the GAL.56, this was fortunate to be first flown, in mid-November 1944 towed by a Whitley, by one of the world's most experienced glider pilots, Squadron Leader Robert Kronfeld, who was General Aircraft's chief test pilot. Anyone else would probably have crashed on the first take-off, because the effect of rising out of the ground cushion was so violent that, to quote Captain Brown, 'Loss of ground effect would cause it to dart sharply back into the ground, and no amount of backward elevator movement could prevent this at speeds up to 80 mph IAS.'

In the immediate post-war period many tailless aircraft were frightening pilots in at least nine countries, but I cannot imagine anything more terrifying than the GAL.56 – and Farnborough tested only TS507 with the mildest sweepback of 28°. Of course, design of flying machines, at least in those days, was so unpredictable that the more sharply swept Maximum V version might have flown better.

At Farnborough the routine was for the glider to be towed by a Spitfire IX to about 20,000 ft and then cast off. Captain Brown relates the subsequent behaviour of this glider in his aforementioned book, and we can all be thankful that he survived to do this. In August 1947 he must have been very relieved to be able to hand this machine back to Kronfeld at Lasham. Here, soon afterwards, it got into an unrecoverable and fatal spin. Brown comments, 'Although saddened by the news it did not surprise me, for I always had the instinctive feeling that the GAL.56 would one day win the eternal battle of wits with those few who flew it.'

Kokusai Ku-105

It was probably *Punch* that published a cartoon showing a British roadside filling station of the 1940s. An enormous Cadillac has drawn up 'for gas'. The pump attendant asks, 'Would you mind switching off, Sir; you're gaining on me!' Something of the sort applied to the Ku-105.

This big (115-ft span) transport aircraft was based on the Ku-7 assault glider, a sort of Japanese copy of the German Go 242 but on a much larger scale. Power was provided by two 940-hp Ha-26-II engines on the fronts of the tail booms. These enabled the monster to take off by itself, because it was restricted to a weight of only 12.5 tonnes (27,558 lb), limiting the payload to a mere 3.3 tonnes (7,275 lb). Range was estimated at 1,553 miles, cruising at 137 mph.

The Ku-105 appeared in April 1945, by which time Japan's strategic position was already critical. Nine prototypes were built, and plans were rushed ahead to produce a batch of 300 Ku-105s, named *Ohtori* (Phoenix), equipped to carry fuel to Japan from the Sumatra oilfields. It was calculated that on each flight the Ku-105 would burn 80 per cent of the fuel put aboard in Sumatra! Just 20 per cent, or a mere 1,400 lb, might make it to the Land of the Rising Sun.

Perhaps we ought not to be too harsh on this vehicle, born in a time when desperate measures were needed. Concorde, born in a time of no desperation at all, carries almost 10 lb of fuel for each 1 lb of payload, so the Japanese tanker was twice as efficient – or are we again comparing apples and oranges?

One of the few surviving photos of the Ku-105.

AVRO TUDOR

From fifty years on it is hard to believe that, at the end of World War II, we British thought we were world leaders in aviation. In fact, this merely betrayed our ignorance. At the same time, we fully recognised that for the moment we could not compete against properly designed American commercial transports, such as the DC-4 and the Constellation, with converted bombers such as the Halton and Lancastrian. Not to worry. Coming along fast were our own properly designed airliners, led by the Avro Tudor.

Tudor happens to be my middle name, and so I particularly wanted this to be a really fine aircraft, worthy of its great forebear, the Lancaster. Avro's design team, led by Roy Chadwick, could surely be relied upon to produce a real winner? But when the Tudor prototype appeared towards the end of the war, flying on 14 June 1945, I was not especially impressed. Two giant main wheels and a tailwheel smacked of 1935 rather than 1945, especially as it meant that passengers had to board a fuselage tilted like the side of a hill. And for a big 7,000 hp aircraft to be equipped to carry just twelve passengers seemed to suggest that the tickets would be expensive.

In fact the whole procurement set-up was ludicrous. The customer was the Ministry of Aircraft Production, which did not actually operate aircraft and knew nothing whatsoever about civil aviation. The airline, BOAC, was a government instrument which knew nothing about competition, or even whether its services were competitively priced. It carried mailbags for the Post Office, and government VIP and Service passengers whose tickets were paid for. Fare-paying passengers were a rare species. Thus, the Tudor was designed to carry twelve passengers in sumptuous comfort non-stop across the North Atlantic.

But this book is not greatly concerned with economics. The Tudor gets in on much more certain grounds. To be frank, not only was it not in the same class as its transatlantic rivals, but the makers made the proverbial 'pig's ear' of it.

The basic uncompetitiveness stemmed mainly from the choice of four Merlin engines. Chadwick, Bomber Command and many other people had so relied on the Merlin during the war that it never occurred to them that it might not be the right engine for peace. Indeed Canadair deliberately threw out the Pratt & Whitney radials on their C-4 (DC-4M) and replaced them with Merlins. Later Trans-Canada's Gordy McGregor, a tremendous pro-Rolls man, told me, 'It was a strategic error.' Had the Tudor been Super Connie-size, and powered by the Centaurus, it might have been an important competitor on the world stage. But it would also, of course, have had to be a good aircraft.

Sadly, the Tudor was anything but a good aircraft. It is a reflection on the sheer difficulty of local aerodynamic design to note that this exceedingly experienced design team, using a wing and engines with which they were very familiar, should have created an albatross that hung round their necks for years until it could thankfully be junked. In the words of Captain E.M. 'Winkle' Brown (in *Wings of the Weird and Wonderful*) even the original prototype 'suffered from directional and longitudinal instability, pre-stall buffeting at a relatively high speed, violent rudder oscillation at moderate angles, severe take-off swing, loss in performance from that estimated, and a tendency to bounce on landing'. This was all apart from the fact that by reason of its basic design and powerplants it could never be a competitive aircraft anyway.

Despite all this, it was Britain's only available 'flagship of the skies'. On 21 January 1947 a highly publicised ceremony took place at Heathrow Airport, then just a few tents pitched on a sea of mud, at which Princess Elizabeth, the future Queen, named the fourth production aircraft *Elizabeth of England*. Hailed as the lead aircraft of BOAC, the Tudor simply had to be got right. Boscombe Down, the Aeroplane & Armament Experimental Establishment, were called in to help, surely an indictment of a major manufacturer's development and flight-test capability? A totally unnecessary element of tragedy was introduced to the programme on 23 August 1947 when the prototype of the Tudor 2, with a fuselage stretched from 79 ft 6 in to 105 ft 7 in, crashed on take-off, killing everyone on board including designer Chadwick. The cause: in final preparations someone had swapped over the aileron cable connections, telling nobody they had been tampered with and leaving no written record!

Apart from the much larger vertical tail the Tudor 4B didn't look very different, but over 300 modifications had at least made it an acceptable flying machine.

I won't go into the exceedingly complex story of how the Tudor was gradually brought up to the stage at which, if you were generous, you might consider it acceptable to the pilot. Some aircraft seem to have everything go right, while the Tudor was perhaps the ultimate example of everything not only going wrong but resisting all attempts at rectification. In preparing this note I compiled a dossier of 186 modifications and numerous juicy quotations, but the Tudor is not worth such comprehensive treatment.

Suffice to say there were three sizes of fuselage: the short Mks 1 and 3, the long 2, 5 and 7, and the intermediate 4 series. Some of the 186 modifications were externally obvious, notably the greatly enlarged vertical tail and extended inboard nacelles. Gradually and haltingly the Tudor was made somewhat better. Back in March 1946 BOAC had caused a stir by letting it be publicly known that they had demanded 343 modifications to the Tudor 1, but many of these were concerned with details of furnishing. The serious stuff concerned the aeroplane itself, and on 11 April 1947 BOAC cancelled its order simply because it was obvious the Mk 1 would never have the range to operate on the North Atlantic. Later Qantas and SAA cancelled because the high-capacity Tudor 2 was clearly never

going to have the hot-and-high performance needed to operate on their routes.

BSAA, Don Bennett's line to South America, tried very hard indeed with the Tudor 4 and 4B, which were probably the best of a bad lot. Sadly, on the night of 29/30 January 1948 *Star Tiger* simply vanished somewhere near the so-called Bermuda Triangle, and on 17 January 1949 precisely the same thing happened to *Star Ariel*. So BSAA gave up, though for a while it operated some survivors as freighters.

I flew as a passenger on two Tudor 1 sorties on the Berlin Airlift, without incident. But later, on 12 March 1950, a stretched Mk 5 crashed at Cardiff Llandow. The eighty casualties made it Britain's worst air accident up to that time. The cause was ascribed to incorrect CG position. By this time the Tudor was beginning to mature. Indeed the same aircraft, on the Berlin Airlift, had taken off with the elevator locked; Don Bennett landed it on the trimmers!

In my opinion, the Tudor could never have been of any importance on the world scene. What actually happened is that the programme degenerated into a plethora of different versions, most either used for a very short period or else never used at all. Production stopped in 1948, and even at this time derelict Tudor hulks were littering the landscape.

BRITISH HELICOPTERS: BRISTOL SYCAMORE, CIERVA AIR HORSE AND PERCIVAL P.74

At least until recently, there were always 'rogue' specimens of every type of production aircraft. For diverse reasons these individual aircraft exhibited much poorer flying qualities, worse flight performance and generally inferior behaviour than the norm. In writing a book such as this it is important to try to avoid damning a type in general because of the bad qualities of one particular example, but even though some were much worse than others, the first subject of this chapter had a bad reputation.

Late in World War II the autocratic family board of the Bristol Aeroplane Company decided to form a helicopter department, and over the next

Though this Sycamore HR.13 was better than earlier versions, brute force was still needed on the collective, which made every take-off dangerous, and to move the trimmers the cyclic had to be gripped between the knees.

Today large helicopters use three engines to drive one main rotor, whereas the Cierva Air Horse used one engine to drive three.

twelve months built up a talented design team led by Raoul Hafner. The logical way to begin was to design a relatively conventional four-seat machine, the Ministry raising experimental specification E.20/45 to cover it. To avoid trouble, the prototype, with Ministry serial VL958, was fitted with a Pratt & Whitney R-985 Wasp Junior engine of 450 hp. The type number was 171 and the appropriate name was Sycamore. Alan Marsh made the first test flight on 27 July 1947.

As the Sycamore had many good features it is a pity it also had many bad ones. Certainly the best part was the main rotor, with three blades made largely of wood. It was aerodynamically outstanding, and as it spun at up to nearly 300 rpm, with 287 available in normal flight, it had abundant kinetic energy and made autorotative landings following engine failure particularly easy. Against this could be set a host of shortcomings which perhaps to some degree stemmed from lack of familiarity with helicopters built elsewhere, such as in the USA.

For example the Sikorsky S-51, designed earlier, had powered controls which eliminated stick forces other than those of stiction and friction. In contrast, the controls of the Sycamore were exceedingly heavy, making piloting a very tiring job, and the collective lever in particular quickly became so hard to move that in many Sycamores the pilot had to retrim strongly nose-up before attempting to come to a hover. This in turn meant that one had to exert sustained heavy forward pressure on the cyclic stick in cruising flight. No pilot likes to be locked into a situation where neither hand can be freed even for a moment.

To retrim the Sycamore the pilot had to rotate traditional hand wheels, which themselves were hard to turn. Invariably the pilot was left desperately wishing for a third arm, so that he could retrim without letting go of either stick. (In contrast, the cheap little Hiller 360 or HT.1 (HTE) could be retrimmed by a thumb switch on the cyclic.) But all these were merely incidentals, as were such things as the nose-high attitude in the hover. The real killer was the virtual impossibility of raising the collective in one firm movement. With any helicopter the lift-off has to be firm and positive, and if the machine is allowed to dither at the crucial time it can quickly encounter ground resonance which can turn into catastrophic instability. One of the Sycamores to do just this belonged to Farnborough's Aero Flight. It crashed on lift-off. Flight Lieutenant Ken Hough, an experienced test pilot, was killed and Rolls-Royce's chief test pilot Harvey Heyworth injured. Squadron Leader Ron Harvey, a courageous test pilot who considered a particular Sycamore lethal, once asked a Farnborough colleague what he thought of the Sycamore; the reply was, 'Please! Not while I'm eating.'

Bristol went on to spend many years fiddling with tandem-rotor machines which began almost by using two Sycamore rotors on a fuselage reminiscent of a railway coach. These eventually produced the Belvedere, which would have been much more useful if it had been appreciated that the compact and lightweight turboshaft engines could have been tucked up above the cabin to drive straight on the main gearbox. Instead they were mounted vertically inside the cabin where the payload might have been!

Mention of Alan Marsh inevitably reminds one of the Cierva Air Horse. This was a giant for its day, distinctive in having three rotors all driven by a single Rolls-Royce Merlin. From 1996 it seems absolute nonsense: today we would prefer to have one main rotor driven by three engines, as in the EH 101 and Super Stallion. Fifty years ago the world's body of experience with helos, especially large ones, was very limited. The first Air Horse made its first free flight in Marsh's hands on 8 December 1948, and despite the seemingly clumsy configuration the flight trials went quite well. The monster had fully powered controls, and many other advanced features. I include the Air Horse here because eighteen months later a crucial part, the front-rotor swashplate drive link, broke with the helicopter at about 500 ft. Such a failure was unsurvivable, and Squadron Leader 'Jeep' Cable and test engineer J. Unsworth were killed.

Any engineer or pilot will confirm that they like to have redundancy in the vital parts of structure, so that, if anything breaks, there is always another load-path to hold things together. In helicopters this is difficult to achieve. Indeed it is common for the entire machine to be stopped from falling out of the sky by a single nut – picturesquely called the Jesus nut – at the very top of the rotor hub. With three clutches, three sets of output gears and three sets of swashplates and hubs – every item potentially a killer – I would not personally have liked to fly an Air Horse for a living. Indeed the feeling in the Ministry of Supply at the time was that for larger machines (they suggested 15,000 lb gross as the limit) it was highly desirable to eliminate

The Percival P.74 proved to be outstandingly safe, because it never rose from the ground.

mechanical drives entirely, and instead use a 'gas drive' with some form of jet propulsion at the tips of the blades. Fairey built the Jet Gyrodyne and then the impressive Rotodyne with pressure jets at the blade tips in which fuel could be burned for take-off and hovering, causing a noise like a large steam locomotive toiling slowly uphill.

For the Rotodyne, D. Napier & Son produced a special version of the Eland turboprop in which a shaft drive to an auxiliary compressor provided the high-pressure airflow fed to the blades. They also designed a much smaller engine with a similar layout, called the Oryx, to power the Percival P.74. This was highly regarded by the Ministry as the right way to go. As the gas drive imparted no torque to the fuselage, apart from trivial friction which tended to turn the helicopter the same way as the rotor (instead of in the opposite direction), only a very small tail rotor was needed to point the way the pilot wanted to go.

I often visited Napier, and on one occasion heard that a panic had ensued when it was discovered that an Oryx compressor was missing! It transpired that a keen fitter had locked it in his personal toolbox, which gives an idea of what a small unit it was. Nevertheless the whole engine, complete with aux-

iliary compressor, was 7 ft long and about 20 in in diameter, and on one side a huge mixing box was added where the hot gas and fresh compressed air were combined before being fed to the rotor. Incredibly these engines, instead of being put above the fuselage, were mounted vertically up each side of the cabin, making a nice hot deafening barrier between four front passenger seats and four more behind.

Hunting Percival Aircraft did a lot of rig testing at Luton and then, in April 1956, borrowed Ron Gellatly from Fairey Aviation to begin flight-testing the first P.74, XK889. He soon asked colleague John Morton to join him as co-pilot, because it needed their combined strength to move the controls. Then followed over three months of agonising attempts to overcome a seemingly endless succession of problems. Finally they had full power on both engines and maximum gas delivery to the three blades, but the P.74 showed no inclination to rise. When he first encountered the beast Gellatly was very concerned to find that, in the event of a dire emergency, he had to unstrap, leave the cockpit, walk the length of the cabin and get out of the door at the back. He need not have worried; the P.74 never got off the ground!

LEDUC RAMJETS

This is not a story of bad design, but of a perfectly sound idea which, persisted with over many years, did nothing but consume money and effort. In 1929 Whittle had an idea for a totally new propulsion system which would make aircraft go faster. After seven years of failing to get anyone interested, he eventually obtained just enough money (not a penny of it from the government) to build an engine, and the rest is history. In France at the same time René Leduc had an idea for a propulsion system that might make aircraft go faster still. After thirty years, with masses of money from his government, he gave up.

Many people wonder how we might do better in what is called technological forecasting. This is a science or art in which you attempt to predict what new ideas or discoveries will come along, and when, and which ones will eventually be put to practical use. Leduc's life was devoted to the ramjet, a method of propulsion which, unlike Whittle's, was not new. The ramjet or athodyd

had been proposed by such visionaries as Marconnet, Chanute and Lorin, all of whom, like Leduc, were French. Basically, the ramjet resembles a turbojet with all the working parts taken out. Air is rammed in at the forward-facing inlet, further compressed and slowed in a suitably profiled duct (a diffuser), heated by burning fuel, and then expanded and greatly accelerated through a propulsive nozzle. The simplicity of the scheme is obvious, and like the turbojet the ramjet can propel aircraft faster than sound. The chief drawback is that a ramjet cannot start from rest, so a second propulsion system has to be provided for take-off and initial acceleration to high speed.

This was always self-evident, but Leduc still saw in the ramjet 'the aeroplane of the future'. From the outset he never thought of it as an engine to be attached to the aircraft in the same way as other engines. All his patents and designs were for aircraft whose fat fuselage *was* the ramjet. Of circular

Leduc's 1953 vehicle, the O.21, perched on its Languedoc carrier aircraft.

Access to the O.21 cockpit was achieved by sliding the entire nose-cone forward.

section, the fuselage formed a continuous duct from nose inlet to tail nozzle. As his early designs were subsonic, the front portion of the duct was divergent, forming a diffuser, to slow down and compress the air. The aft section was convergent, to expand and accelerate the flow. The fuel was added as far upstream as possible, but after the flow had been brought to the highest pressure and lowest velocity attainable.

In the early 1930s Leduc conducted simple experiments with bench models whose thrust could be measured whilst compressed air from a hose was blown through them. In 1935 he claimed to have made a model ramjet which generated a thrust of 8.8 lb at an airspeed of 671 mph (nearly Mach 1). I believe the only way he could have tested this would have been to have blasted it off in free flight by a rocket, and then there is no way he could have measured the thrust.

At the 1938 Paris *Salon* he exhibited a model of his proposed Leduc O.10 aircraft. For the first time the world saw a 'needle nose' containing the pressurised cockpit pointing out from the circular nose inlet to the fat ramjet fuselage, to which conventional wings and tail were added. Leduc said this 'machine of the future' would generate 14,000 hp, enabling it to reach 1,000 kph (621 mph) at a height of 30 km (nearly 100,000 ft). Then the war intervened.

Leduc carried on with the O.10 throughout the war, receiving limited amounts of funding from the Vichy Government, and after liberation he was able to set up a growing design and factory organisation at Argenteuil, Paris. There the O.10 was constructed with remarkable rapidity. A shiny stressed-skin machine, it had a centrebody in the inlet which seated a pilot and observer in tandem, with a small APU (auxiliary power unit) to drive the fuel pump and generator. Fuel was fed to 500 burners arranged round the leading edges of five tubular ducts of increasing diameter in the centre fuselage. Leduc estimated that the thrust would reach 3,527 lb at 560 mph at low altitude. An SE.161 Languedoc was fitted with large dorsal trunnions to carry the O.10 aloft. The first separation and glide back were made from Toulouse Francazals on 21 October 1947. On 21 April 1949 it was claimed to have 'reached 423 mph on half power', and on a later flight to have 'climbed at 8,000 ft/min at a height of 11 km'.

Two further aircraft were built to the same basic design. The second was almost identical to the first, but the third, called the O.16, was fitted with a small Turbomeca Piméné turbojet on each wing-tip, to provide auxiliary power during the descent and landing. Leduc never built the planned catapult to launch the O.10 or O.16

from the ground.

Next came the O.21, one third larger and more powerful. Still subsonic, the O.21 was planned to have a Marboré turbojet on each wing-tip, so that it could (just about) take off by itself. It was also intended to have two 20-mm cannon. In the event, the only significant change was that the single-seat cockpit was far in front of the air inlet, which was obviously a better arrangement. The O.21 made its first free flight from the Languedoc on 16 May 1953. At Mach 0.85 the thrust at full power was claimed to be 13,228 lb (6 tonnes), the same as the gross weight.

By this time Air Ministry funds permitted the construction of the more advanced O.22. Bigger still, and with swept wings and tail, this was intended to take off by itself with much better acceleration from a SNECMA Atar turbojet mounted downstream of the cockpit centrebody, upstream of the white-hot zone of ramjet combustion. The O.22 took off on Atar power from Istres on 26 December 1956, and made more than thirty successful flights on the power of its turbojet. The ramjet was estimated to enable Mach 2 to be reached, theoretical thrust at this speed at low level (if the structure were strong enough) being calculated to be 132,280 lb. But by 1957 the Air Ministry could see that it was never going to lead to operational squadrons, and cut off funds before the ramjet could be tested.

The history of aviation is liberally sprinkled with ideas which were tested, found to work and then abandoned. Another example is the Short-Mayo composite aircraft. What I am saying is: these were all ideas which, in the cool light of day, ought to have been recognised for what they were – nonstarters, successful or otherwise.

PLANET SATELLITE

Time after time in the history of aviation a new type that has looked marvellous has turned out to be the proverbial 'can of worms'. In 1947, when I was still in the RAF, I saw a drawing of the most fabulous light aeroplane one could imagine. It was called the Planet Satellite. Though the world was being flooded with cheap ex-Service aircraft – such as airworthy Tigers at £25 – the Satellite looked so wonderful that people with enough money seemed certain to buy it.

The fuselage was perfectly streamlined (no qualification needed). In the nose was the fully glazed cabin for a pilot and three passengers. Dual controls were fitted, and on each side was a downward-hinged metal door with inbuilt step, and an upward-hinged (or sliding) Perspex panel, giving easy access to both pairs of seats. The low-mounted wing housed a tank on each side. On the wing was mounted the 250-hp Gipsy Queen 32 engine, with fan-assisted cooling using air taken in through a flush inlet above the fuselage. An 8-ft tubular shaft drove the variable-pitch pusher propeller at the tail. Ahead of the propeller were the sharply dihedralled tailplanes and elevators and a ventral fin and rudder. Simple pneumatics operated the large plain flaps and tricycle landing gear, the main units of which swung forwards and inwards into the fuselage. With an estimated range of 1,000 miles cruising at 191 mph, with four adults and baggage, the Satellite looked like what it was:

about three generations later than the competition, which consisted of such things as Procter 5s and Austers – or even Pipers and Cessnas.

Of course, I did not have the slightest chance of being able to afford a Satellite, but I watched its progress with benevolent interest. When the real thing appeared at the 1948 SBAC show – held for the first time at Farnborough – I became quite excited. It had not flown at that time, and I looked eagerly in the aviation press for news of the start of flight testing. It was to be a long wait.

The Satellite was the brain-child of Major J.N.D. Heenan. In the immediate post-war era he concluded that the world could use a well-designed four-seater, and it seemed possible to build an aircraft that ought to capture most of the market. Not being a traditional hidebound aircraft designer, he started from first principles. He wanted high performance, which meant beautiful streamlining. He wanted a quiet cabin, so he put it in the front, and the engine as far in the back as possible. For safe operation he specified a reasonable wing loading, large flaps and powerful brakes. An extra, not necessary but perfectly sound in concept, was to make almost the entire structure from MgZr (magnesium-zirconium alloy). These alloys are noted for their low density, in the region of 1.75, whereas aircraft aluminium alloys lie around 2.9. This means that, weight for weight, the MgZr part is thicker and therefore needs less underlying structure for it to be stable in compression or torsion. The Satellite structure was thus amazingly simple. Stringers were conspicuous by their absence, and Heenan needed fewer than 400 drawings for the whole aircraft, compared with about 3,000 for a conventional lightplane.

Heenan was no fool. He was determined to get everything right first time. For example, he did comprehensive tests on the little-known MgZr alloy, investigated chromating and priming, tested the engine cooling system, checked that rain would be shed immediately from the Perspex nose panels,

and had a specimen section of wing put through exhaustive fatigue tests. Planet Aircraft was formed in a very professional manner, and Group Captain H.J. 'Willie' Wilson, a recent holder of the World Air Speed Record, was appointed test pilot (later becoming managing director). Construction was entrusted to Redwing Ltd at Thornton Heath, and because they were short of the right kind of technical staff, Mr F.G. Miles was called in at a late stage to advise on the design.

The completed machine, neatly finished in blue and with registration G-ALOI in silver, was taken

When I first saw photographs of the Satellite I wished I could afford to buy one!

to Hartford Bridge (Blackbushe) for flight testing. Many years later Wilson recorded what happened:

After the first hop, which resulted in the undercarriage collapsing, the Air Registration Board called for an investigation of the stressing. After numerous delays the machine was prepared for a second flight. Once more I carried out a hop to about 20 feet, then executed what I thought to be quite a reasonable landing. When, on inspection, it was found that the main keel had broken, that really brought down the wrath of the ARB, who insisted that the aircraft had to be completely restressed. My own view was that we should, in the old phrase, jack up the windscreen and run a new aeroplane underneath.

G-ALOI gathered dust in the F.G. Miles hangar at Redhill for ten years until it was finally broken up for scrap in 1958. The fuselage of the second Satellite was used for the Firth helicopter. Probably wisely, this was never completed. All very sad, because even today the Satellite looks about three generations later than the things private owners actually fly.

FAIREY FD.1

After World War II the British aeronautical procurement machine, successively styled the Ministries of Aircraft Production, Supply, Aviation, Aviation Supply, Technology and Defence (Procurement Executive), naturally scurried about trying to respond to the new level of performance opened up by jet engines. Today most high-speed aircraft are of what might be called conventional configuration, though there are a few tailless deltas and canards. But in the mid-1940s it was widely felt that any jet aeroplane had perforce to have an unconventional configuration. The FD.1 added a challenging extra: tail-standing VTO (vertical take-off).

As in the US Navy, the basic idea was that VTO fighters should take off from small platforms aboard ships. This, of course, is the easy part; the difficult bit is getting back. Perhaps the Fleet Air Arm deliberately ignored this in drawing up specification E.10/47 for an experimental aircraft which, whilst retaining 'qualities suitable for a fighter', incorporated propulsion and control systems enabling it to be fired under quite modest acceleration – say, 2 g – from a steep ramp.

While design effort on the full-scale manned aircraft, later called the Fairey Delta 1, went ahead at Hayes, Fairey also worked on a back-up programme of half-scale pilotless models. These were simple vehicles, with most of the body length occupied by delta wings fitted with elevons (serving as both elevators and ailerons). The tubular body was almost wholly given over to tankage of HTP (high-test peroxide) and hydrazine, a lethal mixture reminiscent of the Me 163. Even by itself HTP is deadly stuff, especially if brought into contact with skin, grass, earth or any biological material. In contact with hydrazine it explodes. These liquids were fed to two Fairey Beta I rocket engines in the tail, with superimposed swivelling thrust chambers.

Control of these chambers was assigned to an on-board autopilot. In 1946 such technology was crude in the extreme. Indeed, in the absence of anything else it was decided to copy major elements of the system fitted to the German A.4 (V2) rocket, with two-axis gyros in a very primitive feedback closed loop. The models were blasted off a ramp at 85° by two large cordite boost motors, thereafter climbing gently away under the thrust of the liquid-propellant rockets. In practice, of course, it was not like this at all, and the author was told by Fairey's F.J. Costigan and P.J. Duncton that for a VTO model actually to behave as planned was almost unheard-of. In contrast, a young Fairey person guarding the orange and black VTO vehicle displayed at the 1952 Farnborough show said, 'We're on the brink of a VTO supersonic fighter.'

In fact the FD.1 was quite difficult enough without aiming to go beyond Mach 1. It was a simple little delta aircraft, with a vertical tail roughly the same size as the wings. On top of this relatively huge fin was a small fixed-incidence delta tailplane. Each wing had a slat, fixed open, over the outer half-span. On the trailing edge were large elevons outboard and small split airbrakes inboard. The crucial bit was that the 3,600-lb thrust Derwent turbojet was to have a special nozzle, designed by Rolls-Royce at Hucknall, capable of being vectored over a cone of 32° included angle. Around the nozzle were four large fairings for cordite boost motors, with sufficient thrust to fire the FD.1 off almost vertically. An anti-spin parachute was housed in a container on each wing-tip, and a braking parachute under the rear fuselage.

Taxi tests began at Ringway (now Manchester Airport) on 12 May 1950, which was over a year late. By this time the Fleet Air Arm had cooled towards VTO fighters, perhaps because it had realised they had to land as well as take off. Starting off in a wave of enthusiasm, they had caused to be created a tiny aeroplane which inevitably filled any test pilot with awe. Just because something is small and simple does not mean it is safe to fly. In the case of the FD.1 one had only to give it one glance to see that it would be exceedingly 'hot', perhaps in all senses of the word. This very fact delayed the start of flight testing, because not even Ringway's runway was long enough. It meant dismantling and trucking the aircraft to Boscombe, where Group Captain Gordon Slade made the first flight getting on for a year later, on 12 March 1951.

He must have been relieved that the VTO idea had by this time gone out of the window, or the flight test programme would have been really hair-raising. I saw the aircraft on several occasions, and even allowing for the effect of its small size it

A Ministry of Supply photo of the Fairey E.10/47 taken at Ringway in August 1950.

landed faster than anything I had previously seen. The braking parachute candled or failed to deploy properly on two of these occasions, and on one Peter Twiss said he burned out the brakes trying not to go off the end of the long runway at Boscombe. The slats were removed, and the rocket mountings were replaced by conical fairings. All this left a nasty little beast which had little span, not much length but plenty of height. Taken in conjunction with very narrow track this made the FD.1 sheer murder in a crosswind or rough air. Someone in the RAF did everyone a favour by failing to correct a swing after touchdown, which left VX350 on its belly.

Prone piloting: Reid & Sigrist RS.4 and Gloster Meteor

With that cheap commodity, hindsight, one can see that perhaps the British Air Staff might have assessed and disposed of most of the 'last ditch' German air-defence inventions of 1944–45 before the war ended. Surely any sensible observer would quickly have concluded that none was relevant to the post-war RAF? Yet the notion of a small rocket-propelled interceptor simmered for ten years, even though it would have had extremely limited range and endurance (each would have defended a single airfield or city) and would have been most inconvenient to operate. For example, if it did manage to regain its home runway, it probably could not be taxied back to dispersal. The rationale behind persisting with such aircraft was the need for the ultimate in quick take-off and climb to kill high-flying bombers carrying nuclear weapons, because every single bomber had to be shot down.

One of the most important point-defence projects was the Bristol 185, which was picked from seven submissions in 1949. This in turn launched the de Havilland Spectre controllable rocket engine and various other new systems and armaments. It also launched a serious research effort into prone piloting, because one of the features of the interceptor was that, as in some of the German schemes, the pilot would lie face-downwards. Among other things this greatly improves the ability of the human body to withstand severe acceleration in the vertical plane (vertical relative to the aircraft), so that a sustained 7g (then considered to be a fantastic level) could be endured with little discomfort. A pilot sitting upright would quickly have blacked out and found it hard to keep a grip on the combat situation. Another advantage was that a prone pilot could fit into a fuselage of about 25-in diameter.

The RAF Institute of Aviation Medicine began a prolonged programme of research into prone piloting. Only cursory attention was paid to the alternative of sitting in a reclining chair in an almost supine posture. Guinea-pig pilots tested various simple rigs, and then began flying a light twin which had begun life during the war as the Reid & Sigrist RS.3 Desford. In 1951 this was converted into the RS.4 Bobsleigh specifically to research prone piloting. The prone cockpit had

A Ministry photo of the Bobsleigh, showing the extended nose for the prone pilot. Test pilots who flew it wondered how the idea had ever got so far.

The Bobsleigh convinced everyone who tried it that the prone-piloting idea was a non-starter, so why spend a much greater sum converting this Meteor?

been added on the nose. So that the poor chap could breathe, especially when under g loads, padded support was provided at the shoulders, as well as at the pelvis and along the thighs. A special pad curved round under the chin to support the head. It first flew in this form on 13 June 1951.

One has to think for only a few seconds to appreciate that there are fundamental problems here. The whole posture is not a natural one for a pilot. His view is so restricted, especially in manoeuvres with his head jammed down against the chin rest, as to make it impossible to engage in air combat with any hope of success. If you have a runny nose, too bad; if you sneeze you are in real trouble. The seat harness is incredibly restrictive, and the seat-type parachute now rests on a rigid structure between the thighs. There is almost nowhere to put an instrument panel, and instrument flying is a major challenge. The normal ability of a fighter pilot to make harsh control movements is replaced by small and unnatural movements of a small stick, which has to be geared up to move the control surfaces in a way that was very difficult forty years ago, while the rudder is driven by pedals

moving in an unnatural sense. In fact, the Bobsleigh had two sticks, one for each hand, driven by small wrist movements, and, as the legs could not move, the pedals were driven by pivoting of the ankles.

The whole thing was such a clear non-starter that, true to British form, someone in the corridors of power thought it would be nice to spend a lot more money and try it on a Gloster Meteor. The last F.8 built by Armstrong Whitworth, WK935, was fitted with a completely new nose section containing a prone pilot position which was supposed to be similar to that of the Bristol 185 (in fact it very soon diverged and became a pure research modification). To balance the extra side area they put on an NF.14 fin. In some ways surprisingly normal, flying 935 was enough to convince any *fighter* pilot that it was complete nonsense. You couldn't even see where you were going in a steep turn, and of course the vital action 'Check Six' – trying to see if any of the bad guys were on your tail – was impossible. Two of my colleagues on *Flight International*, Mark Lambert and Hugh Field, both flew 935. I don't think either was able to take it seriously.

SHORT SB.1

Several of the stories in this book describe how, in the immediate post-war era, designers in many countries were trying to find out how best to design aircraft to fly in the new realm of performance made possible by jet propulsion. As well as swept or delta wings, some thought it a good idea to leave off the horizontal tail. At Short Brothers & Harland, in Belfast, David Keith-Lucas and Geoffrey Hill did a lot of research on a configuration for a jet bomber which combined elimination of the horizontal tail with a special form of swept wing called 'aero-isoclinic'.

As its name suggests, the aerodynamic form and structure of this wing were so arranged that, even in hard manoeuvres, there would be no measurable twisting of the wing, isoclinic implying constant angle of incidence at any given spanwise point. A key feature of the aero-isoclinic wing was that, instead of having conventional ailerons, the entire wing-tips pivoted for both lateral and pitch control, in the first case in opposition and in the second in unison. Thus, it was possible to combine the wing's torsional and flexural axes.

Obviously the next thing to do was to build a simple aircraft with which to test the idea. The result was the SB.1 glider, a minimum-cost aircraft with a wooden wing and stressed-skin fuselage. At the time I asked Keith-Lucas whether the results with a wooden wing would really read across to a metal one, and he looked thoughtful and replied, 'Near enough, I think.' Armed with an anti-spin parachute in the tail, the SB.1 was taken to Aldergrove (today Belfast Airport) and first tested on winch launches in July 1951. On the 30th of that month the glider was towed to 10,000 ft by a Sturgeon. Test pilot Tom Brooke-Smith then cast off and found no particular problem in the subsequent free flight.

The SB.1 then stayed on the ground until 14 October, when, with a longer towing cable, Brooke-Smith again followed the Sturgeon down the Aldergrove runway. On this occasion he found the SB.1 absolutely unmanageable. He told me it was unquestionably the worst few seconds of his long flying career. Though the glider naturally rose off the ground first, 'Brookie' was unable to keep it in the smooth air above the tug's wake. As the combination climbed away from the airfield it was obvious that the glider was not under control. It seemed prudent to cast off. What happened next was that the SB.1 reared up and then plunged down to the end of the runway. Brooke-Smith suffered several crushed vertebrae, one of the most painful of injuries, which put him on the ground for six months.

To say he had had enough of the SB.1 is an understatement. The wreck was completely rebuilt and fitted with two tiny Turbomeca Palas turbojets. Renamed the SB.4 Sherpa, it enjoyed a long and successful career. Nobody at Belfast was able to tell me whether 'Brookie's' crash was solely the result of wake turbulence.

One of the few photographs showing the SB.1 airborne.

ULMER LEATHER: BELL X-1D, X-1, X-2 AND X-1A

This story differs from the others in that it deals with a number of different aircraft of uniquely advanced design, carried through with great boldness and assurance, but which incorporated small pieces of material which caused them to suffer catastrophic explosions.

These aircraft, the Bell X-1 and X-2 series, were built to thrust ahead into the unknown realm of supersonic flight. In many areas their design involved completely new technology. Inevitably, such aircraft posed exceptionally high risk, in structure, aerodynamics, propulsion, stability and control, and systems – and in what is oddly called aviation medicine, because nobody knew for sure how humans would perform at beyond Mach 1. It is typical of the ironic history of aviation that all these factors worked pretty much as advertised, whereas the most desperate danger was introduced by thoughtlessly bringing together materials which had long been known to be lethally incompatible.

To show that the dangers were not exactly unknown, in the summer of 1949 I was an undergraduate working through my 'long vac' at Westland Aircraft at Yeovil. One thing I learned was how to do electric-arc and gas welding. The commonest gases were oxygen and acetylene, and I was repeatedly reminded never under any circumstances to let any organic material come into contact with the oxygen. For example, to oil or grease the valves on the gas cylinder or torch would cause an explosion. I was told, 'There's only one thing more dangerous in this regard than compressed gaseous oxygen and that's liquid oxygen.' This had been common knowledge for many years – knowledge probably gained 'the hard way'.

One imagines all this was known to the citizens of the United States as, immediately after World War II, they led the world into exploring the uncharted dangers of manned flight at speeds faster than sound. Once it was clear, in the weeks following 14 October 1947, that the Bell X-1 really could 'pierce the barrier', contracts were signed for second-generation aircraft, the X-1A, X-1B, X-1C and X-1D.

It so happened that the first to be completed was the X-1D, USAF aircraft 48-1386. This made its first gliding flight on 24 July 1951, in the hands of

the Bell engineering test pilot Jean 'Skip' Ziegler. On 22 August 1951 Lieutenant-Colonel Frank Everest, chief of flight test at what had become Edwards Air Force Base, strapped himself into the X-1D as the EB-50A carrier aircraft (USAF 46-006) climbed through the 7,000-ft level. He was to make the first powered flight, but he reported a low nitrogen pressure. The mission had to be aborted, which meant jettisoning the propellants from the X-1D's tanks. As soon as the jettison switches were closed an explosion rocked the aircraft, and the chase pilot reported flames from the X-1D. Everest quickly vacated the cockpit, and the X-1D was dropped to destruction soon afterwards. What had happened?

Now we move on a few weeks to 9 November 1951. On the vast apron at Edwards, various Bell, Reaction Motors, USAF and NACA crews were busy around the same EB-50A. The big Boeing had just returned from a brief flight carrying recessed into its belly 46-064, the third and last of the original X-1s. The Nos. 1 and 2 X-1s had already flown 156 times, exceeding the speed of sound on many occasions, and a few months earlier No. 3 had made a single gliding flight. The pilot assigned to No. 3 was Joseph Cannon of the NACA.

The No. 3 X-1 was better looking than the first two. Painted gleaming white, it had a stronger cockpit canopy without the numerous frames of its predecessors. Less obvious was that its tanks accommodated more rocket propellants – 437 US gallons of lox (liquid oxygen) and 498 gallons of alcohol – which were fed by a newly developed turbopump instead of by nitrogen gas pressure. The tanks were filled, the lox tank topped up and Joe Cannon strapped in to carry out checks before making the first powered flight. Suddenly there was a colossal explosion. The B-50 crew managed to escape; so too, eventually, did Cannon, though he was injured. The X-1 and the EB-50 were totally destroyed by the explosion and subsequent fire.

Those responsible for the X-1 flight programme in the Air Force and NACA were naturally concerned at such sudden catastrophes destroying two of the valuable aircraft. Investigations continued, but must have been unbelievably incompetent. Perhaps there was an underlying feeling that explosions were a natural result of filling aircraft with such highly reactive propellants, and the fact that in the early 1950s the media were not breathing down anyone's neck would certainly have made things more relaxed than they would be today. Be that as it may, *nothing was done to remove the cause*, and by June 1952 the third-generation aircraft was ready to fly. The Bell X-2 had razor-thin swept wings, a totally new rocket engine of enormous power, and was in almost every respect a completely fresh design. It was expected eventually to reach Mach 3 (2,000 mph).

It was in fact the No. 2 X-2 that was ready first. Ship 46-675 made three gliding flights between June and October 1952, but it took until spring 1953 for Curtiss-Wright to deliver an XLR25 engine. The programme was already running years late, but powered flights at Edwards had to be preceded by ground tests at the Bell plant at Wheatfield, NY, followed by captive flights under the EB-50D carrier aircraft. One of these captive flights, with full propellant tanks, took place on 12 May 1953. At 6 p.m. the B-50 was at 30,000 ft over the centre of Lake Ontario. X-2 pilot Ziegler was not aboard the X-2, but was looking in through the canopy checking various instrument readings. Near him was Frank Wolko of the B-50 crew. Suddenly there was a gigantic explosion. The chase pilot just had time to see the X-2 engulfed by a ball of red flame when his F-86 was violently rolled over and away from the B-50 by the blast. When he was again able to see the B-50 its belly was showering burning debris, the largest piece being the outer half of an X-2 wing. Neither Ziegler nor Wolko were seen again, and little of the X-2 was ever recovered.

This time it was Bell who had to do the investigation, because the X-2 was still in their charge. Aware of the two previous explosions, they had nothing to go on in the third case. Their report said, 'It has not been possible to establish . . . whether the fuels were alcohol and oxygen vapours and atmosphere or balsa wood and oxygen, and whether the fuse was a hot wire, spark, shock or vibration . . .'

I cannot comprehend how it was that none of the hundreds of people who had an interest in finding out what had happened to the X-1D, the No. 3 X-1 and the No. 2 X-2 ever thought of spending a few minutes having a quick glance at the materials with which the lox came into contact. Instead, by late May 1953 the best answer anyone could give to the repeated explosions was that oxygen gas had some-

how leaked and been ignited by an electric spark. This idea sounds sufficiently far-fetched, but then the decision was taken to bring the X-1A (48-1384) back to Bell's plant to have the bundle of pressurised nitrogen tubes replaced by simple spherical bottles. I could not comprehend what bearing the storage of the nitrogen had on the supposed leak of oxygen, though that was the reason for the modification.

The X-1A had already made two gliding and four powered flights in Ziegler's hands. After the modification it was passed to 'Chuck' Yeager, who took it up the Mach scale until on 12 December 1953 he hit 2.44, but encountered hair-raising inertia-coupling (which proved the toughness of both man and machine). In 1955 the X-1A passed to the NACA, the pilot being Joe Walker. His second flight (the twenty-fifth for the X-1A) was on 8 August 1955. Carrier B-29 No. 45-21800 climbed out of Edwards and by 1.42 p.m. had reached the drop height of 30,800 ft to the east of Edwards. Walker, tightly strapped into the X-1A, had completed launch checks and was ready for the drop and motor ignition. Suddenly there was an explosion. It was nothing like as violent as some of the others, but enough to drop the X-1A down from its drag braces so that it just hung on the bomb shackle. Cockpit lights went out, pressures rapidly fell to zero and Walker quickly realised that many other things had happened. The pilots of the three chase aircraft reported a white cloud followed by debris, separation of doors and access panels, dropping of the X-1A landing gear, a fire in the mid-fuselage and a major rupture which exposed the interior of the lox tank.

Walker quickly scrambled back into the B-29, which was not seriously damaged. It was then discovered that the X-1A's landing gear could not be retracted and that the alcohol fuel and dangerous peroxide could not be jettisoned (the lox tank had emptied itself). The only thing to do was to jettison the X-1A, and it was dropped to the desert floor from 6,500 ft. According to Jay Miller (in *The X-Planes*), 'Examination of the X-1A's twisted and burned parts quickly led examiners to the conclusion that something out of the ordinary had caused the destructive explosion.' The mind boggles at the non-brilliance of such a deduction. Meanwhile a Bell Aircraft engineer, Wendell Moore, decided to do some investigating on his own. He had known, as had hundreds of other people in the programme, that joints, pipe

One of the supersonic aircraft which were destroyed by ulmer-leather explosions was the X-1A. The X-1B was remarkably lucky to survive.

connections and bulkhead doors in the lox tank were sealed by gaskets made of ulmer leather. This is leather impregnated with a 50/50 mixture of tricresyl phosphate (TCP, familiar in the home) and carnauba wax, a little over 1 lb of the mixture being absorbed by each 1 lb of leather. Each tank was calculated to have about a cupful of TCP in the gaskets. To me this choice seemed strange, because any chemist would tell you that, in contact with lox, ulmer leather will detonate under a modest impact. Originally inside the leather, the

lethal TCP was squeezed out by tightening the gaskets, and subsequent inspection of other X-1s (notably the X-1B) revealed 'a considerable amount' sloshing about in the tank and in the feed piping.

Moore simply took a piece of ulmer leather, put it in about a spoonful of lox and hit it with a small hammer. The explosion was violent. He then told the hundreds of investigators what had resulted in the loss of an X-1, X-1A, X-1D, X-2, EB-50, Ziegler and Wolko.

YAKOVLEV YAK-1000

Defying gravity with a heavier-than-air machine is obviously difficult, but one might expect that putting wheels on something so that it could run along the ground ought to be the proverbial piece of cake. That there's a bit more to it is shown by millions of supermarket trolleys which suffer from severe shimmy and want to go in any direction but the one you wish. Even big aerospace companies find it hard to put the wheels on correctly. When Hawker tested the P.1127, predecessor of the Harrier, it went up and down on the thrust of its engine with few problems. When they tried high-speed taxi trials the outriggers shimmied violently, leaving a wiggly trail of scrubbed rubber, and the front main gear suffered such oscillation the leg cracked.

Hawker weren't the only ones. More than ten years earlier Aleksandr S. Yakovlev had decided to put *velosipedno* (bicycle) landing gears on his Yak-50 prototypes. The two aircraft performed better than predicted, and almost succeeded in the virtually impossible task of displacing the MiG-15 from the mass-production lines. The only problem was on the ground. The undercarriage wanted to snake off in all directions, and veteran test pilot Sergei Anokhin said, 'On a wet surface it was sheer murder.'

The Yak-50-I was on a taxi test in June 1949, and flew on 15 July. A few weeks earlier Yakovlev's designers had quickly sketched a remarkable experimental fighter to fly at 1,750 kph (Mach 1.65) on the thrust of an RD-500 (Derwent) turbojet, and later to reach 2,000 kph (Mach 1.88) with an afterburner. Given the odd designation Yak-1000, it again used *velosipedno* landing gear, differing from that of the Yak-50 mainly in that the stabilising outriggers were moved in from the wing-tips to a point where wing chord was the same as the length of the leg. Like the later F-104, this aircraft had an overall length getting on for three times the span of the unswept wing.

Anokhin and his colleagues began taxi testing in early 1951. This time, partly because of the axial distribution of masses, with very little lateral stabilising dimension, the directional instability on the runway was dangerous. Bold curving black lines were left by the tortured tyres, and twice the aircraft was severely damaged. In the end the programme was abandoned, without the potentially very fast fighter ever getting off the ground.

Later the bicycle landing gear was coaxed and tamed. Eventually it was used with complete success in the extremely attractive Yak-140 single-engined Mach 2 fighter, and in the long series of Yak-25/26/27/28 twin-engined aircraft. But the Yak-1000 is one of very, very few jet aircraft that were never even able to fly.

The Yak-1000, which Aleksandr S. Yakolev considered his 'only failure'.

GRUMMAN XF10F JAGUAR

The XF10F was probably the worst product ever to bear the proud name of Grumman.

Grumman has a splendid track record of having designed and mass-produced eminently tough, effective and successful aircraft. Thus, the XF10F is an odd man out. It was an early design for a carrier-based jet fighter, the sole prototype (US Navy Bureau No. 124435) being completed in early 1952. It was the result of five years of intensive project study, the whole point of which was to ensure that whatever was finally built was right. The outcome of these prolonged deliberations was an aircraft so stuffed with innovations that problems could be guaranteed. Indeed, I think even a superficial look at the aircraft would have left the observer shaking his head. In a nutshell, it

was the result of trying too hard.

In 1946–47 Grumman was already well into the XF9F Panther programme, and this straightforward carrier-based jet fighter sustained a highly successful production run of 3,367 aircraft, the final 1,985 having swept wings. Just why Grumman and the Navy felt impelled to redesign the F9F is obscure, but in January 1948 this tinkering had resulted in the new designation of XF10F. This worked its way through numerous shapes and sizes, which soon ceased to have any affinity with the F9F, and by mid-1948 the new project was characterised by an extremely portly fuselage, with an afterburning Westinghouse J40 turbojet fed by cheek inlets near the nose, with the ducts passing under the cockpit floor, and a high-mounted wing. Soon this wing was given variable incidence, as in the later Vought F8U Crusader.

Variable incidence would have been bold enough, but by July 1949 Grumman had replaced it with variable sweep. Today we know how a VG (variable geometry) 'swing wing' should be designed. Over forty years ago it was a different matter, and when the XF10F was assembled at Edwards AFB in April 1952 it cannot really have inspired confidence. It had been flown there partly dismantled in an Air Force C-124. This was the only trouble-free flight the XF10F ever made.

Almost every part of the XF10F was unusual, and probably complicated. The left and right wings were pivoted to 'the largest high-strength aluminum-alloy forgings made for aircraft up to that time', and driven by a single colossal hydraulic cylinder 6 ft long. The absence of a redundant or standby drive was explained by the belief that, in flight, if the wings were unlocked they would unsweep to the landing angle of 13.5° by aerodynamic forces. This belief was later discovered to be unfounded. Since the wing roots translated (moved bodily) to front or rear, as the wings pivoted, the complexity of the plumbing and flight controls may be imagined. At the front was a 'roll-top desk' which kept the sliding leading edge faired into the fuselage, while at the back a mass of 'turkey feathers' tried to do the same for the Fowler flaps.

Look where you will, every part of the XF10F was bad news. The J40, of course, was the most serious turbojet failure in history, crippling the US Navy's future planning, but the rest of this particular aircraft was so full of problems that the engine was hardly noticed. According to 'Corky' Meyer, senior engineering test pilot:

Probably the greatest single source of trouble was the aerodynamically balanced horizontal tail. The stick was like rubber; the stick moved, and a finite time later the tail moved. The stick activated the little canard servo plane on the horizontal tail boom, the light aerodynamic forces on this small area then eventually moving the entire horizontal tail. After applying progressively more stick input the tail would finally respond madly and then it had to be corrected in the opposite direction. . . . Various fixes were tried. . . . Nothing did the trick, and I was never to achieve positive control, the tail was always doing its own thing and leaving me wondering how I could catch up with it. . . . On one of the three flights that I made with the larger tail fitted I found myself *completely* out of phase with the tail, the airplane bucking uncontrollably around the sky. I should have baled out, but couldn't get out of the cockpit. I shall never know how I regained control, having not the slightest idea what I or the airplane did to recover.

Of course, this was only a small part of the problems. At maximum sweep the directional qualities were officially recorded as 'so bad that nobody would believe them'. The jet nozzle blasted against the rudder until a large fence was added to keep the two apart, and to try to get some directional control large horizontal fins (called horsals) were added, looking like low-mounted tailplanes. Thanks to cable stretch the pilot had virtually no rudder control, the peak deflection being ±3° instead of the planned ±30°. As for roll control, the complex array of spoilers were so useless and troublesome that they were eventually disconnected. This left just the tiny wing-tip ailerons, which had been put in merely to give the pilot feel, and so the maximum rate of roll was a pathetic 10° per second!

One could go on and on. Literally hundreds of separate items caused problems. Grumman's propulsion expert, Bob Mullaney, said, 'Every flight was a first flight' because something – usually several things – had always been altered. Eventually everyone had had enough, and the first 100 production Jaguars, and eight F10F-1P photo aircraft, were cancelled on 1 April 1953. The entire flight-test contract was terminated on 12 June of that year.

Once it stopped trying to fly, the Jaguar began to prove useful; indeed two were put to good work, the second being the first F10F-1, BuNo. 128311. The first was demolished testing carrier flight-deck barriers. The other became a target for tank guns at the Army's Aberdeen Proving Ground. Thus these truly awful fighter-reconnaissance aircraft became part of history. Anyone who studies them will find it hard to believe that almost the same team of engineers could have gone on to create the F-11F Tiger, and much later the F-14 Tomcat.

DOUGLAS X-3

Like many schoolboys I used to draw aeroplanes in the backs of school exercise books. Predictably, some were the most impressive 'hot ships' I could imagine; speed has always been attractive. Unfortunately, some of the most exciting-looking hot ships have proved to be what the Americans call dodos or turkeys. This is doubly unfortunate because, while you suffer all the costs, technical risks and dangers, you receive none of the expected benefits.

Of all aircraft ever built, I think the Douglas X-3 has a fair claim to be considered 'the hottest-looking ship of all time'. Designed to have sufficient fuel to 'soak' at Mach 2, it had a needle-like nose and a length of nearly 67 ft, but the wing was so small that from many angles it could hardly be seen! The track between the main tyres was a mere 6 ft 9 in. Had it been assigned to the company's El Segundo plant, where the chief engineer was Ed Heinemann, I guarantee it would have performed as advertised.

Instead, the US Air Force placed the contract with the main team, at the Santa Monica plant. Here the design engineers had immense experience with transports and bombers, but in 1945 nobody had any experience of design for Mach 2. They really did a very good job. The sole aircraft built, USAF No. 49-2892, was rolled out in late 1951 and, following extensive ground testing, was flown by company pilot Bill Bridgeman on 20 October 1952.

It was very much a minimum aircraft, though the body was so long there was room for 808 Imperial gallons (970 US gallons) of fuel. The tiny cockpit hardly provided enough room for the instruments or downward-ejection seat, and the two flat transparent panes on each side tapered together at the front to form an extraordinarily acute vee windscreen. Immediately behind these transparencies were the plain inlets to the two Westinghouse J34 turbojets, each supposedly good for 4,850 lb thrust with afterburner, the nozzles being arranged Phantom-fashion about halfway between wing and tail. The tiny wing was the only one ever flown on a manned aircraft with a true supersonic section of the kind called

parallel double-wedge (trapezoidal, or hexagonal), thickness/chord ratio being 4.5 per cent. The available depth was so thin that the hinged leading edge and split trailing-edge flaps were driven by actuators which had to be inside fairings under the wing. The rear fuselage had the form of an upsloping boom carrying the small tail, the horizontal surfaces being powered slabs. All three units of the landing gear retracted hydraulically into the fuselage. Unusual structural features included the use of titanium for the tailplanes and the hot underside of the tail boom, and the fact that the wings were polished aluminium, the rest of the aircraft being painted white.

General handling of the X-3 was satisfactory, apart from the fact that – as anyone today would have been able to predict, noting the way its masses were distributed longitudinally but not transversely – it was tailormade to suffer from inertia coupling. This can be manifest in various forms, but the basic one is that any attempt to roll the aircraft can lead to violent gyrations involving pitch and yaw. Severe inertia coupling was experienced with the X-3 in October 1954, and fortuitously this happened to be at the time when the F-100 Super Sabre programme was in deep trouble, with nobody certain what had caused a series of in-flight break-ups. The X-3 threw the spotlight on inertia coupling, so by sheer chance this rakish beast did accomplish something.

Basically, however, it was a total waste of time. Far from being able to soak at Mach 2 for not less than thirty minutes, this futuristic-looking ship was actually subsonic! In level flight the maximum speed at the optimum height was 650 mph, or Mach 0.95. Bridgeman did once reach Mach 1.21, but that was diving at 30° in full afterburner. It has often been the case that an aircraft was unable to reach its design speed, but the X-3 may have set a record in being unable to reach even *half* its design speed! The one thing it was good at was throwing the tread from its tyres. With a take-off speed of over 260 mph the wheel rotational speed reached almost double what the tyre industry was used to, and it forced Goodrich and Goodyear to develop new tread structures, which came in handy for the B-58.

(Overleaf) Few aircraft have looked so fantastic as the X-3, nor failed to perform by such a margin.

Convair XF2Y Sea Dart

It used to be taken for granted that a combat aircraft designed for operation from an aircraft carrier must inevitably be compromised, and have a poorer performance, in comparison with a rival able to use a two-mile runway. Think how much greater are the penalties if the aircraft has to operate not from land but from the surface of the sea or other water!

In World War I the problem was bypassed by putting uncompromised Sopwith 2F1 'Ship's Camels' aboard lighters towed behind destroyers. During World War II things were harder, and there was no obvious way of avoiding the weight and drag of floats. Probably the best seaplane

fighter was a converted Spitfire IX, which reached 377 mph and proved reasonably agile, but it would still have had a hard time against 109s and 190s. The only birds of this species used in action were Japanese. They had several types of fighter seaplane, but all were easy meat for an F6F or F4U.

At the end of the war the British, having decided in 1942–43 (when a seaplane fighter was really needed) that there was no requirement, suddenly felt they simply had to build a jet fighter seaplane. After all, having no propeller made it easier. The result was the Saunders-Roe SR/A1. There was nothing particularly wrong with it, apart from the fact that any small boy could see it was going to be

The first Sea Dart, the XF2Y-1, prompted Convair to proclaim, 'Other seaplanes are boats with wings, but this boasts the sleek contours of a missile.'

useless. If a fighter is at once bigger, heavier, slower and significantly less manoeuvrable than the opposition, then you will save money and pilots' lives by not building it.

In the United States, however, the Navy has seldom passed up any idea unless it has been demonstrably proven to be unattractive or incapable of fulfilment. In 1945 the Fighter Branch was busy trying to discover how to make fighters that could operate from water and also defeat the bad guys! Commander, later Admiral, A.B. Metsger told me, 'We studied your SR/A1 carefully, and came to the conclusion it ought never to have been started. But that did not disqualify the concept of a water-based fighter.' Another Fighter Branch head, Tommy Blackburn, said, 'We stood way back of the problem and talked over ideas with . . . Martin, Grumman, Douglas, Convair and Vought. There seemed to be no way to build a competitive airplane with floats or with a seaplane hull of any kind we could come up with. But we could not help becoming increasingly excited by the hydroski.'

Hydroskis are exactly like the water skis worn on the feet. At speed they ride across the sea surface, lifting the vehicle by their dynamic reaction. As speed decays, so the vehicle – aircraft or ship – gradually sinks into the water until it floats. The skis themselves have little buoyancy, because they are not much more than curved plates. And, as they are so thin, they can be retracted into the structure of the aircraft. Thus, if the aircraft is correctly shaped, it could reach jet speeds, or even fly faster than sound.

When aircraft had to be propelled by propellers a water-ski design was inevitably clumsy, as we saw in the Schneider Trophy story (see page 61). Clutches and shaft drives were needed to a water screw to accelerate the aircraft to a speed high enough for the fuselage to be raised right out of the water, so that the main propeller could then be started, to give air thrust for take-off. As explained in the Schneider story, the gears had to be changed over whilst transmitting maximum power! With the advent of the turbojet there was no such problem. The main engine(s) could be started with the machine still floating recessed into the sea. Of course, it was necessary for the air inlet(s) to be in a place where bulk water or even spray could not normally be ingested into the engine(s). The pilot could progressively open up to full power, the aircraft soon rising high out of

the water to ride on its ski(s). The great reduction in drag meant that take-off acceleration on the skis would be high, enabling quite short stretches of water to be used. Once airborne, with ski(s) retracted, there seemed to be no reason why a hydroski fighter should be significantly inferior to a land-based one.

A major research programme into aircraft skis was begun in 1946, involving the Navy, NACA, All-American and Edo. Three test aircraft were used, the largest a Grumman G-21B Goose, with which encouraging results were achieved. Accordingly, in early 1948 Convair at San Diego were awarded a contract for two prototypes of a ski-equipped fighter originally called Y2-2 and later given the Navy designation of XF2Y-1, and named Sea Dart. The first, with Bureau No. 137634, was completed in December 1952. Following prolonged taxi tests on San Diego Bay, test pilot E.D. 'Sam' Shannon made the first flight on 9 April 1953.

The XF2Y-1 was an odd-looking tailless delta. At rest the waves lapped over the sharp 60° leading edge and the large powered elevons that formed the trailing edges. The cockpit was in the pointed nose, with a hinged canopy incorporating an acute vee windscreen. Further back, on top on each side, were the inlets to the two Westinghouse J34 turbojets whose nozzles were right at the tail. On top was a very large delta-shaped fin. Underneath was either a large single ski on the centreline or two smaller skis, mounted on sprung oleo legs which also retracted the ski(s) into the underside of the fuselage, or hull.

Eventually five Sea Darts were built. More than 100 different ski arrangements were tested in 1953–55, single skis eventually proving superior. Small wheels on the ski tail(s) enabled the aircraft to taxi thunderously out of the water up a ramp. In the air the Sea Darts handled reasonably well, but manoeuvrability suffered from several factors, one of which was lack of engine power. The second aircraft, completed as the first YF2Y-1, was re-engined with the Westinghouse J46, but even with full afterburner the ratio of thrust to weight was still only about 0.5. Despite this, the YF2Y became the first seaplane of any kind to exceed Mach 1, in a shallow dive at 34,000 ft on 3 August 1954. But three months later, on 4 November, the same aircraft – said to have been taken beyond its design limits in a hard Mach-0.9 turn at low level – exploded in a fireball during a public display.

Perhaps the many problems, such as yawing and

porpoising on take-off, might have been solved. Perhaps good engines might have been found. Perhaps the F2Y could have been made comparable in

agility with other fighters. At the end of the day I still feel this concept was a non-starter, but it was hard to see this when the idea was new and exciting.

CHANNEL WINGS: BARTINI, CUSTER AND ANTONOV

It seems obvious to me that flying machines whose propulsion systems can do nothing except accelerate air directly backwards are unacceptably crude. This crudity reaches obscene levels in modern fighters, whose thunderous engines generate thrust at low altitudes which exceeds the total weight of the aircraft, but pointing directly astern. What a crazy way to fly!

Many inventors have sought to do better, with various methods of powered lift. (Digressing, I had to give a talk at the Fifth Powered Lift Conference in California in 1987. Coming back via PanAm I was invited to the flight deck. The captain looked me up and down and said to his co-pilot, 'He's no weight-lifter, he's an ordinary guy!' He turned to me and said, 'A few days ago we were really

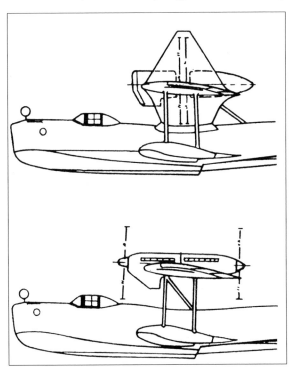

worried to have all these Powered Lift delegates on board. We realised that if each had about 500 kilos of practice weights in his hand baggage we'd go off the far end of the runway.' I said, 'Would you believe, the entire system of today's air transport doesn't allow for that happening, you're right!')

Of course, the obviously successful powered-lift method is the simplest, created by British engineers named Hooker, Marchant, Dale and Lewis. If their Pegasus engine had instead been American it would today be lifting aircraft off the ground all over the world. A quite different, but equally impressive, system is USB (upper-surface blowing), pioneered by NASA and Boeing and seen in the YC-14, QSRA and Asuka – and in a very mild form in the Antonov An-72 and 74. As it has demonstrated the ability to generate lift co-efficients exceeding eight on a wing capable of cruising at Mach 0.8, we may see this obviously valuable technique really being used one day.

At the other end of the scale are the ideas that fail to deliver. We have already looked at propellers inside tubular fuselages. Another is the channel wing. This is the propeller mounted above a wing formed into a half-circle fitting closely round the propeller disc. The theory is that lift is greatly increased by the high-speed slipstream blown across it. One minor drawback is that this augmented lift is achieved only at the bottom of the channel. Everywhere else it acts at an angle, until at the sides the lift forces act inwards and oppose each other!

One of the pioneers of the idea was an Italian, Roberto Bartini. A Communist, he emigrated to the Soviet Union in 1924, and by 1930 was an established designer. He proposed surrounding a propeller by a close-fitting ring, the lower part of which was broadened into an aerofoil. The Central Aero- and Hydrodynamic Institute did model tests and confirmed 'the Bartini Effect'. Bartini then led

Bartini's original scheme for the DAR flying boat was to mount the two engines nose to nose with the propellers close together inside a lifting duct. The DAR was eventually built with conventional tandem engines.

the design of the DAR, a flying boat resembling a Dornier Wal but with the engines arranged nose-to-nose, so that the two propellers were a few inches apart, inside such a duct. At the eleventh hour it was agreed that the extra lift was less than the weight and drag of the duct, and the DAR finally flew, once the ice had thawed in 1936, with ordinary tandem engines.

The greatest exponent of the idea was Willard R. Custer. I first saw a picture of one of his aircraft in March 1948. It looked faintly like a stubby monoplane with two large underslung engines, but these were really the channel wings, with a propeller inside each. This aircraft was said to have been flown during the recent war. Custer then produced the CCW-5, supposed to have flown at Oxnard, California, on 13 July 1953. This was a Baumann Brigadier light twin, grossly modified with a channel wing on each side. The engines were Continental O-470s of double the original power at 280 hp each. Custer said the CCW-5 had taken off at 70 per cent power at near maximum weight in less than 90 ft, climbed at 3,000 ft/min and flown 'under perfect control' at 11 mph.

According to the 1956–57 Jane's, 'Custer Channel Wing Corporation was formed to develop . . . aircraft . . . to take off in a few feet, hover, permit forward speeds in excess of those of conventional aircraft, and will allow an aircraft to slow down, hover and land vertically under full control.' I can only say such a fantastic claim would never have appeared in that annual under the editorship of John W.R. Taylor or his successors. At the time I was technical editor of Flight. I was sorely tempted to explain that the whole thing was nonsense, but my superiors would not hear of it (so I just ignored it). McGraw-Hill were made of sterner stuff, and their Aviation Week did one of the biggest debunking jobs I have ever seen in print. Of course, none of the planned production CCW aircraft appeared.

Surprisingly, it seems that otherwise reputable people have felt impelled to see if they can make the channel wing work. For example, Hanno Fischer in what was then West Germany read Custer's claims and set about designing a somewhat different machine in which the two engines – 250-hp Lycomings – were geared to a single propeller inside a long-chord duct above the fuselage, in an arrangement strongly reminiscent of Bartini's DAR. The lower part of the duct formed the channel wing. Built by Rhein Flugzeugbau as the RF 1, it had a performance almost certainly poorer than if the engines had driven ordinary tractor propellers on the wings. It first flew in August 1960 and, provided the gears and clutches worked properly, could just reach 290 kph (180 mph). RFB later moved on to simple short-chord annular ducts around pusher propellers, with no pretensions at added lift, and the result is seen in today's Fantrainer, which is the cheapest way of making a pupil at least imagine he is flying a jet.

Much later, in the 1980s, the extremely professional Ukrainian OKB, named for the late O.K. Antonov, held an open day at their design centre in Kiev. Parked on a low loader was an odd reincarnation of Custer's CCW-5, though looking much faster. A placard said it was the An-181. Eventually a picture appeared in a Polish magazine. I asked general constructor Pyotr Balabuyev about it. He pondered for a few seconds and said, 'I think we should not have exhibited that.' I got the impression it never even flew.

(Previous page)   The Custer CCW-5 did at least have some proper wings, but Custer's claims were fiction.

JET LIFT 1: THE BEDSTEAD AND SUCCESSORS

In addition to the turbojet, the turbofan (front fan and aft fan), afterburning and jet deflection, young RAF test pilot Frank Whittle studied schemes for vertical take-off and landing (VTOL). He saw at once that, with development, the gas turbine would make possible engines giving far greater power per unit of installed weight than the best piston engines, and that various types of VTOL aircraft would be possible.

Equally, after World War II Dr A.A. Griffith saw that his employers, Rolls-Royce, would be pleased if he invented aircraft requiring not just one engine but anything up to 100! He began to think about supersonic transports being lifted off the ground by batteries of specially designed lightweight turbojets, used only at take-off and landing. His employers were indeed pleased, and in 1951 got the Ministry of Supply to pay for two research rigs to explore the basic problems of stability and control of vehicles supported solely by thunderous columns of hot gas. Officially designated TMRs (thrust-measuring rigs), they were better known as Flying Bedsteads.

Utterly unlike any previous flying machines, they consisted of the simplest possible framework to mount two Rolls-Royce Nene turbojets pointing towards each other, so that their gyroscopic effects cancelled out. Their jetpipes were turned 90° downwards, to give lift rather than thrust. One pipe was in the centre of the rig, in line with its centre of gravity. The other was divided into two, to end in two half-size nozzles, one on each side. Thus, if either engine should fail, though the machine would crash, at least it would crash upright rather than in violent tumbling.

Round each engine diffuser was a collector manifold for compressed air, which could be bled off at a rate equivalent to an astonishing 3,600 hp. This was piped to a central chamber from which valves, controlled by the pilot's stick, fed air as

With autostabiliser switched off, the 'Bedstead' was probably the most dangerous flying machine ever tested.

required to downward-pointing nozzles at the front, back and on each side of the rig. The front and rear nozzles, which were extremely powerful, controlled the pitch attitude of the rig, and by using pedals to swivel these nozzles the pilot could also point the rig in any direction. The smaller side nozzles controlled roll.

It will be appreciated that everything depended on keeping the device balanced on its three jets of hot gas. Tricky was hardly the word for it, and someone commented, 'Nothing comes down faster than a jet-VTOL upside-down!' The pilot who had for many months been involved in the development of the TMR had second thoughts when it was ready for his attention, and he politely declined to fly it. The job was thus assigned to a Farnborough test pilot, Squadron Leader Ron Harvey. He was delighted at the challenge.

To say he needed to concentrate is an understatement. As soon as he moved the stick, the big bleed flow through the control nozzle(s) reduced the flow available for lift, so he had to open the throttle (but how much?). Coming down to the ground, pulling back the stick in an aeroplane results in an immediate change in angle of attack and hence lift, arresting the sink, but opening the throttle in the Bedstead merely had a second-order effect, in that it controlled not rate of descent but rate of change of descent. Even the Nene took some time to spool-up. Coming down too fast, one could open the throttle wide in a panic and still crash.

But perhaps the most terrifying feature of all was that, instead of having big, easily castoring wheels, the Bedstead's four legs terminated in wheels reminiscent of a tea trolley. When Harvey first climbed aboard a Bedstead he felt extremely high above the ground, totally exposed and on something that felt top-heavy. Landing with a ground speed higher than about 3 mph would result in the whole thing overturning. If it rolled over he would be dead, because, despite his recommendations, nobody bothered to protect Harvey with a strong overhead arch until he had finished the test programme and handed over to the Rolls-Royce pilots. Then a crash protection arch was built in, but the rig still crashed and killed one of the maker's pilots.

Harvey began testing the first Bedstead on 3 July 1953. He carried out the entire flight-test programme, often flying in manual with the autostabiliser switched off. As he recalls, 'Judgement of height was difficult. Near the ground one had better reference, but that was dangerous at any speed, due to the certainty of rolling over if one touched the ground accidentally. At higher altitude, say 150 feet, I felt very high indeed. I was very much aware that a mechanical defect or a piloting error would be very fatal.'

So why build such a desperately dangerous flying machine? Simply because there was the glittering prospect of going on to build aircraft able to rise vertically on the lifting power of dozens of simple lift jets. Of course, there would be problems. One would have to cater for sudden loss of thrust from engine failure, and the more engines you have, the greater the likelihood of that happening. Loss of a lift jet would mean that another on the opposite side of the centre of gravity would also have to be shut down to avoid dangerous control problems. But designers continued to be mesmerised by the possibility of doing away with giant airports, and also of designing aircraft wings for cruising flight, instead of the far greater challenge of take-off and landing.

After a while designers realised that, at least for the foreseeable future, there were not going to be any Mach-4 passenger airliners taking off on 200-plus tons of lift from deafening batteries of turbojets, but they still believed in the basic idea, especially in Britain. Here Bristol Siddeley and Rolls-Royce saw that, if the simple turbojets were replaced by turbofans with a high bypass ratio, the same lift could be obtained for much lower fuel burn and a small fraction of the noise. On the other hand, they increasingly realised that a limiting factor was the sheer bulk of the lift system, and these lift fans made the matter worse.

Despite all the problems, Hawker Siddeley was not the only company to be captivated. Drawings here show the HS.140 executive jet and the HS.141 airliner in the 100-seat class, both intended to achieve VTOL from high-bypass RB.202 turbofans (in the first case one, and in the second sixteen).

It was a lovely idea, but – in the proverbial cold light of day – a non-starter. For one thing, it proved difficult to reconcile the aircraft size, fuel capacity, empty weight, range and cruising speed, to say nothing about costs. For another, the notion that there could be such a thing as a small city-centre airport for VTOLs proved to be elusive. Quite apart from the vexed question of noise, it was easy to prove that such an airport would have to be nearly as big as a conventional one. At least the brochures were cheaper and less dangerous than the hardware they described.

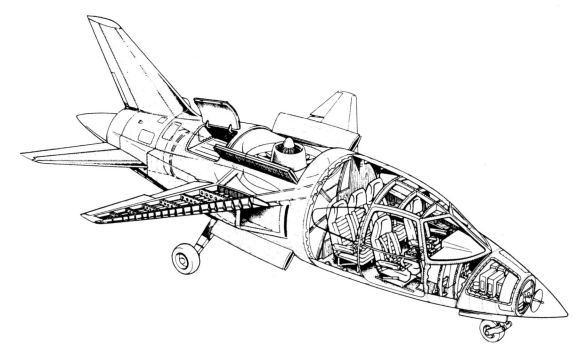

The Hawker Siddeley HS.140 was a projected VTOL bizjet.

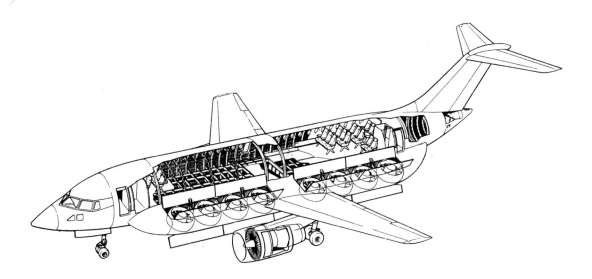

The Hawker Siddeley HS.141 was a projected VTOL jetliner.

Propeller lift

The first examples of propeller VTOL to fly were the XFV-1 and XFY-1. These two unique creations were not necessarily 'bad' aircraft – people like Lockheed and Convair usually knew what they were about – but they suffered from the laws of nature. They were prime examples of talented design teams trying to meet a requirement which any objective observer might think doomed to failure from the start.

It may have been the fault of the wild schemes thought up by the Germans in 1943–44 to try and stem the onslaughts of the Allied heavy bombers; some of these were mentioned in the story of the BV 40 (see page 118). Even more 'far out' than this glider fighter were all manner of piloted devices which were intended to stand upright on their tails pointing at the sky in order to make a VTO. A few were meant to be VTOLs, by coming back to perform a landing, while others simply separated off the bits thought worth recovery, such as the pilot and maybe the engine, and fitted these with parachutes.

The problems are obvious. Quite apart from those associated with the design of the aircraft, there was the need to get the thing to its take-off site, stand it on end and get the pilot up into the cockpit. Then he had to start the flight in a reclining seat, so that he was strapped in head downwards (a few had a prone pilot, in which case he was almost in an upright position), take off, push over into forward flight and shoot down enemies. If he was flying one of the VTOLs he then had to fly back to the starting point (nobody really addressed the navigational problem) and then carry out the difficult part. First, he had to slow down and 'translate' from fast wing-borne flight to hovering flight supported by the propulsion system. He then had to let down vertically on to the correct spot, with imperfect controls, looking back over his shoulder and juggling the throttle so that he landed with rate of descent close to zero. With an ordinary aeroplane, pulling back the stick results in an immediate vertical acceleration, for example to reduce rate of descent. Opening the throttle of an engine results in a delay while thrust builds up. Then there is a further delay while this extra thrust slows the rate of descent. It's like a hot-air balloon. We all know about the doctor who said, 'Take the pills ten minutes before you feel the pain coming on. . . .' Extra thrust *gradually* changes a too-fast descent into a hover or a climb. The obvious result, except with a pilot very experienced on type, is a rapid descent, frantic firewalling of the power lever, upward zoom, closing the throttle . . . ending in a crash or running out of fuel after too long pretending to be a yo-yo.

The Germans had a fair excuse: they were desperate. But after the war the US Navy was not particularly desperate, except perhaps to fight the newly created Air Force for funds and political power. But in their relaxed frame of mind they thought it would be nice to see if they could use the exciting German technology to create fighters that could operate from small areas of deck, such as the fantail of a cruiser or even on a merchant ship, in order to protect these vessels against air attack. In spring 1947 they began a long-term research programme with airframer Ryan and engine-builder Allison, in the course of which, on 31 May 1951, Allison 'flew' an upended J33 turbojet restrained only by loose cable tethers. This can claim to have been the first jet VTOL flight.

Ryan went on to build the X-13 Vertijet, but this was for the rival Air Force and powered by a Rolls-Royce engine. Back in 1951 something happened that nobody in the US Navy has ever explained to me, even though I discussed it not long afterwards with two heads of the Fighter Branch in the Bureau of Aeronautics. The decision was taken (by whom seems to remain a mystery) that in the immediate future no turbojet was ever going to appear sufficiently light, powerful and fuel-efficient for the total engines-plus-fuel weight for a suitable mission to make a VTOL jet fighter practicable. Anyone will tell you that, for a given weight of engines-plus-fuel, you can get more lift-off thrust from a turboprop. Accordingly the Navy went back to Allison and said, 'Make a turboprop powerful enough for a VTOL fighter.'

This was the crunch point. It matters little whether Allison succeeded with the planned T54 engine or not. The fact remains, how in the 1950s could a turboprop fighter ever have been taken seriously? How could it hope to catch jet bombers? How could it hope to win in air combat?

Here the pilot of the XFY-1 is in the cockpit with no ladder, so there's only one way to go . . . upwards!

The rest of the story can be quite brief. Lockheed built two examples of the XFV-1 Salmon (BuAer 138657/8), first flown in the conventional aeroplane mode from Edwards by Herman 'Fish' Salmon on 16 June 1954. Convair built two examples of the XFY-1 Pogo (BuAer 138649/50), first flown in the VTOL mode by James F. 'Skeets' Coleman at San Diego on 1 August 1954.

I inspected both and talked to both pilots. There is no suggestion either aircraft was particularly difficult or badly designed, and both in fact made transitions. The Convair did what it was designed to do: lift off vertically, transition to wing-supported aeroplane flight and then transition back to hanging on its eight-bladed prop for a vertical landing. In contrast, Lockheed doubted that the interim Allison XT40 coupled turboprop, of alleged 5,500 shp, was sufficiently powerful for VTOL, so it did the rather pointless thing of tearing off down the Edwards runway – 'Like the proverbial scalded cat,' said Salmon – transitioning to prop-supported hovering flight and then changing back to wing-supported mode for a landing at 135 knots. This was the mirror-image of what it was actually intended to do.

What puts these interesting machines into this book is that as air-combat aircraft they were *obvious* non-starters. Both test pilots agreed, but said things like, 'But they flew nicely . . . we learned a lot . . . well, Americans like to play with new toys.'

What may be even stranger is that engineers who ought to have known better schemed tail-standing vehicles as civil transports! One of the illustrations here comes from a paper read in 1952 by Raoul Hafner, who has already appeared in these pages as

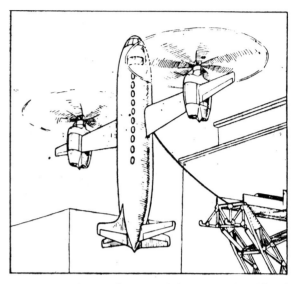

In 1952 Bristol seriously proposed this as a VTOL airliner!

the perpetrator of Bristol's first helicopter (see page 125). He seriously suggested that upwards of fifty passengers should strap in to pivoted seats in an airliner with its fuselage vertical. It would then drone up into the sky on the power of its turbine-driven prop-rotors, the propulsion system being broadly similar to that of today's more sensible V-22 Osprey. On arrival at the destination the pilot would somehow transition back to the vertical attitude and hover in mid-air, hoping that the passengers all managed to rotate through 90° relative to the cabin. The sketch shows the convertiplane 'hovering at full power whilst being hauled in to a mooring structure'.

Another visionary was Count Helmut von

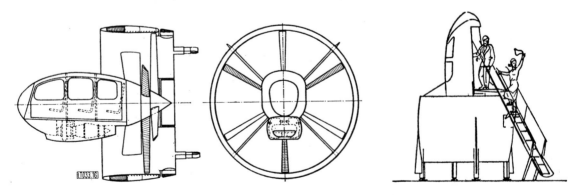

The Bureau Technique Zborowski called this the Hanneton III (two 600-hp turboshaft engines). They thought the world was waiting for private VTOLs.

Zborowski. At a conference in Duisburg in 1954 he proposed various forms of Coleopter, which in effect were vertical turbojets or turboprops with a surrounding annular wing. SNECMA in Paris took up the idea, and via a series of Flying Atar vertical turbojets actually progressed to testing a full-scale *Coléoptère* in 1959. Few people were really surprised when on 25 July 1959 it crashed, the pilot fortunately ejecting. Drawings show Zborowski's proposed turboprop private-owner version. I find the girl waving goodbye rather touching, because we may be sure she would not have had the benefit of an ejection seat.

VEB Type 152

Out of the blue, in 1958, photographs and brief details appeared of the roll-out at Dresden of a previously unknown four-jet civil airliner. Everything about it was unlike what might have been expected. For example, as it had a high wing it had to have 'bicycle' landing gear with outriggers to stop it tipping over, like a B-47. Called the VEB 152, it was said to have been designed by a Professor Brunolf Baade. It made its first flight on 4 December 1958.

So far as I know, nobody at that time thought of making any connection between this strange passenger aircraft and Junkers bomber projects of World War II. Such a connection would have appeared tenuous until, twenty-five years later, the existence was revealed of a 'missing link'.

The missing part of the story was published in 1983 in a Moscow magazine article about an apparently all-Soviet jet bomber called the Alekseyev Type 150. The design bureau of Semyon M. Alekseyev had previously been known only for small tactical aircraft, notably twin-jet night fighters. Now we learned from official historian I. Sultanov that he was also responsible for a large bomber, though credit for the basic design was given to the Central Aero- and Hydrodynamic Institute in Moscow, many of whose staff were named as important in the programme. No Germans were mentioned, though late in the story the name of Baade appeared as one of the people who assisted.

One had to know a bit more about the subject to realise that this was a rewriting of history. Baade, along with several hundred other 'potentially useful' German aircraft engineers, had been deported to the Soviet Union in 1946. They were taken to

The Alekseyev Type 150 had a perfectly sensible layout for a bomber.

In contrast, the VEB Type 152 was a non-starter as a passenger transport.

Podberezye and set to work as two design teams, called OKB-1 and OKB-2; Baade was in the latter under A.Ya. Bereznyak. In 1945–46 Baade, Hans Wocke and other former Junkers designers had sketched a twin-jet bomber, the EF 150. In 1948, OKB-2's immediate task complete, a contract was placed for a prototype of this bomber, as the Type 150. In the same year Alekseyev, whose own OKB had been shut, was placed in charge of OKB-1 and -2, whose work was henceforth co-ordinated.

Work went ahead, and the bomber was flown by Ya.I. Vernikov on 14 May 1951. It was a perfectly sound aircraft, which achieved a speed of 930 kph (578 mph), and exceeded the required speed at sea level of 790 kph (491 mph) by 60 kph (37 mph). Unfortunately, waiting for the Lyul'ka AL-5 engines had brought it into the same timescale as Tupolev's bigger and more powerful Tu-88, which was clearly more capable and went into production as the Tu-16 (called 'Badger' by NATO). The final nail in the Type 150's coffin was that on the sixteenth flight, on 9 May 1952, it stalled during the landing approach, causing damage which was never repaired.

In 1953 OKB-1 and -2 were closed. The Germans were allowed to return to the then DDR (East Germany), where they made it possible to start an aircraft industry. They helped set up the VEB (publicly owned enterprise) group of aviation factories. The biggest, at Dresden, concentrated on the Type 152, a civil version of the bomber. Though nobody saw the link with the EF 150, several observers, including myself, pointed out that the configuration of the Type 152 was an excellent one for a bomber, but ridiculous for a passenger transport. The useful space under the passenger floor was largely eaten into by the front and rear main landing gears, but not by the wing, which imposed a large overhead obstruction along the centre of the cabin. Bicycle gear is the last thing you need for a civil jet, which wants to rotate on take-off and then land with a considerable degree of flexibility – the bicycle aircraft must be flown off and back on in precisely the correct (almost level) attitude. A further point is that the Type 152 had almost the same wing as the bomber, with a low aspect ratio and very broad tips, which again is just what you don't want for cruising efficiency and long range.

Yet another minus feature was that, whereas the Soviet bomber had been powered by two well-developed Lyul'ka engines, the 152 was fitted with four engines of lower thrust (6,940 lb each) specially developed for this aircraft by another VEB at Pirna. Called Type 014, a continuation of German wartime designations, it was said to have been specially designed for good fuel economy, but in fact it was typical of 1945 technology, and completely outdated fifteen years later. Take-off specific fuel consumption was 0.85, compared with around 0.6 for contemporary Western airline engines. It was also outdated in its thrust/weight ratio of three, compared with nearly five for Western engines of the period. Thus the crucial parameter, the total mass of engines plus fuel, was uncompetitive, resulting in short ranges and small payloads – quite apart from the modest cruising speed of 497 mph.

Above all, airlines need to have absolute confidence in their equipment. They buy only from people with a long track record, and the product must be not only fully competitive in all respects but both it and its engines must be something on which total reliance can be placed. The Type 152 stood out a thousand miles as the wrong product, by the wrong team. One could absolutely guarantee that it wasn't going anywhere, even before, on 4 March 1959, DM-ZYA stalled at a height of about 1,000 ft and exploded on impact.

By that time it had been redesignated Type 152-I. The 152-II was redesigned to have four-wheel bogie main gears retracting into compartments extending aft from between the jet nozzles. The Dash-II made just two flights, the first on 26 August 1960, before the whole programme was cancelled. Optimistically, three more aircraft were in final assembly, with parts of fourteen more following. According to *Air International* the programme was stopped because of 'severe economic difficulties'. That's the kind of reason governments love to think of to explain cancellations. This one was a non-starter from day one.

BRISTOL 188

On 3 May 1962 the magazine *Flight International* published one of my last major articles written as technical editor. It was on the Bristol 188, and carried the subtitle 'A Versatile Research Aeroplane'. Perhaps now I may be able to apologise for this mistaken statement, but I can derive some comfort from the fact that I wasn't the only one to be taken in. Chris Barnes, author of the 'Putnam' *Bristol Aircraft Since 1910*, called it 'a technical advance of inestimable value in the practical approach to supersonic transport operation'. Other people were taken in as well, including the British Government. The long-suffering taxpayer was not consulted.

The final Bristol aeroplane was almost a re-run of the Douglas X-3 (see page 145), though it was ten years later, took four times as long, cost (as far as I can discover) fourteen times as much and was even more useless. It was in early 1954 that the Ministry of Supply issued Specification ER.134

A prodigious amount of effort and money went into the Bristol 188 after the supersonic aircraft it was intended to support had all been cancelled, so it didn't matter that it never got anywhere near the hot-soak conditions it was designed for.

(Experimental Requirement) for an aircraft to assist in aerodynamic and, particularly, structural research for highly supersonic flight. To accomplish this it had to soak at over Mach 2 for at least thirty minutes, to enable temperatures throughout the airframe to stabilise.

A year later Avro began work on the 730 reconnaissance aircraft, later developed also as a bomber and missile carrier. This outstanding aircraft was one of the many cancelled at the stroke of a pen by Duncan Sandys in April 1957, because of his belief that military aeroplanes were somehow obsolete as a class. To support it, the ER.134 was made even more challenging by being required to cruise at Mach 2.6 (1,720 mph), which in turn ruled out the use of aluminium alloys from the structure. It was also a requirement that the aerodynamics of the wing and engine nacelle should as nearly as possible duplicate those of the Avro 730. A.V. Roe were themselves already supporting the 730 by the 731, a three-fifths scale research aircraft.

The contract for the ER.134 aircraft was awarded to Bristol, the type number being 188. In 1956 Bristol Aircraft Ltd was formed, upon the division of the firm into aircraft and engine companies, something which should have been done thirty-six years previously. The newly formed Bristol Aero-Engines had a fine turbojet in the Olympus, and this could have done the 188 a bit of good. This was far too sensible for the Ministry mandarins, who decided it would be nice if the much smaller and lower-powered de Havilland Gyron Junior could be completely redesigned into a new version, the PS.50, with a modified compressor, 2,000°K afterburner, variable nozzle and new control system. Thrust with maximum reheat was to be 14,000 lb.

Around these engines Bristol Aircraft designed large and complicated nacelles with movable centrebodies in the inlets and a host of controllable flaps and valves to let air in or out. The nacelles were actually wider than the very slender fuselage,

whose length of 71 ft was more than twice the span of the very thin wing, whose ailerons had enormous horn balances! At the back was a fin of impressive acreage, on which was perched a tiny tailplane. Any similarity to the Avro 730 seemed to have been forgotten.

Dominating the entire programme was the cruise Mach number of 2.6, which meant that the structure had basically to be made of stainless steel. This probably doubled the time taken to build the aircraft, and certainly far more than doubled the overall cost. Partly by perfecting a jointing method called puddle-welding the feat was accomplished, five years behind schedule. This delay was despite a large proportion of the airframe being subcontracted to Armstrong Whitworth, to assuage their mortification at not being awarded the original ER.134 contract.

The first Bristol 188, XF923, was rolled out for pre-flight tests on 26 April 1961. Snag followed snag, and many thought the axe would fall before they could get daylight under the wheels. At last taxi testing got under way in February 1962. Still almost nothing worked properly, though the ever-loyal Chris Barnes's book says delays were due to 'crosswinds and other unfavourable conditions'. Bristol is hardly an area of incessant typhoons, and British breezes hardly bother an aircraft whose take-off speed is 295 mph. At last Godfrey Auty got airborne on 14 April 1962. At the Empire Test Pilots School dinner that year he was voted 'man most likely to eject in the coming year'.

In fact, he didn't have to – because the two Bristol 188s spent almost all their time on the ground. Having failed by a tremendous margin to get anywhere near holding even Mach 2 for half an hour, let alone the unattainable Mach 2.6, there was nothing useful they could do. But the tale of the last aircraft built at Bristol can at least end on a happy note. Originally the Ministry had wanted *six*.

Jet lift 2: Dassault Balzac, Fairchild/EWR-Süd AVS and Rockwell XFV-12A

The possibility of lifting aeroplanes vertically off the ground under the direct thrust of jet engines matured just in time to find an answer to another possibility: that of conventional airbases being wiped off the map by nuclear missiles. Obviously, no amount of hardening of above-ground aircraft shelters is going to provide an adequate shield against such an attack, to say nothing of protecting the base personnel, whereas dispersing the aircraft throughout the forests and towns could make the enemy's targeting problems quite difficult.

Accordingly in the late 1950s NATO issued NBMR (NATO Basic Military Requirement) No. 3 calling for a multi-role tactical strike/fighter able to operate away from known airfields, plus NBMR-4 for a jet-lift transport to support it by bringing food and drink, fuel and ordnance. The possibility of massive multinational orders naturally excited the main Western aircraft and engine firms, and in 1961–66 jet lift was all the rage.

Rather sadly, the house of cards eventually fell apart, because while NBMR-3 and NBMR-4 could suggest objectives, no government actually had to buy anything. The waters were muddied by the fact that the winners were British, and Her Majesty's Government had solemnly decreed in 1957 that manned fighters and bombers were an obsolete conception, and that no more would ever be needed. (Stated bluntly like this it is hard to believe this actually happened.) Meanwhile the countries that didn't win went away somewhat hurt, and said they wouldn't play.

The French said that, even though their Mirage III-V hadn't won, it was 'of equal merit' to the winning British Hawker P.1154. To support the Mirage III-V, Dassault rebuilt a Mirage III prototype into the Balzac 001 jet-lift test bed. Its Atar engine was replaced by a smaller Bristol Siddeley Orpheus, and amidships, between the air inlet ducts to the Orpheus, were placed eight Rolls-Royce RB.108 lift jets. This aircraft made its first free flight on 18 October 1962. On 10 January 1964 it crashed, killing its pilot. It was repaired, and crashed, again killing its pilot, on 8 September 1965.

Rolls-Royce naturally wanted to keep ahead in jet lift, and were irritated that rival Bristol Siddeley, working with Hawker Aircraft, found a way to build a jet-lift warplane, the Harrier, with just one simple engine. Eventually they came up with a brilliant jet-lift engine, the XJ99, developed in partnership with Allison. This was picked for what the Americans and Germans hoped would be the ultimate tactical warplane, to (as a Fairchild Republic vice-president put it) 'lick the pants off the British Harrier'. That US company was teamed with EWR-Süd, of what was then West Germany, in creating this wonder aircraft. It was called variously the US/FRG or the AVS, from Advanced Vertical Strike.

It was everything the Harrier was not. Where the Harrier had a simple wing, the AVS had a variable-sweep 'swing wing' with complex high-lift systems. Where the Harrier had one engine, the AVS had six. The two main lift/cruise engines had vectoring

The hovering Balzac, which twice demonstrated its lethality.

Fortunately, the US/FRG AVS never got much further than artist's impressions.

jet-pipes, with afterburners. At the front were two pairs of XJ99 lift engines, which not only had complex provisions for hovering flight control, but could then be retracted away inside the fuselage. In the end this technical marvel ground to a halt, unflown, in 1968.

The main US sponsor for the AVS had been the Air Force, but the US Navy was also irritated by the success of the British Harrier, and when in 1969 this aircraft was actually ordered by the US Marine Corps they could bear it no longer. Obviously, this upstart, subsonic, simple, cheap and altogether maddening Limey product – which, they said, 'couldn't carry a box of matches across a football field' – had to be knocked out of the picture. After wondering how best to do this, the Fighter/Attack Technology programme was launched, to create a basis of know-how for a highly supersonic single-seat all-weather fighter/attack prototype to operate from simple decks, with neither catapults nor

arrester wires. Industry was informed that innovative ideas would be welcome.

In 1972 the task was assigned to North American Rockwell, with a design called NR-356, the Navy designation being the strange one of XFV-12A (strange because it fitted neither the F nor the V number sequence). To save money and time, the XFV-12A used parts of other aircraft, including an A-4 and an F-4. The whole scheme was based on a complex lift system energised by diverting the entire gas flow from the single Pratt & Whitney F401 main engine, which in full afterburner was rated in the 30,000-lb class.

The enormous gas flow was to be discharged through two full-span pipes along the forward canard and two more along the aft main wing, these surfaces being opened for take-off and landing to form a series of spanwise ejector ducts. These ducts were to entrain a very large airflow – hopefully with an augmentation ratio of 7.5 to 8 –

The full-scale mock-up of the final form of the spectacularly unsuccessful XFV-12A.

which, on being accelerated downwards through the ducts, would multiply the lift created by the original flow of high-energy gas. The objective was a thrust-augmentation ratio of 1.6; thus, if the lift from the hot jets was 20,000 lb, the gross lift actually achieved would be 32,000 lb.

Control in hovering flight was to be provided by pivoting the spanwise ejector flaps. These could squeeze the jets or expand them, or swing them bodily to the rear or ahead. Differential deflection could control the aircraft in yaw, to point to left or right, while (for example) squeezing the canard jets and expanding the wing jets would pitch the aircraft nose down. On the wing-tips were fins and rudders, which were the chosen places for the main landing gears! Once climbing away, the XFV-12A would gradually transfer the gas flow to the main propulsive nozzle. As the aircraft accelerated forwards, so could the wing and canard ducts be closed off, to provide ordinary aerodynamic lift.

Conscious of the amount of new ground to be explored, Rockwell carried out prolonged testing using a variety of costly full-scale rigs. In 1975 the company boldly announced, 'First flight is scheduled for April 1976.' Company President Jim Tichenor told me, 'It'll make the Harrier as dead as the dodo.' It didn't happen, and as year followed year the company began to talk about delays caused by funding limitations. What they didn't like to say was that it didn't work. Pressed, they explained that they failed to achieve the desired augmentation ratio in the ejector ducts, but there was more to it than this. So, like the AVS, yet another complex wonderplane never got off the ground.

RSRA/X-wing

This final story is by no means a simple tale of a 'failed aeroplane'. Indeed, though the X-wing was to fly as an aeroplane, it was to take off and land as a helicopter. It serves as a case history of a perfectly sound and extremely attractive idea which is proving so difficult to realise in practice that, even though it has been a huge project of NASA, the sights have been lowered dramatically and the time schedules have gone 'out of the window'.

It is also yet another story of how good ideas are thought of in Britain, tinkered with in a half-hearted way, and eventually handed over to our American friends. What normally happens next is that US technological might simply tramples the problems to death and leads to commercially sold products which we in Britain then purchase. So far this particular tale has not followed this pattern. I

This is how the Sikorsky S-72 RSRA (Rotor Systems Research Aircraft) looked originally, with a conventional main rotor.

was vexed when we gave up and handed the idea to the USA. Now I am beginning to think we were well out of it!

The concept is that of a new form of rotor which, as the helicopter accelerates to a high forward speed, can be slowed down and finally stopped. In the basic X-wing aircraft the rotor then serves as an unusual form of fixed wing; in alternative schemes it can be retracted into the airframe and the lift provided by a conventional wing. To achieve this always appeared a challenge; now we know it is one of the toughest things ever attempted in aviation.

What everyone wants is a vehicle that can take off vertically from a small pad, with little noise, fly somewhere at, say, 500 knots, and then land vertically and quietly. A Harrier can do much better than 500 knots, but the noise and fuel burn in the jet-lift mode are very high. A helicopter imparts general acceleration to a lifting airflow up to 100 times greater, so the VTOL problem is solved; but it cannot cruise even at 200 knots, let alone at 500. So what we want is a helicopter which for translational (A to B) flight can turn itself into an aeroplane.

Of course there are many possible arrangements of what are sometimes called convertiplanes. The Fairey (Westland) Rotodyne was a pioneer exam-

ple of a twin-turboprop fixed-wing transport which also had a large rotor added. The V-22 Osprey is an impressive tilt-rotor machine, whose rotors can turn into propellers with their thrust axis horizontal. The tilt-wing machines are close relatives, while there are a limitless number of arrangements in which engine power can blow air through slits to augment the lift (sometimes by factors exceeding ten) of a normal wing. If we can accept a modest take-off run then the EBF (externally blown flap) and USB (upper-surface blowing) can result in excellent aircraft devoid of the awesome complexities of rotors.

In 1954 what was then the British National Gas Turbine Establishment began investigating high-lift systems in which high-volume, high-pressure airflows are blown through narrow slits along the span of wings and rotor blades. Ian Cheeseman concentrated on lifting rotors, and initially studied 'blades' of circular section. In other words, each blade was a tube, with high-pressure air blown in sheets from fine tangential slots around the upper surface, plus one underneath. This kind of CCR (circulation-controlled rotor) gave outstanding results, and no difficulty was experienced during tests in which vertical take-off was followed by stopping the rotor in the fore/aft direction, leaving the aircraft as a conventional jetliner. Cheeseman later went to the University of Southampton, where he developed more efficient rotors with blades of oval shape, but of course in Britain there was no money for proper hardware development.

Inevitably the CCR moved to the USA, where the US Navy and Lockheed-California confirmed and extended the British work. A major advance, previously suggested by Cheeseman, was to use a flattened oval blade profile with just two blowing slots, one along the top of one edge and the other along the top of the other edge. Thus, the aerodynamics would be roughly the same no matter which edge was leading and which trailing. When stopped, such a rotor could be used to give lift even during high-speed cruising flight. I always thought a two-blade CCR of this type preferable, but American work apparently showed the superiority of the four-blade 'X' form, which when stopped has two blades swept forward at 45° and two swept aft at 45°. Obviously the forward-swept blades pose severe structural problems, especially as the objective was to cruise at 500 knots (575 mph). The X-wing is attributed to

Robert Williams of DARPA (the Defense Advanced Research Projects Agency).

In 1983 everything seemed ready for a major programme. DARPA and NASA embarked on a joint programme to establish all the technologies and both the hardware and software necessary to support a flying X-wing prototype. The NASA/Army RSRA (Rotor Systems Research Aircraft), the Sikorsky S-72, was the obvious candidate aircraft on which to test the X-wing stopped rotor. Sikorsky was awarded contracts which involved gross modification of both S-72 aircraft, the second being intended actually to fly the X-wing.

To say that a lot of advanced technology was involved is the understatement of the century. Even designing and making the enormous wide-chord blades was something never before attempted. Pratt & Whitney produced the unique Coanda-flow compressor, driven by two 1,500-hp T58 engines, to feed compressed air through another unique device, the pneumodynamic plenum drum with forty-eight butterfly PCVs (pneumatic control

This greatly simplified sketch of the main elements of the X-wing will give a faint idea of why the control complexity transcended that of any previous aircraft.

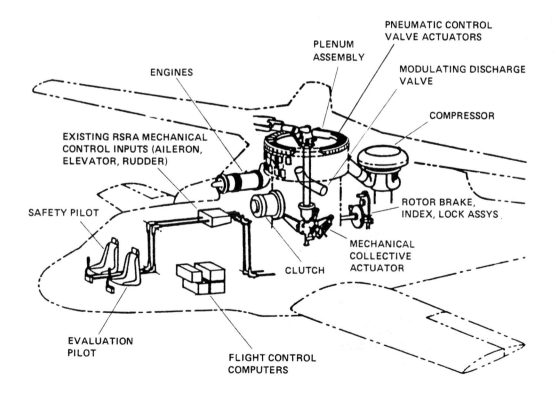

valves), twenty-four for the leading edges and twenty-four for the trailing edges. In the rotary-wing mode, from 0–150 knots, blowing would be applied to the four blade trailing edges. In the conversion mode, from 150–200 knots, blowing would be applied to the trailing edges of the advancing blades (the ones moving forward against the oncoming air) and to both edges of the retreating blades. In the fixed-wing, or stopped-rotor, mode, from 200–500 knots, blowing would be applied to the four trailing edges, two of these having originally been leading edges.

It does not seem particularly complicated, but in fact any operational X-wing aircraft requires a redundant digital FBW (fly by wire) or FBL (fly by light) vehicle management system more complex than that of any previous aircraft, and fully equal to that of the Space Shuttle. There is simply no room here to outline all the tasks to be performed, but they essentially include all those of a helicopter other than blade pitch control, plus all those of a high-speed aeroplane, plus such extras as air supply modulation, vectored thrust and many inter-system management interfaces. The original requirement was for twenty high-speed (20 MHz) microprocessors, with over 200,000 lines of installed software code, plus sixteen high-speed serial data links and two complete MIL-1553B data bus systems!

In December 1987 I visited the X-wing programme at NASA Ames Research Center. I was delighted to learn that the first test flight had just taken place, on the 2nd of that month. 'Ah,' said Dr James A. Albers, Deputy Director of the Aerospace Systems Directorate, 'but the X-wing was not fitted.' I found a general atmosphere of gloom, which was intensified by the fact that a few days later the original contract funding expired. Sikorsky naturally stopped work, and the RSRA aircraft were placed in storage at NASA Dryden Flight Research Center.

As I said, it would not be quite right to describe the X-wing as a failure, merely as something which turned out to be more complex than it had at first appeared, and which in consequence ran out of money. NASA's latest broad-brush perspectives on future aircraft give it the briefest of mentions, tucking it away along with many other possible forms of high-speed rotorcraft.

Today a lot of work is still going ahead, but it is in the nature of model testing and simulations. Even these are complicated and expensive. Any resumption of flight testing will be preceded by testing of the actual X-wing in the mighty NFSAC (National Full-Scale Aerodynamic Facility) at Ames. Several factors have led to down-grading of the target performance (for example, in maximum speed to a mere 200 knots, with a possible extension to 210, which is slower than a Westland Lynx). Several hardware failures included one of the main gearbox (inadequate lubrication) and of the plenum cylinder (intense heating caused by titanium sliding on titanium). More difficult to cure was a failure of a main-rotor flexbeam, essentially the X-wing main spar, which was then repeated with a second specimen at less than the design loading. Yet a further problem is debugging the software, which has never ceased to grow and now far exceeds the planned 200,000 lines.

In August 1991 Dr Albers brought me up to date on this difficult concept:

The primary objective of the RSRA/X-Wing program was to demonstrate the process of conversion from rotary-wing flight to fixed-wing flight and back using a circulation-controlled X-Wing rotor. The RSRA was chosen as a test bed for the X-Wing rotor since it already possessed many of the required attributes. Note that the process of transition (hover to forward flight) could not be addressed, since the RSRA/X-Wing eventually had a gross weight in excess of the rotor's lifting capability.

The very-high-speed stopped-rotor flight regime was also beyond the scope of the program. The 210-knot speed limitation for stopped-rotor flight is not due to the X-Wing rotor, it is instead due to the presence of impending sonic airflow on the advancing tips of the RSRA tail rotor. The X-Wing rotor itself had a design flight speed of approximately 350 knots. The maximum speed of an operational X-Wing aircraft is projected to be above 400 knots.

But it's all a long way off. And that's typical of modern aviation. At the start, in year one, you think you'll get the production aircraft certificated in year eight (or whatever). But at year eight your best prediction has gone back to year fifteen. And at year fifteen you've forgotten about it, because it was cancelled at year twelve. It's much easier just to write about it!